The Gangster's Butler

I can't promise
it's easy reading,
but wanted you to
have a copy !! :)

The Gangster's Butler

HOWARD SCOTT WILLIAMS

ISBN: 1545591733
ISBN 13: 9781545591734
Library of Congress Control Number: 2017906547
CreateSpace Independent Publishing Platform
North Charleston, South Carolina

Introduction

This book is about one reporter's experiences on a few major news stories in Los Angeles during three exciting decades after World War II, until 1976. It is a book of surprises, even for other reporters who worked the same stories.

Does 1976 seem like a long time ago? Think of JFK, Elizabeth Taylor, Howard Hughes, Mickey Cohen, LBJ, Sirhan Sirhan, Marilyn Monroe, Lana Turner -- and many more. The names can produce news today, even if they are dead.

This is not a rerun of big stories in newspapers or on television. Those are available in libraries. These are inside stories, a first-person memoir from jobs at United Press, two newspapers and CBS-owned KNXT, Channel 2, Hollywood.

For a non-journalist reader, this book tells what it is like to be a reporter. The work place is usually not the newspaper office. (Except when Gangster Cohen walked into the City Room hunting me). A reporter is a visitor on somebody else's turf, often without an invitation. He or she has to adjust and describe a new situation, from Skid Row or the White House.

Post-war L.A. was booming. The future of newspapers looked dazzling. The Times Mirror Corp. opened a visionary afternoon newspaper, the Mirror. In thirteen years it was dead. Buried. Television news tore the newspaper business apart, inch by column inch. It created a new galaxie of stars and sucked in the blood supply of newspapers -- advertising. Viewers stopped buying newspapers to read on rides home from work. News with pictures and sound was waiting in the living room. Movie studios, once feared near collapse, moved into TV. The surprise loser was public transportation. People no longer rode streetcars to go see movies in theaters. Evening bus and rail schedules were cut by a third or more.

Politicians saw what TV could do for *and to* candidates. Office holders and seekers, were joined by defense lawyers and judges at every level, and decided they had to control this demon. Armies formed on both sides. We began "peace" talks in Los Angeles, then statewide.

The assassination of Sen. Robert F. Kennedy in 1968 crossed frontiers. Requests from the local and world press for seats to cover the trial of Sirhan Sirhan outnumbered seats in the bullet-proof courtroom two to one. Who would be left out? Seven people from newspapers and television stations around the state met with two L.A. judges to find a solution.

It was technically simple, but had never been tried before. By default, I was handed the project. An expanded version was used by a Virginia Federal District Court for the first 9-11 case, in 2006, to serve families in five states.

After thirty or sixty years, memories can be fallible. Witnesses to an event may describe it differently even moments later. Police and lawyers see that constantly. However, journalists are trained to observe and report accurately.

In those days there were five newspapers in downtown Los Angeles.

Five reporters would cover the same big story.

Five City Editors routinely compared what their reporters did with the stories written by the four other reporters. Stories might differ in style, but in their comparisons the City Editors checked facts. None of the editors liked to find errors in their reporters' stories.

The system bred accuracy by experienced professional reporters. TV news on film began to join the comparisons. It was all a benefit to the public.

Some of the details of stories in this book were known by only a few people and did not appear in newspapers. Research for this memoir tapped many sources including file cabinets full of yellowing clippings and hundreds of notes. Clues are here for further digging. The files even contained a picture and story about my wife, Ann, who with another ticket agent at the Brown Derby's immediate neighbor, Western Airlines, was robbed by a gunman. He was arrested later, and the girls ID'd him in an LAPD line-up. News can hit anywhere.

All of us in journalism had great stories. That was the joy of the job.
Howard Scott Williams

THE GANGSTER'S BUTLER

Between the end of the World War II and Vietnam, few Los Angeles personalities made headlines as often as Mickey Cohen, the city's leading gangster. Judy Garland, Bing Crosby, Bob Hope, Richard Nixon, Clark Gable, Eddie Cantor and a few local politicians were regulars. Cohen kept up with them by starring in a continual circus with policemen, lawyers, hoodlum hangers-on, pretty women and the dead bodies of associates.

Sometimes, Cohen's activities became *personal* stories, bizarre sidebars that I left out of the newspaper.

* While he spent days in court fighting a traffic ticket, Cohen sent congratulatory notes to my wife in a hospital maternity ward.

* In court again, fighting a more serious charge of battery after a short bar fight, Cohen barged into the Mirror News City Room and demanded that I help him. I could have, but the City Editor told him to get out....

* Days later, after Lana Turner's daughter killed Cohen's bodyguard, that City Editor sent me to Mickey's apartment to ask for his help. While there I played butler for two women in the apartment.

Those details never got into my stories in the newspapers. Many months later I told part of the butler episode elsewhere. That part was "borrowed" by a colleague who put it in his own book as "fiction." The real story is all here. (See Letters chapter)

Covering Cohen was easy. Unlike his peers in the rackets around Los Angeles, such as the Sica Brothers and Jack Dragna who were unreachable and avoided the press, Cohen liked to be associated with reporters. He remembered names and was always polite. A new reporter could have Cohen's home telephone number and an invitation to "Call me anytime."

Reporters covering Cohen sometimes got close enough to discover that he was a cleanliness freak who constantly took time out to wash his hands and took long, long showers. However, the press didn't really know what he did for a living day by day.

The United States Senate Kefauver Committee held hearings in Los Angeles on organized crime, in late 1950. The hearings would have limited star appeal without Cohen. His appearance there was a lesson in Washington's appreciation for my employer, United Press. A member of the Senate committee tour group tipped me that Cohen would testify the next day. I could not disclose the source. We included that news item in our overnight story to UP clients. In the morning, the first question to the committee staff came from Tom Caton of the Herald Express:

"Will Mickey Cohen testify today?"

Answer: "Well, I don't know."

Question: "United Press said he will be here?"

Answer: "I don't know."

Caton was one of best reporters in town, and he and his boss, City Editor Aggie Underwood, didn't like being beaten on a story or any part of a story. Aggie kept closer contact with Cohen. It paid off for her later.

Cohen did show up. I introduced myself and got his calling card. Then I called my wife, so she could see the action. She worked upstairs in the same Federal Building. Cohen was standing alone at a break, so I introduced her. Mickey said, "Your husband is a very good reporter." He hardly knew who I was.

After admitting he had been a gambler, Cohen testified that he maintained his current style of living by borrowing money from friends. A bank officer was reported to have left his job after Cohen testified he borrowed more than thirty-thousand dollars without a promissory note.

Police usually said Cohen was a layoff bookie. Small bookies who took too many high-odds bets could lay off some of the bets on Mickey, for a price. He had goons who could help bookies collect debts. It was fancy living for a kid who grew up poor in Boyle Heights.

Cohen was born in Brooklyn. His family moved to Los Angeles. Later, Mickey moved east and, still young, became a medium-level professional boxer, a featherweight, in Cleveland. His life changed after that. He became a bookie and was reported to have been in business with Al Capone in Chicago. Back in Los Angeles, Cohen was rumored to work with Bugsy Siegel, the eastern mob front man who built the Flamingo in Las Vegas. Siegel was shot to death in 1947, killed by a bullet through a living room window of Virginia Hill's home on Linden Drive, Beverly Hills.

Cohen as a Target

Cohen escaped death a few times by pure luck or insider information. In conversation he referred to five attempts on his life. His front for years was a men's clothing store which, in its final version, was located on the Sunset Strip. Cohen went to the restroom in his store, and while he was out of sight someone shot up the place from outside, killing an associate in the store, Hooky Rothman.

In another shooting on Sunset Boulevard, in July, 1949, Mickey and a party of people that included a State Attorney General's investigator were shot at from a vacant lot across the street when they walked out of Sherry's Restaurant about three a.m. Mickey was wounded, his bodyguard was killed and two women were wounded, including a Los Angeles Mirror columnist, Florabel Muir. There was an investigation. What was a well-connected state official who knew Buffy Chandler, wife of Times Publisher Norman Chandler, doing at a restaurant with a gangster? The explanation was: "Official business."

Cohen, of course, could not imagine who fired the shots. He was interviewed on radio and said that a "mad dog," was responsible. It sounded so good he repeated it: "Yeah, a mad dog." He probably knew who did it. Are you listening, Mad Dog?

Until that time, Mickey Cohen was just a headline to me. In 1949 I was writing news for the United Press radio "split," our scheduled times to interrupt the national radio wire and transmit local news. That job consisted mainly of rewriting stories done by other Los Angeles UP staffers for Southern California newspaper clients. Rewriting meant changing the stories into conversational radio style. It was a good way to learn about Los Angeles newsmakers by osmosis. Later that year I began covering all beats in the Los Angeles Civic Center for UP, including Federal and County agencies, courts and grand juries. Mickey Cohen was a regular part of life on the beats.

Cohen lived on the west side with his petite red-haired wife, LaVonne, who appeared to enjoy a sweetly unaware existence. Aside from a small bomb going off in bushes in front of his house, the Cohens fit in with the quiet neighborhood. His headlines were created elsewhere. Her toughness surfaced when they divorced.

Cohen's image was not tarnished when some thugs who became known as the Seven Dwarfs beat up the operator of a small television repair business in the Wilshire District. They were Mickey's guys, but it was the police who looked bad because they caught the Seven, held them in the local police station for a while that day and then, inexplicably, let them go. The beating victim was rumored to be an unsavory neighbor/businessman in a friendly part of town, a guy who got what he deserved. The incident might have been forgotten, but an amateur photographer took pictures of Mickey's guys being busted outdoors. When no stories showed up in the newspapers, the stranger called the Times and offered photographic proof. The Times ran pictures, the man kept the negatives. Cops had a lot to explain. Some were charged, but they were acquitted.

At a subsequent investigation, Cohen testified that he went with a Times reporter to buy the pictures. Cohen said he gave the reporter two-hundred and thirty dollars, all the cash he had. The reporter went to the cameraman's door and returned soon with the pictures. The picture taker said the reporter only paid him thirty dollars. The reporter left the Times.

Who were the seven? What did they do? Months later I saw one of them dealing in a Las Vegas hotel casino.

Another Cohen escape occurred in 1959 at Rondelli's Restaurant on Ventura Boulevard. Jack "The Enforcer" Whalen, a lower-level hood, was shot to death late one December night, causing a dozen patrons in the restaurant to scramble for cover. Mickey was there and was reported to have gone to the men's restroom, or ducked under a table. Either way, he was present but not harmed. The shooter eventually got a one-to-five-year term for manslaughter. Decades later an acquaintance who had nothing to do with the news business or crime told me that he saw Cohen deliver the shooter's pistol to the restaurant owner in a paper bag.

As Cohen's notoriety boomed, the police grew tougher. When Mickey drove somewhere, anywhere, he was tailed. He complained about it to the news media. He stopped at Hollywood Boulevard and Vine Street to get a newspaper. He got out, bought the paper and returned to his car. A cop wrote a traffic ticket. It was illegal to stop in a red zone. He said he was being harassed, fought the ticket and hired a top lawyer, Rexford Eagan, who worked with Jerry Giesler, a famous show business attorney. The trial took days, and Mickey lost.

The Cohen Personal Touch

During trials, it is often routine for participants, but not jurors, to mingle and chat outside or inside courtrooms until they are told the judge is about to take the bench. This occurs before the day's work begins, again at mid-morning recess, also after lunch and again at a mid-afternoon break. Those are good times for reporters, because they can, while chatting, find out who will testify what and obtain background information that enhances stories.

During Cohen's "red zone" trial, on July 8, 1957 my wife gave birth to our son, Darin, late at night at West Valley Hospital in Encino. I was up until midnight calling family and friends. Actress Marie McDonald, another newsmaker acquaintance, lived a short walk from the hospital. Marie, a new mother, was separated or divorced at that time from husband Harry Karl, identified in headlines as "Shoe Magnate" because he owned a lot of stores. Marie had talked about pregnancy problems before carrying Karl's daughter. She was one of those I had notified by fone when Ann's doctor said Ann was finally pregnant. I didn't call Marie this time. She was kidnaped early in the year. Her infant girl was at home but was not kidnaped with Marie. After she was released by the kidnapers, she was upset by a story I did. (See McDonald chapter). At the hospital the next morning, Ann and the baby were fine. Then I went downtown for Cohen's trial. I gave the good news to the group outside the courtroom. Cohen joined reporters in offering congratulations and politely asked where Ann was and how she and baby were doing.

Ann had met Cohen at least twice, but he would not have remembered. One occasion was in the Federal Building during the Kefauver hearings. The second time was in the old terminal at what became LAX. Cohen was catching a plane at night to go fishing in Mexico. Ann went along to the airport to see the departure. We joined a couple of reporters in a booth at the airport café before Cohen arrived with his travel party. He stopped at our table to say hello. We let him pay the check for coffee.

When the "red zone" trial was recessed that July, 1957 afternoon, Cohen handed me a three-by-five-inch card and asked me to deliver it to Ann, the new mother. In his neat handwriting was a note:

My sincerest best wishes to
Both you and your newly
arrived little doll. Hope to see
you Ann, and the baby some day.
Mickey Cohen

At West Valley Hospital that evening, Ann was hurting from Caesarean surgery, so she was not up to the humor of the moment. Our son was in an incubator, normal for a Caesarean.

The next morning she was smiling. She pointed to a small table. On it was a copper planter box about the size of two shoeboxes end to end, filled with living greenery. It had been delivered after my visit the night before. She handed me a pale blue envelope. Printed in the upper left corner was the name, MICHAEL'S GREENHOUSES, INC., with an address on Exposition Boulevard. Mickey's "front" business in those days was a nursery. On the envelope flap, in blue ink, was printed "Michael Cohen." Inside was a sheet of blue stationery, with a hand-printed note:

DEAR ANN
    MY BEST WISHES FOR YOU
I AM SURE THE BABY IS A DOLL
HOPE YOU ARE FEELING WELL
MY BEST TO YOU AND HOPE
TO SEE YOU WHEN YOU COME
HOME
MICKEY

They were already on first-name basis. Ann said she was a celebrity among the maternity ward staff, but, of course, she did not get together with Mickey. Did this gift from Cohen imply that a favor was expected in return? It was not mentioned months later when Mickey needed my help.

Cohen was not always friendly with the press. He probably learned to be nice to the press during his days as a pro boxer. A well-known fighter on a card could be worth a little extra money. He was not big or tough or menacing. He walked lightly, even gliding in a way like some boxers I've seen. They don't telegraph their intention to move. The ex-professional boxer had nothing to prove. He acted casual, but he was wary much of the time and missed little.

Reporters waited all one afternoon, mostly sitting on the floor of an empty corridor, while he testified before a Federal Grand Jury in downtown Los Angeles. I don't recall what it was about, but his date with the Grand Jury had been prominently mentioned in the newspapers.

The press did not get insider reports afterward in Federal matters, like we did from a County prosecutor. The reporters would try to get Cohen to talk. He always did, if only to deny there was any reason for him to be in the news.

The Grand Jury departed. The legal staff went home. Reporters asked a secretary where was Mickey? We were told that Mr. Cohen was still in the Grand Jury room.

"Testifying?"

"No, he's alone." That was strange.

"Can we go in?"

"Go ahead," we were told. Strange, indeed. Four or five of us went in.

Inside the formal, wood-paneled room, Cohen sat in a chair, slumped down, arms across his midsection. The usual alert smile was missing. He told the reporters to go away, he was not going to say anything. The reporters pressed. Mickey said he had taken an oath of secrecy, so leave him alone. The newsmen (all men) asked what was wrong. They guessed he wanted to say something, but what?

He admitted, pouting, that he was unhappy with what had been written about his impending interrogation by the Grand Jury.

What didn't he like?

Go away, he said, the press would get nothing more out of him.

A reporter took one more time at bat and told Mickey that if he had a complaint this was his last chance to tell his story, because we all had to leave. Cohen slowly straightened up a little and suddenly pointed at one newspaperman, vigorously.

"How do you think my mother feels when she reads in your newspaper that I'm a 'blue-jowled gangster'?"

Then he left.

Cohen's high living, carefully recorded by tails, finally resulted in a conviction for income tax evasion. He had learned nothing from his former associate, Al Capone, who was so slippery he could only be convicted of income tax evasion. Mickey went to Federal prison. Out again, he resumed his usual style of living. I reminded him of the talk among Cohen watchers that he was inviting another income tax charge. He grabbed my arm, very hard, and demanded:

"Do you know something?"

"You know what happened before," I said. He shrugged.

Cohen went to prison a second time in 1961. The Mirror News folded soon and I was out of the news business for over two years, then moved to Ch. 2 in Hollywood. Newspapers (and radio and television) said that on his second tour in prison a fellow prisoner, reported to be less than balanced, beat him on the head with a piece of pipe, causing enough brain damage to cripple him permanently.

It was a surprise to see Cohen, probably around 1973, waiting inside the lobby of KNXT (later changed to KCBS-TV) on Sunset Boulevard. He was in a wheel chair and was accompanied by a large gentleman who frowned when I greeted Cohen. It took a couple of reminders before the old Mickey began to smile and say, yeah, yeah, he remembered me, and typically ask how I was doing. He did not look well, his face scarred from the beating, and the muscles not quite working. He was there to tape an interview. I led the way toward studio Twenty-three until the producer of the program showed up in the hallway ahead and took him away.

From the back, partly hidden by the tough-looking man pushing him, Mickey Cohen could be seen bent over in the wheelchair, a sadly shriveled little guy going to get a few more minutes of fame.

The Private Eye and a Waiter

At his peak as a news object, Cohen did not seek headlines. They just happened. The guest list for Singer/Dancer Sammy Davis Junior's birthday party early in 1958 at the Villa Capri included a few well known names, but even with Mickey Cohen among them it was a non-story, a small private gathering at a Hollywood restaurant.

Sammy did not need publicity. He grew up in show business, flew to the top of the billboard at a Sunset Boulevard nightclub, Ciro's, and then became a comet over Las Vegas.

Sammy Sr. was celebrating Jr's birthday. (See Sammy Davis Chapter).

Cohen, however, probably wanted to be noticed, but not this way. He was on a campaign to make connections in Hollywood where there was big money. His henchman-bodyguard, John Stompanato, was openly courting Actress Lana Turner. Cohen had been heard to mention "My friend Frank Sinatra." Attending a Sammy Davis party would further the Cohen image of being connected. Sammy's father, Sammy Senior, was there, and Robert Mitchum, John Carroll and Geary Steffan, husband of Jane Powell. Those names were in subsequent stories about one of the waiters, Arthur Black.

The party actually produced two running stories.

One story, an accusation that Cohen slugged a waiter, was covered by the newspapers.

The other story was not known to those who covered Cohen's battery trial. It was only partly disclosed in a company newsletter a year later. The whole story is disclosed here for the first time. (See Much Ado About Letters below.)

The Villa Capri restaurant, where the Davis party took place, was about a block north of Hollywood Boulevard. The Brown Derby, another "moviedom" favorite a few blocks away, was well lighted, and big names might find caricatures of themselves on the walls. Villa Capri was more subdued, cozy, and the lighting was softer. They were both places where stars might show up.

There were differing stories about what happened that Friday night at Villa Capri. The waiter, Arthur Black, said he bumped Cohen accidentally and the gangster slugged him. Some witnesses said the waiter was partly to blame. The waiter went to the police and told them that Cohen hit him. Cohen said his only contact was an accidental bump and he did not hit the waiter. The cops investigated and felt they had enough to arrest Cohen on suspicion of battery.

Whatever might come out, one thing was unquestionable: Cohen did not like to lose in court. Not to cops. He had fought a parking ticket with a smart and expensive attorney, and that was a mere citation, not a criminal case. There was talk that he could no longer afford such costly legal help for this new trial, barely six months after the "red zone" ticket defense. He hired Ed Gritz, at best an unpublicized player in the criminal defense world.

Soon after the story of the Villa Capri waiter's battery case appeared in the papers, Cohen's new lawyer called the Mirror News and said the waiter might drop the charge – for a price. Art White, an Assistant City Editor, told me about the call. The lawyer said it was obvious that the whole thing was a shakedown, and the Mirror could see for itself. White said Gritz would arrive at the City Room in a few minutes. I was to accompany Gritz to the waiter's house and find out what was going on.

I would be "wired."

Gritz showed up, and I went with him in his car. He was carefully upbeat, a gambler on a roll, trying to look unexcited. After a few minutes' drive from the Mirror, Gritz stopped at the office of Hollywood's then best-known private investigator, Fred Otash, a bug expert whom I had met at least twice at noisy news events. Otash was tall and hard-looking, not a cheerful barbecue-and-beer neighbor. In his 1993 book about J. Edgar Hoover, Author Anthony Summers wrote that Hoover met people at the home of Lewis Rosenstiel, a Mafia-connected millionaire whose Manhattan home, Summers said, had been wired "roof to basement" by Fred Otash. That wiring job probably was done not many years before this meeting with Gritz in Los Angeles.

For the lawyer-waiter assignment, I was to carry a wire recorder, a device that went out of style soon but possibly was the best available miniature technology at that time. I knew about it, but had never seen one. For comparison, my personal high-fidelity recorder used quarter-inch tape, had three built-in speakers, was as big as a suitcase and weighed about twenty-five pounds. A year earlier it had preserved the sound of our unborn son's heartbeat. Otash's wire recorder was the size of a pound of butter. It recorded sounds magnetically on wire as fine as fishing line.

Otash gave instructions on how to use the wire recorder. It was about as difficult to figure out as a light switch on the wall: On or Off. I put it in my front left pants pocket, which would be covered by my sports coat. Otash decided the microphone should go in the left breast pocket of the coat. He cut a hole in the bottom of the pocket. The wire, with a small plug for the recorder, ran through that hole inside the coat lining. He cut another hole to exit the coat lining and pulled the wire down a few inches to a belt loop. He wound the wire around the belt loop so it couldn't move out of position, and finally plugged it into the recorder which I then put in my left trouser pocket. My coat covered it all. We tested the switch and recorded our voices. On replay it all came through. Another try and we were ready to go. On-Off. Easy.

Gritz parked in front of an old home that was typical of Hollywood south of the boulevard. It had a tired graying shingle roof, dried up landscaping, a couple of concrete steps to a wide porch. It looked like some my maternal grandfather, Ernest McConnell, an architect, might have designed before World War I. He also did a big office building that about 1990 was designated an historical landmark in downtown Los Angeles. I knew its family history when I worked a block away while attending journalism school at USC.

As Gritz and I crossed the sidewalk, I reached down into my pocket and pushed the recorder's On switch. Gritz knocked on the screen door, and the waiter, Arthur Black, came out of a kitchen and invited us in.

The two men looked alike: average build, short medium-shade brownish hair, similarly shaped faces, serious expressions, and both wore glasses.

Gritz introduced me as his "associate." We sat on a couch facing Black, who was in a chair, leaning toward us, ready to talk. Gritz explained that he understood the waiter was willing to drop the complaint if Mickey came up with some money.

The waiter said yes. If he was compensated for getting beat up, he'd settle and drop the charge. It was like an auto accident, he said. Pay and forget it. They did not agree on an amount, but it appeared Black did not expect much, maybe a few hundred. Gritz said he'd be in touch, and we left. It was over in a few minutes. I hadn't said a word.

In the car, I turned the recorder off. Enroute back to Otash's office, Gritz said he thought that the shakedown was now proven and the case would be thrown out. I didn't see it as being that simple. Was this just compensation for injury? That didn't sound like "shake down" to me. I did not express my opinion to Gritz. The recording would give us the waiter's and the lawyer's exact words, and the Mirror's story that I would write would make no conclusions.

Gritz told me that if Black decided to proceed with the battery complaint, I would be needed to testify about the recording and what was said. I told Gritz that I could not testify. I was just a reporter and couldn't get involved. The newspaper's story would be the end of it for us. That was a generally accepted policy in journalism. Several years earlier, the FBI wanted testimony from reporters who attended a press conference. My United Press boss told them I would not testify, because reporters don't get involved in stories we cover. It was not a firm rule everywhere. The Los Angeles Times let its reporter testify.

When we arrived at Otash's office I took the recorder out of my pocket. We removed the wire and the microphone from my coat. Otash played the recording and it was as good as we had hoped. Otash made a copy on tape, tested it to be sure it contained the conversation, and gave the tape to me.

Gritz dropped me off at the Mirror. Art White had a tape recorder and played the tape for City Editor Hank Osborne. The deadline for the last edition of the day was approaching. Osborne gave me the recorder to help get the waiter's words exactly as given, and I did a short story. It referred to Black's "apartment," possibly a bit of misdirection for the public or other press. The recording was not mentioned, just the conversation.

About an hour later the next edition of the paper was off the press. I called one of the cops on the case and told him what we had in print. I did not tell him about the recording. Two detectives were on the case, W. R. (Bud) Schottmiller and J. B. Close. They were working on a battery complaint. Schottmiller was a familiar face on numerous "publicity" cases, but I talked to Close, as best I remember. The detective said:

"We told him not to talk to ANYbody!"

The policeman was furious and said the waiter sure as Hell was going to continue to press charges.

Arthur Black could not back out now without making big trouble for himself. Gritz and Cohen may have been aware of Black's potential problem, but neither mentioned it to me. This was a criminal action, and accepting payment to drop it could amount to bribery. Cohen, therefore, would want to show that money had been asked for, and if a jury could hear the tape they would be convinced it was a shakedown.

To use the tape, Cohen needed to have the person who made the recording testify that he made it, the circumstances, and swear that the voices were indeed Black and Gritz. In the days afterward, while the authorities proceeded with plans to prosecute Cohen, Gritz called to say he needed my testimony. I told him I couldn't testify unless City Editor Osborne said OK. Our conversations were not disclosed to reporters who covered the case, and I did not go near the courtroom.

One afternoon shortly before the trial actually started, Cohen walked alone into the City Room on the third floor of the Mirror Building at Second and Spring Street.

There was no security then. Anybody could walk in. Press agents often did, going directly to the City Desk with no hurdles in the way. Actors, cops, politicians. All visited. Reporters at desks around the CityRoom did not pay much attention to Cohen, another newsmaker..

From my desk I saw Cohen come in the big door off the elevator lobby. He looked around and pointed at me. I went to see what he wanted. Standing by the door, we talked. He said he needed me to testify. I told him I couldn't, reporters covered stories, they couldn't take sides.

I had been looking for City Editor Osborne, who was away from his desk. Finally, he appeared and I signaled him. He saw Cohen and came right over. Osborne was a wartime Navy officer, a former Chicago newsman, average build, pleasant in looks and demeanor and calm most of the time. He loved a good story.

He listened to Cohen and then told him I would not testify. Cohen argued. Osborne was firm.

Cohen insisted. Osborne told Cohen to "get out."

Cohen left in a quiet, smoking rage. I could feel it.

Osborne told me that if Cohen tried to contact me again I should let him know. Of course!! No one in the City Room was told why Cohen was there.

As the trial wound down, Hollywood names who attended the party for Sammy Davis Junior described what happened at Villa Capri. There was unspecific talk of Lawyer Gritz and a tape recorder in the courthouse. The Examiner had a picture of a recorder, a machine as big as a typewriter. It was an unexplained mystery to readers. We did not report it.

On April third, 1958, Cohen's battery trial was still on. It was Thursday. In the afternoon, Ed Gritz walked into the City Room through the door from the elevators. I saw him and went to find out what he wanted.

Gritz said he was afraid he would have to have me testify. I said Cohen knew I couldn't do that. Gritz said I could go willingly, or.... he tapped his right lapel.

"I've got a subpoena in my pocket, if I have to use it," he said.

He wanted me in court the next day. If he pulled the subpoena out of his pocket and handed it to me, I would have no choice.

"You better talk to Hank," I said.

Osborne was seated at the City Desk. I waved at him, and he came over. Gritz repeated his story. He had to have my testimony, and he had a subpoena.

Hank reminded him that we had been through this with Cohen, and the answer was still No. Gritz argued and almost, not quite, reached for his inside pocket. The conversation ended quickly with a few indelible words by Osborne:

"If you pull that thing out of your pocket, you'll be through practicing law in this town." That line sounded like a Hollywood movie, but Hank wasn't kidding, just exaggerating.

Gritz didn't say anything, frowned, then turned and went out the door.

The trial went on the next day, Friday, April fourth, 1958. I was at home.

Lana and Johnny

At midnight Friday I was supposed to arrive at the Mirror and work as overnight City Editor, handling whatever came along. Usually it meant updating Friday's stories for Saturday's first edition of the paper, fielding a few calls from the Police Beat and perhaps send our radio car to cover something. A reporter and photog cruised throughout the night listening to police radio calls. One night our radio car helped catch a hit-run driver who hit a cop. Calls from our radio car to the City Desk were relayed to me, and I repeated it on another phone to a police dispatcher until a police car spotted our car following the suspect and joined the "parade" on the Hollywood Freeway to make an arrest.

Osborne called from his home in South Pasadena around eleven o'clock, just before I left for downtown. He said to stop by Lana Turner's house in Beverly Hills on my way to the office.

Lana's daughter had killed Mickey Cohen's bodyguard, Johnny Stompanato.

Cheryl Crane, sixteen years old, was trying to protect her mother and stabbed Stompanto. She was taken to Beverly Hills Police Station. Her father, Stephen Crane, went there. Lana was somewhere trying to get Cheryl released. Cheryl was going to Juvenile Hall. One of our photographers had stayed at the house and would wait for me.

Osborne said the City Desk would be manned by someone else that night. I was to pull together details from reporters and photographers working the story. Art White would be in early to coordinate sidebars on what the principal players had been doing. I would write the overall lead story on Stompanato for the first edition. The deadline for copy was 8 a.m., headlines would be written and pictures added to page dummies, and presses would roll by 9.

At Lana's, the Mirror photographer, I believe it was Nelson Tiffany, was standing near the front of the house on Bedford Drive. He was the only person in sight. The action had moved to the Beverly Hills Police Station, leaving Lana's mother, Mildred Turner, and a Beverly Hills cop at the house with the body of Stompanato.

He asked if I wanted to look at the scene? He raised a thumb at a window above the front door. It was one of those white stucco, two-story colonial style places, without the big columns, which are common in the area. I wanted to go up. A description of the bedroom and body would belong in the first or second paragraph of the story. We walked in the front door without knocking or ringing a bell.

Lana's mother was standing at the foot of the stairs in the foyer. She acted as though she wanted to know who we were and why we were there. Reporters learn not speak nor to ask permission because it will often be denied, unthinkingly or automatically, by people not accustomed to making decisions in news situations. A slight pause by a reporter can be long enough for someone to ask, "Hey, where do you think you're going?" A response like "This is a crime scene" was usually enough to cause the person to back off. It was easier if the questions could be could be avoided.

Bluffing works. Lana's mother, a small woman, stood at one end of the first step, blocking half of it. I looked through her, not at her, and walked around her and up the stairs. Tiffany followed. This can happen with cops new on a scene. In that case, we'd stop and explain. And obey. In L.A. the LAPD PR man would help us. Mother Turner just watched us go upstairs.

There was no one in Lana's bedroom with the body. In the new Millennium, television created a big home audience of crime scene security experts. They know the scene is important, may contain evidence and must not be disturbed. That could include footprint impressions on carpets. In those pre-TV-expert days a person involved in a story, or a family member or friend, might be designated by a cop to watch the scene until the Coroner's men arrived to remove the body. A relative or neighbor probably could not tell a reporter from a detective. In this case, the Coroner's hearse was supposed to arrive soon. Mother Turner might have thought the guy without a camera was a "remover." She stayed downstairs.

Anyone reporting on Mickey Cohen's activities in those days knew Stompanato. One did not usually chit-chat and joke with him. He was self-important, accustomed to attention because of his dark movie-star good looks and the aura of suspense his boss Mickey gave to anyone with him. Also, he probably was told by Cohen not to talk to news people. Reporters were not certain what Stompanato did for a living, but "Bodyguard" was often used to describe him, a euphemism for hired thug. Cohen had lost one bodyguard in the still unsolved shooting at Sherry's restaurant on the Strip, so there could be risk in the job. Johnny must be tough.

The bedroom was large, nearly all pink and frilly, a girl's place. It would have been cheerful in daytime. Stompanato was lying on his back by the bed, on the pink carpet, feet toward the opposite side of the bedroom where windows looked out on the street to the west. He was dressed in trousers, shoes, a sweater and a shirt which had been pulled up to show a few inches of his abdomen.

There was no blood except a small amount on a hand towel, altogether maybe enough to cover a folded dollar bill. It looked like the towel had been used to wipe the wound and was dropped next to the body. The fatal wound was small, a neat horizontal cut about an inch wide above his belt. The kitchen knife, which was not there, severed an artery. He died hard and fast. His eyes were closed and he could have been asleep. He was handsome as always.

Later we learned he had an ex-wife and son in another state. Someone would miss him.

The photog had taken pictures earlier, so we went back downstairs. I glimpsed a uniformed cop in another upstairs room. We went out the front door just as the Coroner's wagon pulled into the driveway. They went to look upstairs and decide what kind of problems they might have carrying a body out on a gurney. They were back in a couple of minutes to get the gurney and took it inside.

Moments later a car pulled up in front of the house. The driver stepped out: Jerry Giesler, Hollywood's best-known attorney in criminal matters. He walked up to see us. Anyone who covered Hollywood knew Jerry as a quiet gentleman, a statesmanlike representative of the legal profession, calm, precise and patient, with a flair for sensational courtroom activities that actually were conducted as quietly as a sermon. He had a deceptively harmless air, just another middle-aged man, maybe in his sixties, reddish hair, thin on top. He was not in the least pushy, not a man who would come on strong even under pressure. He told me later, talking in his Beverly Hills area office, that if he had his life to do over he would not be a lawyer. Stress was one factor, he said.

Giesler said he had come to look at the crime scene. We told him he was too late, they were bringing Johnny's body down. We saw Lana in his car, her blonde head down. Jerry said she didn't want to speak with us. He was taking her to a friend's house for the night. Soon, the sheet-covered gurney and its two lifters came out. As they started across from the door to their wagon in the driveway, Lana looked and tossed her head back, eyes closed, the pretty face scrunched up in pain. She put a hand up to cover her face.

Giesler and his client left. The photographer went to call the City Desk on the radio in his car, parked at the curb just south of Lana's driveway. The office reported that Mickey Cohen showed up at Beverly Hills Police department wanting to know what happened to his friend. He was angry at the girl, angry at Lana. That scene was covered by others, so I could go to the office.

At the Mirror, I started on the story. First, I was given the notes that reporters had called in already. Then there were calls to make to the crews out there in Beverly Hills working and the police beat downtown, a couple of blocks from the Mirror building.

Toward morning, Art White came in. After a few minutes he handed me a half-page "book" consisting of paper and carbons, the stuff on which we wrote our stories. On the book were two typewritten sentences. He said they were the lead he wanted to appear on the story. I would write the rest. Above those lines he had typed my byline, although a lot of people had worked on the story.

It occurred to me that my former City Editor, Aggie Underwood at the Herald Express, would never have written a lead for one of her reporters. She stressed that in "Newspaperwoman," her memoir. She had a staff of good writers. There are many ways to write the same story. If the editor "fixed" too many stories, everything in the paper would look the same.

White's lead was accurate. The story told itself. I would not have referred to Stompanato as "Adonis." My story, with contributions from several people, begins with the third paragraph, referring to the body in Lana's pink bedroom.....

Much Ado About Letters

It may appear that the following is of absolutely no importance. The fact is it involved a battle for survival. Most reporters were aware of intense competition, but casual talk in a City Room did not include crucial economics. They chased movie stars instead of counting unsold papers in newsracks. "Exclusive" stories sold few extra papers. Circulation drivers knew more about that than reporters. We all knew "PM" newspapers were failing. The (PM) Daily News closed, and the Mirror became the Mirror News. Some reporters made the move, some lost jobs. Competition was for life.

The Gangster's Butler

During the next two days, Sunday and Monday, I was off, reading about Stompanato in the paper, watching it on television. Monday was a bad day for Cohen. A jury convicted him of battery. When I walked into the City Room around eight o'clock Tuesday morning, City Editor Hank Osborne wanted to talk. That was when I heard about the Lana letters.

Osborne said that Lana Turner had written some syrupy love letters to John Stompanato. After he heard the verdict, Mickey Cohen gave Lana's letters to Aggie Underwood, City Editor of the Herald Express, our chief competition. Osborne said the Herald was going to cover its front page with the letters.

In a later Millennium full of radio and television and web news, a scoop of that nature might seem a bit less than shocking. But this was 1958. It was a time of film star idealism, mostly clear of public scandal. Private lives seemed fairly normal in the papers if courtrooms were not involved. Lana Turner was a unique case.

In a history of the Herald Express, written for the Los Angeles Press Club's 1989 year book, Managing Editor Herb Krauch said his paper had "hundreds of scoops" in his experience, starting before World War I.

"One of the most important of all was in the late 1950s when the Herald Express published exclusively Lana Turner's love letters to gangster John Stompanato," Krauch wrote.

Was he joking? The exclusives lasted only two days, actually just the early edition on each of two days. But, Krauch was serious. The Mirror and the Herald had fought a war for survival for almost ten years. It was not just about pride.

Osborne had been tipped during the night that Hearst lawyers were discussing who owned the letters and whether the Herald and other Hearst newspapers coast to coast could run them. Did Lana own them, or did Stompanato, or his heirs? The public didn't see the legal memos, but they would see the result soon. The Herald was going to run the letters, and Osborne would have to figure out what the Mirror could do to make up for having been beaten badly. First, he wanted to see the damage. He told me that a copy boy was down Spring Street at a newsrack, the first place where the first edition of the Herald Express would be put on sale. It was about twelve blocks south of the Mirror.

There was a long hour to wait. When the copyboy called around nine a.m. it was a letdown. There were no Lana letters. The second edition would be out in a couple of hours. Osborne told the copyboy to stay there. The Herald might still be waiting for legal clearance. They might put a re-plate of the first edition on newsracks as soon as approval was given.

The copyboy's next call came before eleven a.m. The Herald's second edition had the letters. A few minutes later he rushed in with the paper. Hank and I read the letters together on my desk. They were labeled "Copyright by the Herald Express."

Osborne told me to call Mickey and ask if he had any more letters. He said to read the letters in the Herald to Cohen and ask if they are what he gave Aggie, and ask if we have his permission to run them. I had his phone number on his card;

Mickey answered the phone in his Westside apartment. Yes, he knew about the letters. Did he have any more? He said he didn't know. I asked if it was okay with him if we ran these letters, the ones in the Herald. He said he didn't care.

I read a few words to Mickey and asked if that was one he gave the herald.

"Yeah, that sounds like them," said Mickey.

I did the same with the next letter in the Herald, reading a few words.

"Yeah, that's probably one," Mickey said. He plainly wasn't interested in hearing more.

Osborne turned aside, gave orders, and someone began writing the Mirror's story. The Mirror's press room waited for the remake of page one of our second edition.

Osborne wrote a note on a newspaper in front of me:

"Ask if he has more letters"

I asked Cohen, again, if he had any more letters. He said he wasn't sure that he gave them all to Aggie, but he didn't know.

At least he had confirmed he was Aggie's source.

"Ask him to look for more," wrote Hank with a pencil on a newspaper margin.

I asked Cohen if he would look around and tell me if he had any more. He said he might when he had time. Could he could look now? He said not now. Soon? Maybe.

Osborne whispered instructions again. I asked Cohen if I could go to his apartment in West L.A. and wait while he looked. Cohen said sure, come on out. Osborne said go. I had never been there before.

Asking Mickey Cohen for Help

I got my car and headed for Brentwood, across town near UCLA.

At the Mirror, someone wrote about the letters and lifted excerpts from the Herald Express. Our story said that the letters were "released to the Mirror News by Mickey Cohen."

It was maybe eleven a.m when I arrived at Cohen's door, a short distance north of Wilshire Boulevard. The West Gate of Brentwood Country Club was a few a few blocks from Cohen's place. I knocked and waited. The apartment building, two stories high, painted two shades of dull blue, looked new, well maintained, nice but modest, not a lavish gangster palace.

Cohen opened the door. He was wearing a towel around his waist, shoes and a fedora hat. He said he was in the shower and I could wait in the living room.

The apartment layout became of interest later. It was not big. A person entering the front (and only) door would find on the left a small living room with a fire place. Opposite the door a dozen feet away was a door to a bathroom, and to the right of that was an opening to the kitchen. On the far right as one came in the door was a hallway. It stopped at a wall and turned left. A few feet around the turn was a door to a bedroom, and at the end of the hallway to the left was the bathroom where Mickey was showering.

Windows in the living room looked east down down to the street. He had a private staircase. Mickey left me in the entry, an open area which contained chairs, a table and telephone.

Butler at Work

Mickey, it turned out, did take long showers. After about twenty minutes of waiting, the telephone rang. I presumed it also rang in the back of the apartment, the bedroom, and Cohen would answer it. It rang and rang. After a couple of minutes, it was a puzzle. Another minute and it was agitating. It made no sense. I had called earlier and Mickey answered immediately. Maybe the phone wasn't ringing in the bedroom. Who might be calling? The caller obviously knew Cohen, probably knew he was in the shower and thought that eventually he would answer. It continued to ring, seeming to get louder and more insistent. It had to be important. What to do? This wasn't my place. I wasn't even a guest. I was a business visitor, with no other role.

Finally, I decided that if the caller wanted to ring that long, maybe only three or four minutes but seemed like forty, I might help Mickey by answering. The butler role was new, but why not?

"Hello."

"Gimme Mickey!!" snapped a female voice.

She clearly knew I was not Cohen. Now what? I didn't know who it was, but she meant for me to obey.

"Who's this?" I asked, so I could tell Mickey, or tell the caller he was busy.

"LaVonne. Get him!" she ordered.

His ex-wife, and she was angry. I decided to obey and tell Mickey she was calling.

Without another word to her, I walked down the short corridor toward the bedroom, came to a dead end and turned left toward where I could hear the shower running. As I passed the bedroom door I could see a woman, partly under a blanket, dark red hair, face down, snoozing on the bed. On the left, not in the bedroom, was the shower. I got close enough for Mickey to hear me and called:

"Mickey, LaVonne is on the fone."

He cursed. He said he'd come out. I returned to the living room. There was no point in telling LaVonne anything. She would know he was going to answer. We had never met, so there was nothing to say. I waited near the phone. In a minute or two, Cohen came out in the same costume he wore earlier to answer the door: shoes, towel around his waist, and fedora hat. I walked into the kitchen, and from there could easily tell it was a heated conversation. I heard enough to figure what it was about. LaVonne had read in the papers that Mickey was going to pay for Stompanato's funeral, and she wanted her alimony, which she had publicly proclaimed was overdue.

He ended the conversation with: "You can go to hell!" He slammed the fone down and went back to his shower.

Later, the redhead came out in a dark, knee-length robe, barefoot. I was across the room by the fireplace. She went into the front bathroom.

In a few minutes the fone rang again. By then I had figured out the telephone problem. A telephone in the bedroom must have been turned off so Redhead would not be disturbed, and of course Mickey, in the shower, could not hear the phone in the entry ringing.

Oh, well, what else can happen?

"Hello."

A gruff male voice said, "Is Mickey there?"

"Sid!" I said.

It was Sid Hughes, the Mirror's dayside police beat reporter. He recognized my voice. "What are you doing there?" I told him Hank Osborne could explain. We said goodbye.

Redhead was still in the bathroom when, a few minutes later, the doorbell rang. Well? It's just like another telephone, answer it. I went to the door. Mistake.

It was an attractive young woman, dressed in a conservative, pale blue skirt-suit, as though ready to go to a business lunch. I recognized her from a picture with Cohen that ran on an inside page in one of the L.A. newspapers in the previous few days. She was wearing the same small, brimless black hat that was in the newspaper photo. I even remembered her name. Reporters who covered Cohen had to pay attention to such things. This was the latest of women with whom Cohen had been photographed since his divorce. Some were referred to as "girlfriend." It was a loose definition that was applied to any woman seen with Cohen, even Liz Renay, a well-known stripper. Like Liz, some others may have been happy with the designation "girlfriend" just for the publicity. This one was classier. She may have thought Mickey was just a businessman who was too polite to have earned his bad reputation and hoped he could bring some attention to whatever she was doing, which was probably legitimate. That would not be uncommon. Some people thought being publicly associated with Mickey was good publicity.

The door was open just enough to see her. I stood where I blocked part of her view of the living room, but behind me she could see the kitchen and, beside it, the bathroom door. Redhead was still there.

The visitor said she'd like to see Mickey, not "Mr. Cohen."

I told her he was busy. She said again that she'd like to see him. She was firm, not giving up easily.

I said she couldn't see him right now. She didn't have an appointment, or would not have asked if she could see him.

She pushed the door. What to do? This wasn't my place, and her relationship with Cohen, if any, was an unknown. Push back or yield? Pushing might become a battle. Was I supposed to keep people out? I yielded, and she walked around me. She asked where he was and I said he was in the shower, I would go get him. "Wait here" was the unspoken message, and she did. I hoped Redhead heard the talking and would stay in the bathroom.

I went back to the shower, which was still running, and told Mickey that Miss so-and-so was in the living room. He swore again and said he'd be out in a minute.

I went back and told her he'd be out. Then I stood by the kitchen door, ready to try to block the nearby bathroom door if it opened. The situation seems now, decades later, like a scene from a Broadway comedy in which a supposedly hilarious continuing joke is keeping people from bumping into each other. I didn't like the play. Fortunately, Redhead stayed in the bathroom.

Cohen arrived, dressed in a white shirt that was hanging out, trousers, shoes and no hat. He apologized, said he was very busy, and he would call her in a day or two. The woman seemed satisfied, thanked him, and he saw her out. Cohen went back to the bedroom.

In another few minutes, Redhead came out of the bathroom and went to the bedroom. A very few minutes later she returned, dressed in slacks and blouse and shoes. She joined me in the kitchen where I was sitting at a small table wondering why this day did not end. Without saying anything, she fixed some toast and jam. She put the plate on the table and asked:

"Do you play gin?"

Sure.

She opened a drawer and took out a deck of cards. Not talking, she shuffled the cards, let me cut, burned one and dealt. Nobody kept score. She was winning. I told her I was a reporter from the Mirror. She didn't comment.

Mickey came in, dressed, and said he had to leave. Obviously signaled, Redhead got up and left the kitchen.

I asked Mickey if he had looked for any Lana letters. He said he hadn't had time. Later? Maybe, he said.

Sister Lil

He said he was going to Lil's. That was his sister's ice cream parlor on San Vicente Boulevard, not far away in the Sawtelle neighborhood. I said I'd meet him there. He didn't comment. So, I went to my car and drove to Lil's. Cohen was not in sight. I called Osborne on a pay phone. He said to hang around.

In a few minutes a reporter and photographer from another newspaper came in.

My sometimes imperfect memory tells me the reporter was Jack Jones from the Times. The Times man did not have an opportunity to talk with Mickey. It was lunch time, though late, and we sat together and ordered from Lil, who was waiting on the tables. None of us knew her, but we knew who she was. She was small, like Mickey, and had more gray than he.

We did not discuss why we were there. I supposed the Timesmen had seen the Mirror with our Lana letters and the words that told the public Mickey had given us permission to run them. The Times City Editor would have called Osborne to find out what we were doing, and decided to send a crew to Lil's. Not to the apartment. I was the only newsman in the apartment that morning.

Mickey had arrived at Lil's first and spent the time in the back end of the store, probably on a pay telephone located there. He came out and greeted us. He said he'd answer questions if he knew the answers, but he knew nothing about Stompanato's death except what was in the papers. I had no questions. I just wanted him to go back to the apartment and look for any spare Lana love letters. I didn't say that in front of the others. Two little old ladies sat at a table next to ours, spooning ice cream. When Mickey went back to his private back room, one of the ladies, a bit excited, asked Lil:

"Was that Mickey Cohen?!!"

"Yes," said Lil. "He's here all the time. He's a very nice man." She did not mention that he was her brother.

Cohen stayed in the back out of sight and did not come out again until after the Times crew finished their lunch and left.

It was getting toward late afternoon, and it had been a long day. I called the office and told Osborne we had struck out so far. Osborne said go on home and he'd see me in the office the next morning, when the Herald would probably run more letters. I talked briefly with Lil and she said she would tell Mickey I had gone home

The next day was the same, call Cohen, ask if I could come out, go there and wait again to see if he would look for letters. Neither of us thought Cohen would provide us with any Lana letters, but I called. Cohen said he had not had time to look for letters, and I could go to his place if I wanted, maybe he would find time. He was dressed when I got there, but disappeared quickly in the back of his apartment.

Mid-morning he came out of the back of his apartment and said he had to go to the store. I asked if he had looked for letters? He said he had not had time. I asked if he wanted me to go to the store with him and carry things. He said okay if I wanted to. I did, though it was becoming obvious he wanted to get rid of me.

We went out of the apartment, and down the stairs. His car was at the curb.

"Don't you have a garage?" I asked. There were a few individual garages in the building.

"I don't need a garage," he said. "The cops are watching all the time. Nobody would dare touch my car."

It was not a bad neighborhood then, on Westgate Avenue, nor was it bad decades later when O. J. Simpson did not kill his ex-wife at her condo blocks from there on Bundy Drive.

Mickey picked up a dozen items at the small neighborhood store, mainly light-to-carry but bulky boxes of Kleenex. I offered to carry the boxes upstairs to the apartment, and he let me help.

End of An Assignment

He disappeared again in the back of his apartment. It may have been half an hour later when he came out and said he had to leave. I asked if he had a chance to look for any letters, or had he given them all to Aggie? His answer was brief. In a sad and gentle tone, showing disappointment, not anger, he said:

"There aren't any more letters. If you had testified for me, I'd have had to give you some of them."

"Okay, thanks," I said. And not another word came from either of us as I went out the door to go back downtown.

Of course, he had been stringing us along, wasting my time, the Mirror's time. He didn't gloat, he didn't tell me to bug off. But the result was the same. I stopped at a pay phone to call Hank Osborne.

Hank was not concerned. The Herald's scoop was not an earthquake. We had copied the letters, or parts of them. In at least one edition, the Mirror said:

"Tender and passionate love letters Lana Turner wrote to John Stompanato were told to the Mirror News by Mickey Cohen."

The Mirror also had acquired some letters which had been written by Stompanato for Lana. They read like high school compositions on love, and he sure did wish Lana was with him. Neither letter writer could compete with Browning. Hers at least sounded real. Time magazine called Stompanato's letters "fourth grader's work, laboriously scratched in a copy book, and many never sent."

The Mirror also had an exclusive on that Wednesday, a color photo on page one of Lana and Johnny in swimwear, on a boat at a Mexican resort. Good for street sales. Someone said the pictures were on a roll of film found by a Mirror photographer in Stompanato's apartment on Sunset Boulevard several blocks east of UCLA and Westwood Village. The photographer went through a suitcase looking for anything that might relate to what had happened. He spotted a roll of Kodachrome film. There was no film sticking out of the cartridge to insert in the camera and crank ahead after each picture was taken. The photog knew that meant the film had been cranked all the way back into the original cartridge. It was exposed! The photog pocketed it. We could not process Kodachrome. It required special equipment. The Mirror paid to rush it through as "urgent" at Kodak's Santa Monica Boulevard processing facility. That facility was well known to camera users. I had sent rolls of Kodachrome film there from all over the country during WWII days in the Army. Years later, Kodak produced a color film that anyone could process almost as easily as black and white.

If the story was true, and he did find the film and filch it, there might have been legal problems using the pictures. If Mickey had been at the apartment first, as one story went, the film may have been there but he likely would not have known that it was exposed.

The titillation time of Lana's love letters was short, but guesswork on the "mystery" of how the Herald got them continued for days – in other news media, not the Mirror News or the Herald Express. It was largely an insider item, trade business for news people. Time Magazine and others gave it a few inches. Time said with typical authoritativeness:

"Aggie Underwood had guessed that the lovers exchanged letters, and something might be found, so she called Cohen to ransack Stompanato's apartment."

Time did not disclose its source of that knowledge. Considering the well-known fact that police tailed Cohen wherever he went, it doesn't make sense that he would enter Stompanato's apartment and take something. On the other hand, Cohen would want to be sure nothing was left by Stompanato that would implicate Cohen in any questionable activities. Stompanato was on Cohen's payroll, working while entertaining Lana. It would be unlikely that Stompanato would fail to mention the letters to his boss. If so, Cohen knew about them all along, probably had them and offered them to Aggie. However, Herald Express Managing Editor Herb Krauch said, "It was definitely not a case of someone dropping them into the editor's lap." He did not explain what that meant. Krauch was quoted praising Aggie for her enterprise. William Randolph Hearst also praised her. That was WRH Junior. The Chief had died in 1951 (See Herald Express chapter)

Krauch wrote in the Greater Los Angeles Press Club annual that the letters stood out among hundreds of Herald scoops over decades: "Agness Underwood, then City Editor, got the letters through a midnight escapade with Mickey Cohen, at that time the city's top gangster."

A Hearst magazine insert for newspapers said Aggie thought there must have been letters, called Mickey and asked him to look.

Stories changed. Early on, Managing Editor Krauch was quoted by Editor and Publisher, the national newspaper business trade journal: "We don't intend to disclose the source." When Cohen was named as the source, by the Mirror, for instance, Krauch said the exclusive was made possible because Mickey had long been an important source for Aggie. That was true, I knew. I had worked for Aggie, and she maintained her contacts.

Editor & Publisher quoted Aggie as saying "I went after them all Sunday." That statement surfaced the day before Mickey was convicted of battery.

Ownership of the letters and the right to publish them was a question, so it would not be smart to admit details. There was a story that the Herald paid Cohen a lot for the letters. Aggie said they were a gift. Editor & Publisher quoted Aggie on that: "They cost me a dime – a phone call." The Herald denied that any of the letters came from members of Stompanato's family.

We did know why the Mirror did *not* get the letters from Cohen. We had his own words on that, but the story was not disclosed publicly until almost a year later in the Times employee newsletter, "Among Our Selves," known as "Among Our Slaves."

The Editor of the TimesMirror company paper asked me to write something about the most interesting story I had covered. My complicated behind-the-scenes background about Otash, the bug, the waiter, Cohen and the letters had not been previously told. The AOS story was just what Cohen said to me, that the Mirror got beat on the Lana letters because we wouldn't help Cohen fight his battery rap by testifying in his trial about the wire recording. In the short AOS story, I concluded that if we had it to do over again we'd make the same decisions, even though it would hurt. That story ran in the March, 1959, issue of AOS.

My friend and USC Journalism School classmate, Times Reporter Jack Jones, rewrote my AOS story briefly, without credit, in his fictionalized story of a reporter's life in those golden days of journalism, "Barker Bites Back." That was in 1996, and by then we had both retired to adjoining communities in San Diego County, Jack in Carlsbad and I in Vista. We rarely saw each other. The last time was a farewell gathering for a colleague, Paul Weeks. Jones was not well then and died relatively early.

In the AOS story, I did not mention the women in Cohen's apartment. I did not want to identify them. It a sign of the prim times we lived in then. The press did not gratuitously tell about "friends" of newsmakers unless it was pertinent, such as in the Turner-Stompanato affair.

There was no firm industry tradition. Spite might have had a role in ignoring tradition. A few years earlier The L.A. Times Editor was involved in a love nest story, which became public with an emergency ambulance call. Only the Examiner ran a story. One might suppose that the Examiner retaliated for stories, or even review of a movie, related to a movie actress friend of the head of the Hearst dynasty. Such gossip was sensitive, I was told by a Hearst family member. The public record of an emergency call did not disclose much. Two other love nesters, from the Times and the Herald, were ignored. I learned about them later, not from any police record.

In the Cohen story, even a gangster was entitled to privacy. Mickey continued to add to the Stompanato story. He said a conspiracy was behind Cheryl Crane's killing Stompanato. No names were offered. He was upset when, he said, no family member offered to bury Stompanato. Mickey paid a mortuary about $500. A photo of his check for that amount was printed in the Examiner.

At the inquest, it was learned that Stompanato had lied to Lana about his age. He was thirty-two, not forty or forty-two. She was thirty-eight. A bigger surprise was the Coroner's report that the autopsy showed Stompanato had a serious kidney problem and might have died before he was forty years of age. However, just five years later kidney transplants became common. Maybe he could have found a donor while still 30+.

Lana died in 1995. Cheryl was still around, appearing occasionally in desert resort publications. The escapades of Mickey Cohen were unreal in a sense, but in those days a Police Chief and an Undersheriff were indicted by a runaway Grand Jury in silly and unrelated cases which were dropped quickly. Anything was possible.

Afterthoughts and Danger

A definition of good journalism would not cover the assignments given me during the Cohen battery trial and the chase for Lana letters. Questions about ethical standards or legalities did not come up at the time, except regarding printing the letters.

Ethics was not the question when I invited myself to Cohen's apartment while he looked for Lana letters. Less than a week had passed since Osborne told Cohen's lawyer I would not testify in the battery trial. Cohen was not going to help us. It was absurd. But, the City Editor had to do something. Osborne was a smart City Editor. We had a man inside, and nobody else did.

Wearing a recorder to interview the waiter was probably not illegal in itself under 1958 laws, but doing it for a defendant's lawyer in a criminal case was sure to bring objections in court. It was possibly outside ethical bounds just to sit in such a meeting without disclosing who I was representing. Refusing to testify was good journalism, but not fully purifying for a reporter or the paper.

The waiter denied to the other press that he said what we at the Mirror had on tape about an offer to settle. Suppose the police learned about the tape and demanded it? Suppose Arthur Black had been threatened with prosecution? It would likely go nowhere. Journalism's rule was not to testify. It wasn't tested, neither was a good relationship with all of the LAPD chiefs from Bill Parker on..

It was foolish to answer Cohen's telephone, and answering the door was unbelievable. I knew the woman's name, but do not remember it. One of the local newspapers had just printed her picture and name. I had also seen a picture and name of a redhead with Cohen. It could have been the same one in his apartment. I did not believe it would have been "right" even to use the names in the company publication.

People in other, non-newspaper communities asked if it was dangerous spending that time with Cohen. It was a collision of newspaper and gangster worlds. Mickey Cohen was suspected of having people killed, and he narrowly escaped death in a few shootings. Was it dangerous to tell him he would get no help from us at the Mirror?

Funny Man Buchwald

Fellow USC student Art Buchwald had been a regular correspondent after he went to Paris with several USC journalism graduates in 1948. He dealt with, or at least wrote in his humor column about, Mafioso, and he grew up in New York where they were real. I wrote to Buchwald in Paris about the sideshow to the waiter-battery trial and the days at Cohen's apartment. He wrote back:

"I hope that I don't read, one of these days, that you've wound up full of lead, compliments of Mr. M.C." He closed that letter with:

"Now don't go getting yourself killed." Always joking.

I showed this chapter to a former FBI agent. He said, "You're lucky to be alive."

It never occurred to me that I was in danger. Even the waiter, Arthur Black, told the press that he was not worried about being harmed by Cohen, and the Villa Capri owner said Black was going to stay in his job.

Not until work began on this story did I try to find out what penalty Cohen paid for his battery conviction. In a long report on the web I found a list of his legal trials and penalties. If I got the right one, his fine in the waiter's battery conviction was $500. That was 1958. Cohen continued his difficult life and we had no association in my future jobs. The Mirror News folded 1961, and I was out of the news business for over two years, then moved to KNXT Ch. 2 in Hollywood in 1964. It was there at KNXT in 1973 that I last saw Cohen, in a wheel chair, going to be interviewed.

JFK and RFK

Journalism 101: Be prepared: When a reporter deals with a President, or a candidate, it may be history.

The guest of honor at the Greater Los Angeles Press Club dinner was the junior Senator from Massachusetts, John F. Kennedy.

It was May first, 1959, and the Press Club was just one stop that the young Senator made on a calendar full of public appearances prior to a formal announcement that he would run for President in1960.

Experts, which meant newspaper columnists based in Washington -- or whomever they interviewed on the subject -- usually gave Kennedy, a Catholic, little chance, but he was interesting anyway because a Catholic was going to try. The not-so-subtle question was whether the Pope would run the White House. What would Kennedy say?

The dinner was a chance to see him in person, and it brought out a crowd of curious press and spouses, public relations executives and politicians to the Ambassador Hotel Ballroom. It was not an unusually large crowd for a Press Club event, but the fact that 700 hundred people, the number given in the club newsletter, showed up a continent away from his home made it important, at least to his goal of building a favorable national image. The impression he left would depend upon his performance before people who were accustomed to real stars, as in Hollywood, not Cape Cod personalities and politicians.

Chairman/Toastmaster, Joseph M. Quinn, of the Los Angeles United Press International bureau, called to talk about the program. It was not going to be a platform for Kennedy to deliver a political speech and charm the voters.

Quinn said it was going to be a "press conference." The audience would participate. They would write questions on cards. Monitors would pick them up and deliver them to the podium.

He said Bill Stout and I would screen the cards and select the questions to ask.

Stout and I would share the lectern with Senator Kennedy and take turns reading the questions. Whoever asked the question would step away from the mike and, while Kennedy was answering, Bill and I would huddle to pick the next question.

Stout was a popular reporter on CBS-owned KNXT Channel Two, and I was with the Mirror-News, which was owned by the Times, and I had moved from covering Mickey Cohen to running the editorial page. Quinn did not explain how we were picked to play the interviewer role. Joe and I had worked together at United Press for a few years, starting in 1948.

The format was an obvious choice to control self promoters, which we did have in the Club. These hangers-on, none regarded as important in Los Angeles news coverage, tried to attract attention to themselves at Press Club dinners. A "question" might began with a sentence or two explaining how important the interrogator was. Or the questioner could, and often did, make a speech instead of asking something. The press conference format would also keep the questions to a single subject, so that the Senator would be encouraged to speak to that and not drift into something his pre-campaign staff would prefer that he talk about.

The dinner was a typical Press Club affair. Most of the people knew each other. The martinis and chatter were pleasant and table hopping was the rule. JFK was not a big national star yet. He was pleasant, but barely so, I thought. He was a busy, serious man on a mission, and he seemed to me to be impatient and somewhat condescending. That didn't matter.

Reporters become accustomed to dealing with personages who are "more than equals," such as some movie stars, high-level bureaucrats and visiting dignitaries who view members of the press, as someone said, "tradesmen to be tolerated."

The reaction of people meeting reporters usually depends upon the non-journalist. Those who worked with us, publicists and politicians, were fairly pleasant and predictable. People who are strangers to the business are usually surprised. I met a young (thirty?) woman who said: "You're a reporter? Say something clever." I told her it didn't go with the job.

The questioning process with the Senator moved smoothly, and he was affable until I asked a question about his book, "Profiles in Courage." The question was: Did JFK really write the book that carried his name as the author? It had been written on a card, and was selected by Stout and me as one which ought to be asked. We didn't discuss why. My thought was that, although I had not heard an authorship question, if there was a question then JFK would want to answer it. The name on the card was that of a newsman whose name I gave after JFK's response.

JFK was theatrically angry, scornful. He could have brushed it off, but was snappish as he pointed his clenched jaw at someone, unnamed, on the East Coast whom he accused of starting a rumor that he hadn't written the book.

NOTE: When Kennedy's friend and speechwriter, Ted Sorenson, died in 2010, the New York Times obituary said Sorenson acknowledged he had drafted most of the chapters and was paid for his work.

JFK's mother, Rose Kennedy, sat at a table front and center, her chair closest to the lectern. She was enthusiastic at proper times, applauding her son. When it ended, Kennedy hurried off to his other activities.

As we rose from our seats, the press at the head table did a quick reading on how it went. It was a good Press Club affair, we agreed, but did nothing special to help or dismiss the Senator as a Presidential candidate. He was just another speaker. Joe Quinn thought big. A few years later Richard Nixon, no longer Vice President, was invited to a heavyweight welcome home Press Club dinner at the Beverly Hilton. That was Quinn's event.

My wife, Ann, was among those at the JFK head table with the speakers and Press Club officers, and the Nixon dinner. She was never impressed by people "of importance." If they were friendly, she chatted and traded experiences with any of them. When she met JFK, it was hello, how are you, nice to meet you, thank you. He was in a hurry. I asked later what she thought of him. He was in a hurry, she said.

The Candidate in L.A.

That was the only time I saw JFK. He was back in Los Angeles the following year, 1960, for the Democratic convention. It requires a team to cover such an event. Reporters were assigned to contestants or the delegates. Years later the public heard rumors that the late JFK had slipped away to meet with Marilyn Monroe. If it was common talk then, I didn't hear it.

A reporter from the Mirror News, Carter Barber, tracked me down at the Biltmore Hotel convention headquarters one afternoon. There was a rumor that the Teamsters Union was going to back Nixon. The timing of this news was suspected of being an effort by to derail Kennedy's nomination. Labor was supposed to be in the Democrats' pocket. Walter Reuther, President of the United Auto Workers, was a liberal, trying to hold onto Big Labor's political power in Washington. His devotion to JFK was unquestioned. The Teamsters were atttempting to become the dominating Big Labor power. They could control a lot of disguised labor union money and use it to support more business-oriented (truckers) causes and candidates.

Reuther was lodged at the Statler Hotel nearby, but Barber said the Mirror News City Desk hadn't been able to find anyone who could confirm or deny the Teamsters rumor. He was sent to ask me, since I had written a daily column on labor unions. Were any Teamster sources handy? Could we find Pierre Salinger, Kennedy's press spokesman, and a former newsman? He was "not returning calls."

We stopped first at Salinger's office in the Biltmore, a small, crowded, cheery room with windows enough to make it light and warm on that summer afternoon. No formalities. Just walk in. Pierre was sitting at his desk, no coat, white shirt, relaxed behind a pile of paper. He had to know the answer to the big Teamster question. However, he told us he couldn't verify the rumor, and if it were true, the news would be released by the Teamsters. Ask them.

The rest was out of some New York saloon columnist's book. I told Barber to follow me and we'd talk to the Teamster's political spokesman in person. We left the front door of the Biltmore on Olive, turned right and went south, crossed Sixth Street and kept going on the West side of Olive. Far down the next block, we entered Cook's restaurant. It was a popular place for downtown businessmen. But we weren't there to eat, nor to drink at the bar, which ran along the right wall from the entrance. We went past the bar and along an empty corridor that was paneled in dark wood like a large law firm's offices. The wood panels went on for about 60 feet in a dimly lit hallway that seemed to go nowhere except to a large back door with afternoon sunlight leaking through cracks around it. Push a cross bar and the door would open to an alley.

Maybe thirty feet short of the door was an opening on the right. The dark paneling led right, then left, a zig-zag that suddenly opened into a room about 50 feet square. There were no windows in this cave. Against the far wall was a small bar, with a bartender behind it. There were tables along the left wall, seating a few customers.

In the middle of the room were two or three tables. At one table, alone, sat a gray-haired man in a gray suit with a glass on the table in front of him. He looked tired, a veteran of many wars, occupying his usual command post. Anyone who wanted political talk from Teamsters Joint Council 42 could check Cook's Back Bar in the afternoon, and he would be at that table. I had seen him there before, more than once, and knew his "office" hours. I told Barber that this was the man he wanted and introduced them.

Barber asked about the rumor of Teamsters endorsing Nixon. The man said yes it was true.

Well! Carter had to get a pay phone. There was one in a corner, near where we came in. I sat down, declined a drink, and waited for Barber. He came back and said the Mirror's City Desk told him that the formal announcement had been made about 10 minutes earlier, which was about the time we left Salinger's office. By now it was old news.

Cook's Back Bar was an institution, a hideaway that most people in Los Angeles didn't know existed, even those who dined in the popular restaurant up front. The Back Bar was not a regular place to eat. It was an unpublic place, open to anyone to drink, or deal. The nearby exit to an alley was probably a business asset.

Power Places

Clifton's Cafeteria across the street was well known as a political "must," but Cook's quietly moved into the power base after the War. The Los Angeles Athletic Club, a block or two away, also had a power base of prominent members. Jonathan Club a couple of blocks west had the money crowd, except for those who ran everything and belonged to the nearby California Club. I met Otis Chandler at the California Club after he had become Publisher of the L.A. Times. I was entering the California Club through the kitchen via a back door. Otis was taking the same route to go out. I told him it was my shortcut to avoid walking around the building to the main entrance. Otis said he parked his sports car in the back with the employees to avoid the cowboys who would pick up his car at the front entrance and take it to the basement garage. Otis loved his cars.

The Democrats' convention was a giant mixture of delegates dragged into formal meetings in the Sports Arena south of downtown, close to the Coliseum and the University of Southern California campus. The television audience could see the action better than anyone inside the new Arena.

The major difference in actually being there was that the visitor or participant could feel the crowd, the noise, the confusion and the inescapable boredom of speeches, huddles, mini-conferences and repetitive guessing about what the key players were doing at the Biltmore or Statler.

Reporters could go anywhere, if they had the right kind of pass. Few passes were given out to the prized "front row," which was on a kind of mezzanine, a temporary floor built to the side and slightly below the platform that contained, at various times, all of the speakers, their entourages, and assorted honored guests. When the time came, JFK would be a few yards away from the press.

Those who occupied the somewhat exclusive press section looked across the room at a balcony. The front rail of the balcony seemed higher than the press mezzanine, but beneath them all was the delegates' floor. On the balcony rail, which went around that part of the floor, were draped banners carrying the names of would-be Democratic Party Presidential candidates. The balcony was packed with partisan noise makers. One who stood out, yelling, waving, leaning over to flap the banner hanging from the rail, was a former classmate at USC's School of Journalism, Russ Burton. The name on the banner he shook to life was Adlai Stevenson.

Was it going to be electrifying to see JFK, the probable winner, on that speaker's platform a few feet away? Would he show? It had been a long day, it was late, the program was dragging on without any end in sight. I had to take a bus back to the Mirror News to get my car and drive home to San Fernando Valley, and return to the Mirror News the next day.

History would be made regardless of my presence, and the rest of the team was there to cover Kennedy. Most of them had not met JFK. I had. So, I called the office and left for home.

Endorsing Nixon

My last post on the Mirror News was Chief (and only) Editorial Writer. As the November, 1960 election neared, I had not yet brought up the subject of the Presidential election at the morning Editorial Board meetings, a small group of five or six Mirror editors whose daily work involved local and state government more than national affairs. The matter of an endorsement was settled soon in an unexpected way.

The Mirror News' Publisher, Arthur Laro, was quiet and thoughtful, a soft-spoken gentleman who was brought from the Houston Post to see if he could turn around the twelve-year-old money-losing newspaper, one of four dailies in Los Angeles. Earlier, in our private talks, he had told me of getting a call in Houston from a head-hunting outfit. He was asked if he'd be interested in another position. He said it would depend. He was then asked if there was any place he would NOT want to move to, and he said he answered, "I don't think I'd want to move to Tulsa." And so he came to Los Angeles.

We didn't talk about it, but I presumed Nixon would be the candidate the Mirror News endorsed on the editorial page. The Times endorsed Nixon. The Mirror News was absolutely independent of the Times on editorial policy. Still, I could not be sure. We would decide soon at an Editorial Board meeting. I had to propose something. Before that happened, Arthur stopped at my desk late one morning and said, "I guess we might as well do an endorsement of Nixon tomorrow." I asked if he had any special comments, and he said no, so I wrote one, he approved, and it was published. That was the only time in my brief remaining time on the moribund Mirror that the Board was bypassed.

A barely remembered event occurred later which was a big surprise. I believe that on the morning of election day the Mirror contained an editorial on Page One by Norman Chandler, our owner at the Times Mirror Corporation. Norman blistered Kennedy and his Rat Pack friends in Hollywood and Las Vegas. Norman supported Nixon. I knew nothing about it until the paper arrived from the press room.

Did I like Nixon? Not especially. I had only met him twice briefly before that election. Did I prefer him over Kennedy? Yes. Why? I don't remember. My editorial might explain.

It should have.

When President JFK was shot in Dallas in 1963, I was temporarily out of journalism. The Mirror had closed early in 1962. In the days of mourning afterward, I heard that a recording of the 1959 Press Club program with JFK was broadcast more than once on the Los Angeles public broadcast radio station. I never heard it. Maybe it is in a presidential library.

In 1963 I joined the world in watching the Dallas story of JFK on television. In 1968 I stayed late at my KNXT office to watch the California primary electon returns and saw the RFK story break.

In my memories, each man was an Ambassador event: JFK in 1959 and RFK in 1968 -- the same hotel and the same ballroom. I never met Robert F. Kennedy, and saw him only once in person, at a meeting in Arlington, VA, in 1967 where he was one of several speakers.

JFK's assassin was alone, hiding in a Dallas office building, but fled and was caught later, then was assassinated. RFK's assassin, Sirhan Sirhan, was grabbed by witnesses at the Ambassador. An RFK worker, one of whom was my USC journalism classmate, Jesse Unruh, was with RFK and saw it happen. RFK's killer wanted a show-case trial (see Sirhan). That trial would pull several of us into television courtroom history.

ELIZABETH TAYLOR'S FIRST (SECRET) DIVORCE HEARING
Journalism 101: The Dean of the beat knows all

In the 1940s, Reno was known as the divorce capitol of the nation. The competition, Las Vegas, was a small town surrounded by barren desert and remained that way, frozen by World War II. After 1945, it became a neon "strip" that offered the Hollywood crowd a place to go for easy divorces without parading a lot of messy personal stuff in public. It was much closer than Reno.

The rest of the nation slowly joined the Nevada drift toward "Women's Rights." California law accepted "cruelty" as a valid reason for divorce. Then California said "Mental" cruelty was enough. Nevada lost some of its special advantage. However, California still required a judicial proceeding to establish "mental" cruelty, which had many definitions.

Courthouse junkies in Los Angeles knew where to look for entertainment in divorce court. A book on a counter in the County Clerk's office listed the parties in a lawsuit, plus pre-trial motions, notice of hearings and, finally, the trial date and place. Movie stars' private woes remained on display in California's open courts until "mutual consent" became the divorce law.

Elizabeth Taylor was a surprise entry in this emotion parade. She was a stunning Hollywood beauty who first turned the world's head when she was eleven years old. She married handsome Nicky Hilton just after her 18th birthday. They honeymooned in Europe for three months, the happily-forever marriage of a movie princess and a hotel heir. Who could believe that "mental cruelty" would cause her to file for divorce before her 19th birthday? The world would know soon. Her day in court could be interesting.

Oh my, she was beautiful. Her smile could have brightened any sunrise. Instead, on this day, her brooding eyes focused on a distant world that was invisible to the rest of us.

She went meekly where she was directed, taking a seat on a straight-backed chair that was thinly upholstered for minimum comfort. It was a business meeting, and she was dressed for it in a blue-gray suit and a somber expression.

The court clerk directed traffic to assigned chairs. Lawyers, two for her, one for him, were up front with the court reporter.

A few newspaper reporters and one wire service reporter from United Press were in a single row of seats. Those seats were filled.

A photographer took pictures of Taylor walking in, then he stayed in the background. A bailiff stood by the door.

Counsel for the parties identified themselves to the judge, the witness was sworn, and questions began. Elizabeth remained seated. She confirmed her name and said that she was married to Hilton the previous May, less than eight months ago (it now being January, 1951.)

Was it a happy marriage?

No.

Why was the marriage unhappy?

She raised a handkerchief to her face to absorb tears. It was the first real emotion she had displayed. She looked at the floor, silently. Everyone waited. The lawyer measured her readiness and finally prompted her:

Was he cruel?

She raised her head. "Yes."

How?

He was "indifferent," she said, hesitantly, and he "used abusive language." A lawyer had probably planted those words in her mind sometime earlier, helping define the problem concisely before she told the story in court.

That was not enough explanation to establish mental cruelty, but Elizabeth said nothing more. She lowered her head, the white hanky catching tears.

Gently. the lawyer repeated repeated the question. Indifferent? Abusive language? Could she give examples?

She looked at the lawyer, tears on her cheeks, then gazed at the floor again.

The lawyers looked at each other and at the judge. The unspoken question was what to do now? Call a recess? They had barely started. Liz would have to speak because by law more details were needed. Mental cruelty was sufficient reason for divorce, and was broadly interpreted, but she had to be say something specific.

They tried again. Her voice was barely audible. The court reporter, a few feet away, said she couldn't hear a word. The judge encouraged Elizabeth, like a friend. He suggested that she pretend his court reporter was hard of hearing.

That didn't help. She said nothing and continued to look at the carpet.

It was not a case of stage fright. There was no one from the public there, except a few reporters and a photographer, to share the painful, private memories of this gorgeous young woman.

Elizabeth Taylor fans might have swooned and cried with her. They would have wanted to be with her, had they had known. However, the date and place for this event had not been publicized. The facts were there in the record available to anyone, but.... There was no "audience." Just a few reporters.

The trial was not held in a courtroom, not in the usual sense. This Hollywood news story took place in a judge's chambers, his office, not in the adjoining courtroom over which he normally presided. Technically, this was the courtroom. A judge could even move his courtroom outside to a public street corner in the course of seeking information. Today his office was in use briefly for a "Short Cause" hearing, and the proceedings were being recorded.

It was an unimposing room, maybe thirty feet square, with a desk and chairs, a few extra chairs this day for the anticipated press. A large window admitted sunlight into a hallway outside the open door. There was no public traffic in that hallway. Judge Thurmond Clarke's desk was "the bench" today. A chair near his desk was for the witness. There was no place in the room for the public if any showed.

Was Elizabeth Taylor Hilton getting favored treatment? No, not in a legal interpretation. Her lawyers were able to reduce the possibility of a spectacle, a public trial. Privacy for Liz was arranged in advance, by the court's own rules. The lawyers simply told the court, in a formal *public* record, that the divorce was not contested, but there could be a minor point of difference that might be settled in a few minutes before the judge in a "Short Cause" hearing. Who would notice the request for such a hearing in the pile of motions received in the County Clerk's office and recorded by hand in a book which the public could examine?

Following Rudy

A person not trained in the minor details of courtroom proceedings would logically presume that a Short Cause discussion would take place in the courtroom, with a lawyer standing at the counsel table, and that it would not be a hearing at which the star would testify. Not even reporters

(I was one) who covered the beat and saw the public record caught the meaning.

The lawyers who represented Elizabeth Taylor and Nicky Hilton probably asked Judge Thurmond Clarke to help them keep it a low-decibel affair. There was no legal or ethical reason to refuse such a request, if no rules were broken, but Judge Clarke knew he could not elude the press. The Times reporter would find the Short Cause notice and ask about it, and maybe he did.

An arrangement was made, obviously. On the morning of the Short Cause hearing, the Times man, Rudy Villasenor, told the other reporters on the courthouse beat about the hearing and that Miss Taylor would be there.

He said that if we wished to cover the event we should stand by. Shortly before the principals arrived, the reporters would be told it was time to assemble in Judge Clarke's chambers. The reporters and a photographer would go in together. They were also told by the Times man that it would be helpful if the reporters did not find it necessary to mention where the hearing took place. It was enough to say, "in court."

Reporters on nearly every beat with a press room located in a public building in downtown Los Angeles operated as a "syndicate." There were no "scoops." They shared. It was mutual protection approved by City Editors who knew that on some days there could be more than one story on a beat at one time, and cooperation among the reporters made more sense than sending second reporters from several newspaper City Rooms to help. Another advantage was that reporters who would be absent while seeking medical care or creating hangovers could be protected. A reporter for one paper would call another paper's city desk with a story. A rewrite man would write the story.

The syndicate was at work today. In this case, the Herald Express reporter, a rare loner who didn't work with the syndicate, was informed.

He could not be "in court" that morning, but his paper would be given the story.

None of them anticipated Liz Taylor's inability to talk. The lawyers had told the judge that both sides agreed to terms of the divorce. There would be only a brief explanation, or something. In effect it was all over except for Liz's description of "cruelty." Thinking about it "in court" made her cry.

There was some soft bantering between the lawyers and the judge. Suppose a lawyer posed a question. Liz could agree, or not, with a minimum of words, if any. A nod would do. The lawyer would say to her, "If you could say it, Miss Taylor, would you state that Mr. Hilton was very critical?" And she would say yes, or else the record could show that she nodded. In other circumstances, this could be called "leading the witness," meaning tell her what to say, but Hilton's lawyers would not object. The judge accepted this compromise.

It worked well. The mood even became a bit light as the testimony in the form of questions and nods went on. Liz, never smiling, "testified" that Nicky was critical and had left her alone frequently to go partying, even on their honeymoon. Her tears emphasized that this was cruel.

A Helpful Judge and Neighbor

In a few minutes the divorce was granted. Elizabeth and the lawyers departed, and the reporters went back to their press room to write or call in the story. The United Press story, a few paragraphs written by someone I telephoned at the UP bureau a dozen blocks away, was not printed by the Los Angeles newspapers, who had their own reporters, but it was in the New York Times, for instance, with the (UP) dateline. The Associated Press was not there, but they could use the Times story.

Newspaper readers anywhere may have seen references to an "audience," or a "courtroom," but readers did not know about the judge's chambers, nor that the audience was only a few reporters. Liz's testimony, accurately described including tears and nods, was the story, as it would have been in any location.

Another factor in the matter of Elizabeth Taylor v. Hilton was the trust that developed between reporters and judges. This worked with most judges or prosecutors, and many lawyers. Confidences were protected. The Times man may have learned about the "Short Cause" plan from the judge. The words "courtroom" and "audience" were in the news reports, but there was no other description. The reporters did not include how the trial was, in effect, kept secret from strays who might have wandered into the regular courtroom if the trial were held there.

Judge Clarke (we in news called him "Thurmond") was handsome, trim, with an easy smile. He was experienced. A celebrity case was not new to him, and he was friendly with the press. He had been well educated in how to deal with news people. His "instructor" was Rudy Villasenor, a jovial, short and solidly built gentleman from the Los Angeles Times who covered Superior Courts civil courts for three decades. Rudy knew the law. What would have happened if a member of the public learned of the hearing and looked for it in the courtroom? I can only guess, but surely the citizen would have been directed to the judge's chambers and admitted without question. trial. He'd need a chair.

Why was the Times given this liaison duty today? Rudy sometimes rode to work with his Pasadena neighbor, Thurmond Clarke, whose "office" was about a block from the Times.

Judy

It was much different with Judy Garland a few weeks later in another building.

She arrived to find a group of reporters and photographers waiting in a courtroom, plus a few curious public outside the rail. The press crowded around. They asked Judy to sit in the witness box and pose for pictures, which she did while chatting amiably with them. She didn't talk about what went wrong with her marriage to Vincent Minnelli. That would come out in a few minutes, after the judge signaled the clerk with a buzzer that it was time to proceed. She wasn't asked about her stressful life, which led to a suicide attempt the previous year.

Until the judge was ready, it was gab time with energetic Judy, who, like Elizabeth Taylor, had become part of Hollywood as a young girl. Judy was also nearly ten years older than Liz, and it was her second divorce. Experience helps.

Taylor Times

I never saw Elizabeth Taylor again, but Hollywood is a small town and trails do cross at unexpected times. She married Michael Wilding, an actor, and after two children divorced him and immediately married Mike Todd, a colorful character in show business on two coasts who made his greatest fame as producer of the movie, "Around the World in Eighty Days." Prior to that, Todd was involved with another Hollywood beauty, Evelyn Keyes.

In 1957, six years after the Hilton divorce, a newspaper friend of Hank Osborne, my City Editor, wanted to find out what the discarded ex-husband, Wilding, thought about Miss Taylor's marriage to Todd. This was routine Hollywood/New York journalism. Her ex-husband might pop off.

Wilding had not been easy to find. He did not answer calls relayed by his agent or friends. Then he walked in, an unexpected visitor to the front yard of Marie McDonald's home at 17031 Magnolia Avenue, in Encino. The actress had been kidnapped out of that house the night before. Reporters and photographers stood in the driveway all day, waiting to learn more from police, or anyone. Wilding told the group that Marie was a friend, and he thought he might find out more by going to her house than he had learned from newspapers or radio reports.

After a few minutes I was able to talk to him alone and tell him why I had been trying to reach him. Wilding said he thought the Taylor-Todd marriage was going to be happy.   It was a throw-away line that followed the surprise wedding of Taylor and Todd. Wilding was not going to say anything bitter.

Todd's personal press agent, Bill Doll, whom I also interviewed, mentioned that his wife-to-be had survived an airliner crash in the Chatsworth Hills, at the West end of San Fernando Valley, in 1949. It was remarkable because about half the three-dozen passengers in the DC-3 lived.   Five months after that conversation with Doll, his client Mike Todd died in a plane crash in New Mexico in March, 1958. Taylor was a widow.

The closest I ever got to to Taylor again was a hillside nightclub in Puerto Vallarta. She and two-time husband Richard Burton had used the place as a movie set. They were not around.

Rudy Chased the News Whenever

While doing their jobs of informing the public, reporters often have easy access to people and information that the public can't get reach or see as effortlessly. Every day Rudy Villasenor went behind the counter of the County Clerk's office and examined all of the original papers filed by lawyers in civil cases, so he would not miss developments in cases he was following. Any member of the public could go to the counter and request the same papers on specific cases. The difference was that Rudy might be busy all day and still have to check for new filings before he went home. He had a key to get into the County Clerk's office after hours.

In the year or so I worked the downtown beat for United Press I joined Rudy many evenings after five o'clock when he made a final check of the filings. We skimmed all of the new, blue-paper-bound motions, complaints, pleadings, demands and briefs on cases old and new. It became easy to decide in seconds whether a paper had any relevance for our readers.

Not all court records were available that easily. Courtrooms were in numerous places around the County. There was duplication. Los Angeles County covered more than 4000 square miles, and the citizens, with lawyers, needed local facilities. Downtown had a Hall of Records which also housed the County Board of Supervisors and some courtrooms. Criminal Courts were in a separate Hall of Justice. Federal crimes were tried in Federal Courts, a block north of City Hall. Even City Hall had a few State courtrooms. New Courthouses were built to keep up with the increase in population and court business. The machinery of news gathering was busy and complex, but it also had its personal elements, just like any job, and reporters were a valuable public resource which the digital age has not replaced.

Bleeding for Up

During World War II, the United Press was one of the most exciting "places" a journalist could work. UP Correspondents went everywhere that American soldiers were fighting.

I was in the Army Air Corps, in WWII, trying to join the Aviation Cadet program. At the Air Corps center in Miami Beach, after a few days of written and physical tests (coordination, balance, reflexes) I qualified. I was sent to Smyrna, TN, to await – something. Weeks later a few of us were moved to the University of Tennessee in Knoxville. I met another cadet candidate on a truck going from the train to the campus. He had worked in the headquarters office at Smyrna, and he remembered my name. He said I was one of only two men from Miami Beach, out of 2000, who had perfect scores (Stanine 9s) for pilot, bombardier and navigator. Like the others who went to UT, I was on hold, waiting to join a cadet class. We took classes in English, public speaking, science, and ten hours dual flight training. I also met a beautiful senior with a little bit of a southern accent.

Finding a Career

After UT, the wait to become a real cadet continued at one base after another for a year, mostly in clerical jobs. I listened to the radio day and night, following the war in Europe. I had planned to study chemical engineering, but the reports from war zones convinced me that I should be a foreign correspondent. I know my decision to go to the University of Southern California was the result of listening to USC-UCLA football games when I was in high school. The two ideas came together in December, 1945, when I was discharged in Alabama and took my first classes in the USC School of Journalism on January 2, 1946. On February 2, 1946, I married that wise and lovely girl I had seen graduate magna cum laude from UT in 1944.

Journalism School was good training for newspaper reporting. Wire services were mentioned only as something that a newspaper could buy for coverage of national and foreign news. We were not encouraged to aspire. A weekly paper was the goal. We were taught nothing about being a foreign correspondent. With a journalism degree in June, 1948, I started grad school in International Relations during the summer and stayed there in the fall. Professor Ross Berkes led me toward a future in the State Department.

Ann and I had no telephone. A postal card arrived from Elizabeth (Ted) Jones, of the USC faculty. United Press was looking for a reporter.

If I was interested, I should call Bill Payette, the Los Angeles Bureau Manager. He hired me in October, 1948. I quit grad school.

United Press, I learned quickly, was a big family of talented colleagues writing stories to file on teletype wires, local and cross-country, or the world. UP people were in constant personal contact, known to each other from their daily bylines, messages on the wires and telephone calls. A reporter in Sacramento might receive a message on a news wire or a telephone call requesting a story about a piece of legislation which was of interest to a client newspaper in San Diego. News wires to New York were always spewing out stories, printed on rolls of yellow teletype paper, interrupted occasionally by messages.

New York might want a story from Los Angeles. The story would be written and "punched" on a paper transmission tape, ready to go. A telephone call or, usually, a message on the wire would notify Los Angeles that it was time to send the story. Push a button and the waiting tape would transmit a story to New York and clients.

If nothing happened, someone in N.Y. might press a key to ring a bell in L.A., reminding that it was time to push that "send" button.

If L.A. still did nothing, the New York operator could punch his upper and lower-case teletype keys rapidly. That made the entire cluster of teletype keys on a machine in Los Angeles jump up and down, Bangity Bang! That was a noisy, physical contact, not just a voice or bells.

There were large bureaus in New York and Washington. Unipressers also moved to bureaus all over the world. We became comrades when we competed with the Associated Press, which was a wire service created by newspapers. Members of AP shared their news only among themselves, but an AP newspaper could buy UP and have both services. It was a joyful moment when UP beat the AP on a major story. Editors most often used whichever wire service story arrived first on the teletypes. Winning the play was good for renewal contracts. Other competitors such as Reuters or International

News Service (INS) didn't count for much. UP took over INS and became UPI in 1958.

Working for Fun and Little More

UP was a great place to work except where it counted, making a living. UP reporters worked in an atmosphere of cheapness, chiseling, squeezing and denial. Expenses were slashed or denied. Overtime often was not approved if there was a way to deny it. UP also hired young and cheap beginners like me, then let them sink or swim.

Employees constantly complained about "Downholding." That was "cablese," a combination of words, used with a limit on the number of letters per word, developed to use fewer words when correspondents sent their stories by expensive cable at so much a word, to a bureau from which a story could be transmitted on a UP wire to a client. I never learned much cablese because I didn't go to a foreign country for UP. A correspondent "Unipresser" might have to "uppick" a story or "downhold" expenses. They may have put up with "downholding" in order to keep a fascinating job. Adrenaline is addictive. Old Downholders continue to use cablese when communicating with each other.

I got my first lesson on this stingy company's policy when, after three years, I was promoted to Bureau Manager in Phoenix. About two months later a DC-3 crashed in the mountains east of Phoenix. Aboard were the crew and nineteen cadets. We outran AP by being well ahead on the search for wreckage. I talked to a witness by calling him down in a mine. He had heard the plane before going to work. There were three of us in the bureau, competing with eight in the AP bureau, and the AP also had access to all the output of the Phoenix newspapers. I called in one of my two guys that night to work overnight, so I could get a little sleep and come in very early.

Any good feeling about our performance was scuttled a few days later when I got a call from Fred Green, an executive in the San Francisco regional headquarters, and he told me I should not be putting in for overtime for the guy who worked all night. I told him we had routine work to do, only three of us to do that plus cover the crash, and someone was needed to staff the bureau that night. Green said: "That's what you are there for." Managers worked all hours.

Decades later, UPI died despite brave restarts with questionable "fronts." Only the name survives, barely and with no real news organization. Alumni of the organization have a lively international organization, the Downhold Club, a reminder of the company's stinginess. The DH Club is connected by a members-only email system, hosted for years through Google. About 400 Downholders are in daily contact, from Seattle to Shanghai, Anchorage to New York to OZ. When big stories break anywhere, Downholders have personal experiences and insights to share. That makes it a fascinating read every day. They were important in news coverage around the world, and tried to make UP the best.

When I started at UP, Payette, the L. A. bureau manager, put me to work writing radio wire copy, and gave me a book on "how to write radio." I took carbon copies of stories that were written in newspaper style and converted them. Radio is conversational. Informal. The way people really talk. That kind of writing is used throughout this book. Don't worry about complete sentences. Long sentences might run the radio announcer out of breath.

A newspaper story might say:

"Millionaire playboy-pilot Howard Hughes bought the historic Paramount Studios lot in Hollywood today because Hughes said he wants his own place to make his own movies instead of renting the offices and sound stages his company has been using at Paramount for years."

A radio wire story might start out:

"A big day at Paramount Studios. Howard Hughes bought it to make his own movies."

UP sent local stories to scores of radio stations all over Southern California. Newscasters could take the UP copy off a teletype machine and read it. I heard them on my car radio reading stories just as I wrote them. It's helpful, hearing copy read. New York radio produced full fifteen-minute news scripts, known as "Rip and Read." Rip it off the teletype, fill in the blanks such as the station call letters and the announcer's name, then read.

The floor plan of the United Press Bureau in L.A. provided some extra chances to learn about reporters and newsmakers. UP occupied an area about 1500 square feet on the third floor of the Daily News building at Pico Boulevard and Los Angeles Street. Desks and typewriters and at least four noisy teletype machines occupied the center. Around the perimeter were private offices for the bureau manager, business manager and the Acme Photos office. Acme soon became a formal part of UP. A walk-through at one side of our room led to the Daily News City Room. We used it constantly to pick up carbon copies of stories written by Daily News reporters. We could ask their reporters in person when we needed more information. Along that same side of the room were offices of the Daily News Real Estate Editor and the Religion Editor. We saw well known newsmakers and their press agents going to both.

In another part of the UP area were desks for the Hollywood specialists. United Press had three reporters who worked full time on Hollywood. Virginia MacPherson wrote a day wire column, Aline Mosby wrote a night wire column (for tomorrow's paper), and Hal Swisher wrote a Hollywood column for the radio wire. These columns were sent by wire to New York, then to clients around the world.

A separate Hollywood operation was run by Henry Gris, who worked with foreign clients and local members of the Hollywood foreign press corps. Henry and a helper sent special mail packets to clients. It was a small operation, but it was a birthplace of the Foreign Press Awards which became the Golden Globes. Eventually the Globes gained some acceptance. Any publicity that reaches trade papers and potential ticket buyers is good publicity. Some American papers had their own correpondents/ columnists. I did part-time work for some of those publications while at the L.A.Mirror. I got a call from one which I didn't recognize, a supermarket scandal rag, and for them I called Clark Gable's widow. She softly declined to be interviewed. Later I realized why. Assignments for New York or London papers, which I did, got a better reception from stars.

After a year writing radio at UP I was moved downtown to the District Attorney's press room to cover the Civic Center. That included all the beats in several Civic Center buildings, such as City Hall and the County Board of Supervisors, Federal courts and IRS, State civil and criminal courts, Los Angeles police, the Sheriff, County Jail and the Coroner. The Coroner had his own jury room, morgue and a viewing room to identify dead victims of accidents or crimes. Victims entered the building through a ground-floor hearse reception area equipped with hose, slabs and drains to clean up blood. A Coroner's Jury sometimes was convened to find, formally, if a death was accidental, a homicide, or uncertain. The District Attorney could accept the verdict or take action, including refer the case to a Grand Jury. A few top floors of the Hall of Justice were occupied by hundreds of County Jail prisoners. The jail had its own elevator to deliver prisoners to courtrooms. I used that elevator to interview prisoners in jail or get a haircut by a prisoner working for extra change. No razors were used, although all of the prisoner-barbers were innocent and said they did not belong there.

For stories on those beats, the Associated Press usually relied on its member newspapers, but they were friendly competitors on many stories. A UP reporter on the scene could move something fast to our wires without waiting for the Daily News desk and reporters to produce copy. Downtown was a place to learn beats by following veteran reporters. The names of prosecutors, read about so often, came to life, just like judges and jailers. Also, the Mayor and Council and Supervisors. The name of a journalism professor on the Arraignment Calendar in criminal court was investigated. A transcript of his preliminary hearing was found and read. It went no further.

Shortly after the Korean War began in the summer of 1950, I was moved off the Civic Center beat and back to the bureau. On July fourth, I was told to go to Riverside on a story. I knew what it was. My younger brother, Ernest, who joined the Air Corps after I did during WWII and went straight into a cadet class in California, was a B-29 bombardier in the Twenty-Second Bomb Group. He was going to Korea. Newspapers and newsreel companies sent reporters and cameramen to March Field in Riverside County to cover the Group's departure.

I went there for UP, and steered the other newsmen to Ernest's crew who were loading personal luggage into their B-29. No other crew received as much attention. About forty-five years later, I was surprised to find out, during casual conversation, that a sometimes golf partner in Vista, CA, a neighbor whom I had known for the last 20 years, was in the same bomb group. He remembered my brother and others.

UP's Los Angeles business manager, Joseph M. Quinn, who sold United Press services around Southern California and Arizona, was sent to Korea as a correspondent when the war started. He was a veteran reporter from Buffalo, N.Y. and had been a tank commander in World War II in the Pacific. Six months into the Korean War, we got a new bureau manager, Frank Tremaine. He replaced Bill Payette, who was promoted to chief of a different UP division, working out of Dallas. Tremaine told me that Quinn wanted to come home. I could have that job covering the war if I wanted it.

Here it was, the thing I had trained for. A foreign correspondent, finally. Tremaine had some advice. He had been a UP correspondent in Honolulu on December seventh, 1941. He covered the war in the Pacific. He gave me a choice. He said I had promise and could move up in UP. If I went to Korea, my wife of about five years would have to live in Japan. I would seldom see her. Also, I would not make much money. War correspondents worked seven days and seven nights and were paid in bylines and a limited amount of fame.

If I stayed in Los Angeles, I would no doubt be moved to a small bureau as manager, then would move up to a larger bureau. I'd make more money than in Korea. I accepted his advice, which had unexpected career-changing results. LeRoy Hansen, a classmate at USC who had been hired by Payette soon after I began working there, took the job covering Korea. Years later he became an editor of U.S. News and World Report, a competitor of Time Magazine.

In less than a year I was transferred to Phoenix as Arizona Manager. Joe Quinn briefed me in L.A. and soon visited us in Phoenix. He took me along to visit clients. He became a good friend. Later, in L.A., he moved into City politics and became a Deputy Mayor and owner of City News Service, a small, local wire service.

The Phoenix bureau was in a room that was a shortcut between the City Rooms of the morning Arizona Republic and the afternoon Gazette. The Associated Press also had its offices at the other end of the wall between the two City Rooms. We each had clients elsewhere, with UP being strong in radio stations. AP had most of the Arizona newspapers. UP was a three-man bureau. AP had eight people. AP was entitled to all the stories produced by reporters on the Republic and the Gazette. UP was entitled to nothing. We paid reporters to tip us, and some felt sorry for us and dropped a word or a note on a desk while walking in one door and out the other. We paid correspondents around the state, but I had only a tiny budget for that.

At the State Capitol, Governor Howard Pyle had been a news broadcaster on KOY, the leading radio station in Phoenix and a UP client. I found him alone in the office one afternoon, probably a holiday because not even his secretary was there. He invited me in, for a purpose it turned out. He was reading a paper on his desk, and explained what it was. I don't remember the details, and have not spent hours in a library hunting the story. But, I recall vaguely that the paper he was studying was a commutation of a death penalty to life imprisonment. That may not be exactly correct, but it's how I remember it, and the Governor obviously wanted someone to witness his signature on the paper. I had nothing to sign, just watched as he signed it. Pyle's only comment was that it was not a vicious case.

The Arizona Attorney General's office was a focus of attention suddenly when I was tipped that the AG was planning a "secret" pre-dawn sweep of a small town on the Utah border, Short Creek, later renamed Colorado City. After many months of investigation, the state was going to arrest and take into custody a group of husbands, wives and children of Fundamentalist polygamist families.

Someone in the press tipped me that this secret "raid" was coming in a few months, and I would need background, so I went to see the Assistant Attorney General. He was peeved that the word had reached me, and said I would blow up the whole operation, which was being put together like a military exercise with a lot of law enforcement and equipment to handle scores of people they would arrest or hold. I did not mention the matter to anyone, but began to prepare to cover the story, if it occurred, by reading many AG files on alleged crimes, including forcing female children into marriage, sometimes to very old men.

Arizona Troubles

After eleven months of working 18 hours a day, seven days a week most of the time, I was fired.

It was not a surprise. When I arrived in Phoenix in October, 1951, a bureau manager had recently moved to L.A., and his successor had been fired suddenly. Ray Hebert then accepted the job, but quickly decided he didn't want it and was going to the Los Angeles Times. He delayed leaving UP in order to introduce me, his successor, to the Governor, other newsmakers and our UP clients. This was before Quinn arrived to make more client visits.

Hebert told me that there was a big problem which would hit the following September, 1952: Arizona's primary election. Hebert said the vote count on the primary would be impossible to cover adequately. We could not compete with Associated Press, because both Phoenix newspapers and their staffs would be working the election, and all their information would go to AP. Nothing would go to UP. Hebert said UP had stayed in competition in past elections by hiring some college students to visit polls, and by faking numbers in stories about the election results.

I also heard the same story from clients when Hebert escorted me around to meet them. We charged extra for election coverage and the clients wanted to know if we would provide "the usual slide-rule coverage." I said it would be real. It was real, but there was not enough manpower and money to beat the opposition. Our numbers were honest but we fell way behind.

Joe Quinn had tried almost as soon as I got to Phoenix, with no success, to get some help from the Republic and Gazette on election night. I don't know if Joe knew about the phony numbers history. An old Republic editor, whom Quinn warned me did not like UP, denied our request. I set up a new election system in a downtown Phoenix office. It collapsed.

In that September election night we found that AP had put some ficticious vote results on their wire, but we were behind them, which was what mattered. I had been told by Hebert that it would happen, and that someone would pay.

I got a quick notice, delivered in person by Hank Rieger from L.A., that a farewell letter would arrive Monday from San Francisco HQ. Enclosed was a check which would just cover the cost of moving back to L.A.

I wrote some detailed reports for UP bosses. Frank Tremaine told me I should have asked for help. I did, I had called L.A. before the election but got a denial first, finally an admission how things had been run before. It was too late to help.

Ann and I always agreed that my being fired was one of the best things that ever happened to us. I left the UP which was 7/24, and a week after returning to L.A. was reporting for the Los Angeles Herald Express. I just missed going to AP. (See Herald Express chapters)

Ted Jones (Elizabeth) of the USC faculty, told me she had cleared the road for me to get a job at KTLA, an independent (non-network) TV station. She had withdrawn all the other names she had recommend to KTLA. She got the UP version of my firing, which she said was not at all bad, and told KTLA to hire me. She even told them they should pay my expenses to go there from Phoenix for the interview, because I was an experienced reporter. I did see the manager and anchor at KTLA. The manager, a local television legend already, Klaus Landsberg, said news would never be a big budget item at KTLA, despite some historic coverage he had done, and also that I was way over-qualified for their job. They would pay only $90 a week. I called AP, for money, and in a day was hired -- on the Herald. Ted Jones married and moved to Tucson. We visited them there later.

Herald Express – Short Creek Leak

As I settled into the Herald Express in L.A., the Short Creek matter was developing in Arizona. It was an extremely sensitive subject in Governor Pyle's office. I got a call in L.A. from Governor Pyle's executive assistant, Harvey Mott, a former Managing Editor of the Republic, who had become a personal friend during our year in Phoenix. He told me what they were doing to keep the story from becoming a circus. They wanted whoever covered the story for major news outlets to have the facts, but they couldn't do that in advance of the arrests. Because I already knew the background, they wondered if I could go to Arizona and cover the story for my newspaper, the Herald Express. I suggested to Mott that he write a letter and lay out his proposal. He wrote an official letter from the Governor's office asking for help.

My City Editor, Agness Underwood, was uncertain. Mott was coming to L.A. soon, so he said he would come by the office and talk with Aggie. She told him it wasn't a story that the Herald would cover, but Hearst's International News Service had a bureau in the Herald building, and they might be interested in what Mott had to say.

Finally, it was arranged that INS would hire me for one day to work in the INS office with their teletype operator, receive reports from Arizona and write the INS story. My source would be a reporter I had hired at the UP Phoenix bureau. He was no longer at UP, but would help INS.

Those who planned the operation thought that the residents, before they could all be arrested or placed in custody, would run – on foot – across the adjacent state border into Utah. That was one reason for secrecy. The raid took place as planned, but the people of Short Creek had been tipped and were waiting patiently in the schoolyard when the officers and others arrived at dawn. Mott wrote a letter to me which said that my INS (ex-UP) reporter had decided to play "lone wolf" and go into Short Creek hours before the official raid. He tipped everyone that "the law" was on its way. Mott said it did not make much difference, except it let the polygamist leaders gather the families around the center of "town" as they were taken into custody. There were no problems.

It was all very quiet in the press. Short Creek could not draw attention away from a major headline event: The Korean War ended that day.

United Press Goes On

Hollywood was a big source of stories from the Los Angeles bureau. Aline Mosby's biggest story probably was about Marilyn Monroe. I was told it was she who broke the story that Marilyn said she posed nude for those famous calendar shots because she needed the money.

It was somewhat ironic that after the Monroe story Mosby became a celebrity in the L.A. journalism crowd for her first-person, inside-the-ropes coverage of a nudist convention in a neighboring county. To work that story, a reporter had to disrobe or stay outside. She was gathering mental notes for her UP story at poolside, dangling feet in the water, when two similarly unclad newspaper photographers appeared. As one of them told it, she promptly dropped her hands to cover up. Finally they all got over their nudity and went their own ways, and we heard that no pictures recorded it.

A few years later, Mosby left the Los Angeles bureau suddenly and went to Europe for United Press. She spent some time in Moscow and Paris. Mosby was replaced as Hollywood columnist by Vernon Scott, a classmate of mine from USC journalism school. I heard and verified in a court record, that she had sold stories to a short-lived scandal magazine.

I did a lot of Hollywood reporting later. It was as interesting as the people involved. It varied. Stars are not especially interesting when all you hear is a casual hello at a reception. In retirement, going through notes, I found one written to a reporter on the New York Post which said I had met Monroe on three occasions. Only one was worth mentioning, and that was in Beverly Hills Municipal Court. (See "The Blondes" chapter)

The United Press Days had been special. It is still fun to meet with members of the Downhold Club on email. The unhappy part of it is that the cheapness of Scripps ownership left some very hard workers with scarcely enough to live on in their old age. Some others made it big. A quick computer search will find many names, and save me the embarrassment of leaving out some who should be mentioned, like Walter Cronkite who left to join CBS News; Joe Galloway who received a Bronze Star for heroism while covering the war in Vietnam and wrote two books about the war; Tony Hillerman who wrote classic Indian mysteries, and the guy who "runs" the Downhold Club, a technical feat in which others shared the work, Tom Foty of CBS Radio News.

Many went into academia. There are hundreds of stories about UP alumni. "On the Road," the Beat Generation story, was written on a roll of UP teletype paper. CBS News Anchor Dan Rather's bios list UP or UPI as a place he worked, but the connection is uncertain. Many women are Downhold members. Many Downholders are still working somewhere.

At a book signing party in North Hollywood for Helen Thomas, the White House reporter, I had an interesting time listening to two women Combat Correspondents who spent time in Vietnam, Tracy Wood and Maggie Kilgore. Wood and eight other women wrote a book, "War Torn," about their experiences, mostly grim, covering the war.

Tracy Wood was a constant booster/advisor in my efforts to write this memoir. Her initial reaction to a few chapters:

"Finish it. Finish IT!!"

J. Edgar Hoover and Other Howard Hughes Mysteries

When Howard Hughes was hiding from the world in the middle 1970s, shielded by a mysterious team of male "nurses," the news media of that era had little information to report.

Hughes enterprises seemed to run normally, but all the press had to report about the hidden ruler of the kingdom were minor rumors or factual crumbs. Those were passed on to the public with intense frustration.

It was a major news opera without a script.

It was made worse by criticism from many sources that the news media, all of us, were wasting air time and newsprint by speculating about a crackpot. KNXT broadcast an editorial defending the heavy coverage. Hughes was, to the news media, a missing person. However, few businessmen provided a larger number of employee paychecks in California. Hughes was news.

Before the Second World War Hughes sought attention. He made big movies. HJis airplane racing was a dangerous hobby. His problems with hearing made contacts increasingly difficult. In 1949, Al Kahn at UP told me he could call Hughes at home, and Hughes' sound magnifier made it possible to talk. Hughes' world was still big. Years later he bought Paramount Studio.

Few people saw Hughes in person. Telephoned invitations from press agents to meet Howard became legend. A reporter might get an invitation late at night, perhaps be flown somewhere and find him in a dark and remote place.

He moved to Las Vegas and was seen no more. He moved into a hotel. He spent millions on Las Vegas real estate. He communicated with the world through a spokesman. His mental state was debated. He married a reclusive movie actress and leaked the story to just one news person. He withstood a legal battle over his Nevada casino gambling license despite refusing to appear in person, which was required of mortals and gangsters. Stories about his uncut hair, long fingernails, and assisted living with male nurses added to the mystery.

Hughes had a large and obedient publicist army, the Carl Byoir Company, which had a sometimes strained but successful relationship with the press. Hughes business often dealt in classified government contracts. Secrecy was the rule, except for strange, temporary leaks. Employees carried loyalty and tight lips into comfortable retirement.

Some things got away from all of this control. That was why J. Edgar Hoover, chief of the FBI, wrote a letter which followed – by two years – a routine assignment for three people to update an old Hughes story.

Hoover's welcome letter was the conclusion of an effort to make sense of a Hughes "experience" that started with a call from a Carl Byoir publicist to Frank Tremaine, Los Angeles bureau manager of United Press, inviting coverage of a new stage of an old story. Tremaine took the call, then told me to go to Culver City with a couple of other newsmen, Brooks Honeycutt from ACME photos, which was located next to the United Press office, and Don Dwiggins, a reporter for the Daily News, whose building housed UP as a tenant.

The details of what happened because of that trip are perhaps boring. It was silly unless you consider that those were "McCarthy Days," which meant frequent newspaper and television earthquakes, mostly in Washington, when Senator Joseph McCarthy and his allegedly subversive targets collided. Subversive? Newsmen? Seriously? Someone thought so. Or, someone used that kind of threat to practice censorship on us.

The fact was that three of us who went out on the old story were investigated for possible "violation of the Espionage Act." This was a nervous time in McCarthy's 1950s America. By coincidence, I met and chatted with Senator McCarthy poolside over drinks in Phoenix about the time this whole episode was settled. The subject of Espionage Act did not come up. McCarthy himself was probably not aware of our Hughes event.

The telephone call Frank Tremaine received in 1950 was an invitation from Hughes' own PR company to cover the rollout out of an experimental helicopter, a giant craft that could carry heavy loads of military gear, if it worked.

The chopper was towed out of its hangar at the Hughes Culver City plant near the south end of Marina Del Rey. It was parked where thousands of motorists had an unhampered view of it every day. Those passersby could have done what we did, which was what we were invited to do, take pictures and tell people about the latest Hughes military project. The effect was no different than rolling it out before a grandstand full of people. But, we three, who went there at the request of Hughes public relations people, were accused of making public something that was "classified."

UP put two stories on its news wires. One is dated 1950, the story I called in. At the bottom is the notation by the writer, "pc", who was (Ms.) Pat Clary. Pat took my (hw) call from the airport and wrote the story at 1125 am.

The other story, which I found later in the UP's office files, was written and transmitted on the UP national "daywire" in "(1949)", a year before we went to Culver City. The signature at the bottom is "lh225atimesexamdickdavisfoned" meaning it was written by Lincoln Haynes, the overnight editor at the UP office, at 225am with information from the L.A. Times, the Los Angeles Examiner, and was confirmed with Dick Davis, a Carl Byoir publicist. It was Davis who called Frank Tremaine at UP a year later to invite coverage of the rollout, the public's first look at the helicopter.

We got our pictures and then went to the airport office and asked for the Hughes public relations man. We were met by an Air Force officer who would give us no information. Restricted, he said. We pointed out that the big bird was parked by the busy public highways and also was visible from the Loyola University campus on a south-side hill. His answer was the same: classified. We pointed out the incongruity of his position, but he had his orders. We left.

Six months later, I was covering a hearing in the Federal Building in downtown Los Angeles. At recess a man asked if I was HW and said he was from the FBI. He asked if I had been in Culver City that helicopter rollout day with Honeycutt and Dwiggins. I said yes, and I asked what it was about. He said we were being investigated for possible violation of the Espionage Act. Huh? Ridiculous, I said, and told him that the helicopter was sitting out there in public. He said he was just gathering information. Frank Tremaine, who sent me on the story, had been transferred temporarily to Tokyo to help organize coverage of the Korean War. I reported the FBI visit to his replacement in L.A..

Another six months passed. I was making a routine check of Federal offices and walked by the open office door of Ray Kinnison, an Assistant U.S. Attorney. Ray called out to me. I stopped and turned into his office. He asked if I had been in Culver City when the Hughes helicopter was towed out. Sure, why? He tapped an inch-thick folder on his desk and said he had the results of an FBI investigation. It was his task to decide whether to present this case of possible violation of the Espionage Act to the Federal Grand Jury. They would decide whether to indict us.

Ridiculous, I told him, anybody could see what we saw from the street. Ray led me into another office where there was a large map of the L.A. area on a wall. I pointed to the Hughes plant, to the place where the helicopter was parked, and where all the traffic went by with an unimpeded "bird" view. Kinnison said he thought he would recommend that the matter be dropped. As I did with the FBI agent, I asked who started this thing. Kinnison, too, said he didn't know.

Honeycutt and Dwiggins said they hoped the Grand Jury indicted us because they were certain it would make the one who started it look stupid, as he deserved. But who was that? When this started, my wife was working for the U.S. Civil Service manager in his office in the Federal building. She was upset. I wasn't worried, but wanted answers.

By then, the UP bureau manager, Frank Tremaine, who had sent me to Culver City after getting a call from Dick Davis, was back from Tokyo, so I gave him a lengthy written report. He sent all the material to the top

United Press editor in New York, who sent it to the manager of the UP bureau in Washington, D.C., who sent it to J. Edgar Hoover. Tremaine sent all of the response correspondence, including "Edgar's" reply, to me. That was about September, 1951. I was the new Phoenix bureau manager, and about that time met Sen. McCarthy, who was not part of this.

After Tremaine forwarded the correspondence from everybody, I attended a reception at the Phoenix Press Club which involved a Hughes project. I met an Air Force officer there. I told him about the helicopter affair. The officer knew the story. I asked who started it? He said it was an Air Force officer in Ohio who had seen the UP wire story about the rollout and decided he was going to teach UP a lesson for their publication (on teletype machines around the country) of classified material, and he asked for an investigation. Someone in Defense passed that request to the Department of Justice. The FBI got the job of gathering information.

End of story. Most of it. Hughes stories go on.

Getting Personal with Hughes

Years ago my son, who prefers the uninformative title "engineer" for a sensitive defense industry job he had, mentioned something non-specific about classification of material.

Darin, in his own words:

> "I'd just landed a new job at Hughes Aircraft, and was visiting my folks. When I told Dad about the job, he went thoughtful for a second, then said:
> "I probably ought to tell you. I was once investigated for violation of the espionage act."

Dad: Darin's reaction was memorable.

"You WHAT?????"

Darin continued:

"Oh crap! I'd just filled out all of the forms saying there was no reason I'd have trouble working in the defense industry. Oh crap. Oh CRAP!!"
   "But it's OK." Dad said.
   "HOW is that OK?!!!!"
   "I have a letter from J. Edgar Hoover telling me not to worry about it," he said.

(Dad's) turn:

"When I told Darin about the letter, he came down from the ceiling, still a bit doubtful. I got the letter out of a file, told him the whole story, and he asked,
   "But why would they spend so much effort investigating that?"
   I explained: "Who knew it was stupid until they investigated?"
   He wanted and got a copy of the Hoover letter.

I also told Darin about reading a boldly stamped "TOP SECRET" report from a general in Vietnam to LBJ in 1967, fifteen years after the Hoover letter. (I did not quote it) How? I was sitting next to LBJ in the White House while LBJ read part of that secret report aloud to a group of CBS execs discussing that war. It was right in front of me in LBJ's hand and I could read it easily.
   Security conscious son Darin said LBJ should not have let me see it, but agreed the President could declassify it.

Darin closes it:

"So, I told them at work, and handed over a copy of the letter.

"As far as I ever heard, I was the only person at Hughes Aircraft with a letter from J. Edgar Hoover in his Personnel file. And a letter from Mickey Cohen at home."

Television Influence On Elections

Around the country, politicians were inventing rules to control the new world of television. The idea persisted that West Coast voters waited to find out what voters in Vermont or New York did, then went to their polls in San Francisco or Fresno and played the same song.

It was an irresistible band wagon. Critics also jumped on the networks for using exit polls to determine how votes were going and telling who was leading. Politicians also applied the same reasoning to polls, and said surveys before elections were wrong.

CBS President Dr. Frank Stanton suggested that election days be national holidays, and that the polls across the country all open and close at the same time. That idea was rejected or ignored. CBS commissioned two studies at universities in opposite ends of the country to study the effect of east coast returns on western voters. Both said there was no significant vote influence. However, politicians "knew" better.

Founding the California Freedom of Information Committee

The dispute over influence of eastern voter influence was the direct cause of a bad law being passed, and the foundation of the first all-media journalism organization to unite in fighting censorship. (This was a year before the Reporters Committee).

This new group was formed because a California Assemblyman was angry when he heard eastern voter results on his car radio as he drove to a poll to vote for Rockefeller in a Republican primary to nominate a presidential candidate. He was upset when he heard that Back East those people were voting in big numbers for Barry Goldwater, and early returns from California indicated the same thing was happening here. He kept going to the poll and voted for Rockefeller, he said. But, the damage was done as far as he was concerned. He plunged into a plan to prevent it from happening again. He introduced a bill that would take care of the problem -- in California.

The bill said that no partial returns could be released by Registrars of Voters anywhere in California until all polls in the state were closed. The bill passed. Some of us were concerned about how news programs on radio and TV and newspaper deadlines would be affected. I talked to Frank Haven, Managing Editor of the Los Angeles Tines. He agreed. The Times had deadlines to update election returns, and they wanted to tell their readers how the election was going. If this new bill was signed by Governor Pat Brown it could cut off any results. The election coverage would be limited to telling how many people voted so far, which was not really news. The law would apply to purely local ballot issues, not just national elections.

Haven and I contacted Brown separately, asking him to investigate the question before signing the bill, and to not sign the bill. We called other media people trying to get them to do the same. We figured Brown would never sign a bill like that. But he did. It became law.

Two years later, in another election, at the hour California polls closed and votes were being counted, I got a call.

"You're not going to believe this," said a lady I in the Registrar of Voters office. She was sorry but they could not release any votes at 8 o'clock poll-closing time – when our election special on TV would begin. Votes were being tallied already, but results could not be disclosd because in San Francisco, some voting machines broke down. A lot of people there were still in line to vote, and the polls would remain open. It might take an hour or more.

All the counties in the state were muzzled. The news people opened election programs with other stories.

(I was told years later that the rule was changed to let the Secretary of State decide whether to release early returns if the law required Registrars be muzzled for no good reason.)

Meantime, the day after Governor Brown signed that bill, I saw News Director Roy Heatly in a hallway at KNXT, and we stopped to talk about the potential for problem, and what we could do. I said we'd better organize all news outlets in the State -- radio, TV and newspapers -- and even their organizations like California Broadcasters and California Publishers Associations, to combine our forces on any matter of mutual interest so we could let the public and their elected representatives know what we need. Forget competition.

Heatly agreed. We decided to do invitation lists, meet later in the day and combine lists. Roy found a legislative "sponsor" and we set an evening meeting at the home of Senator Tom Carrell in Granada Hills after the year-end holidays. Carrell's AA volunteered coffee service. We invited about 20 prominent local news people.

That was the birth of something we called the California Freedom of Information Committee. That meeting was held on the evening of February second, 1966. When we finished, Heatly and I went by my house, picked up my wife, Ann, and took her to dinner. It was our 20th anniversary. Years later I was booed by some of the women in the audience at the Beverly Hilton when I told that story after receiving a Freedom of Information award from the Society of Professional Journalists, related to starting CFOIC. (Roy Heatly had moved to a Sacramento station by then.)

Bench, Bar, Media Combine

The organization grew rapidly. Judges, lawyers and their own organizations had their own differences with news people and were welcomed. We formed a discussion platform, a statewide Bench, Bar Media Committee, then local chapters were formed in counties around the state.

It did not take long for CFOIC to become an influence with diverse and friendly people working together. We met from Berkeley to San Diego. It was friendly enough that when it was my turn to talk at a meeting in a San Francisco Airport hotel I kidded about "friends" and said Judge Gordon Files, from a court of appeal division in L.A., had threatened that morning to throw me off the airplane. Judge Arthur L. Alarcon and I were co-chairs of the first BBM Committee. I spoke at a State Bar meeting in Northern California with another active L.A. BBM lawyer member, Warren Christopher, who would serve as Secretary of State under President Bill Clinton. (Christopher's name was on a major investigation into the death of JFK.) Alarcon and I drove to night meetings in two other counties to encourage formation of BBM's.

Twice I was invited to speak at Boalt Hall, the UC Berkeley law school. The audience both times consisted of lawyers and judges. I referred to it as the School for New Judges, which was part of the planning. I presented news media opinions about presumptions that juries were swayed by "publicity" and convicted innocent people. I usually challenged legal groups to show us a real verdict of guilty which was reversed, in part because of pretrial publicity, and which got an acquittal at a new trial. I'm still looking. The standard responses responses are Estes, Tidwell and Shepherd. All three examples are full of flaws and deserve more space than this short book can cover. Just one sample here – at Boalt Hall. A new judge came up after the session and said I was wrong about one of those cases that he knew. But then he said, "The confession bothered me." "It should have," I said. The confession was not allowed to be heard in the trial, but small-town publicity was blamed and helped get two brothers a new trial. The same brothers were accused in a tragic carbon-copy pair of murders a few years later, another man shot, another wife's throat cut, as in the first murders. One brother was convicted at the new trial. Some key evidence was not allolwed.

That particular trip had its own sad, unrelated finish. I was driving from Berkeley on the Bay Bridge to San Francisco that evening when a car stopped in front of mine. I braked, the other driver got out, walked rapidly around in front of his car's lights, climbed the rail and jumped. CFOIC's then chairman, Dick Fogel, Oakland Tribune, saw the only witness's name in his paper.

Some of the press-legal disputes were resolved with good will by determined people. Most Bench-Bar-Media Committees faded away. L.A. County worked well for years, then the Committee's focus seemed to fall under a different set of goals and it faded out. Chair occupants do make a difference. The San Diego BBM committee met as recently as the summer of 2016, to hear legal media experts on cameras and their effect in the O.J. Simpson murder trial. The media experts, Linda Deutsch of Associated Press, and a Loyola Law School professor, did not blame TV coverage for the acquittal.

The Freedom of Information Committee changed its name to California First Amendment Coalition. I was not part of that decision and was out of the news business. The "new" organization adopted CFOIC causes, but also took on purely political issues, which CFOIC founders avoided. CFAC does not acknowledge its parent organization. The national Reporters Committee for Freedom of the Press was founded in 1967, a year after CFOIC, and is doing an important job on the Free Press isues.

California's Public Records Act

The last big project of CFOIC was the writing and introduction and passage of a very long and complex bill, the California Public Records Act, with

Assemblyman Bill Bagley of San Rafael as the principal author. It probably had about 100 pages when typewritten in draft form, with more than 100 people contributing ideas.

It was a huge job that was of interest to diverse agencies and causes, from police records, juvenile arrests, to construction plans, public employee laws and sensitive personal family matters. Many of these agencies required exceptions. The result was a workable law, despite differences about how much an agency may charge for copies, and "shot gun" requests from the public, which need to be refined for specific items. A Federal law already had been passed.

These laws are constantly used by the media and the public. Usually, it seems, we hear about somebody requesting copies of federal agency documents under the federal open records act. The records sought may be copies of letters, or something with national security implications, so the requesting agency, a newspaper for instance, has to get a Court order with an interpretation discarding the claim of national security.

I was prepping to retire and move to San Diego County, so watched it happen from far away. Then I spent two decades in elective office and numerous local and County appointive agencies, watching from inside. I could noisily protest when some public officials schemed to defeat the intent of Open Meetings or Public Records laws. Personal interests of officiaals were sometimes involved but hidden. I lost arguments, not always because my version of the law was wrong. Hired counsel supported what the agency wanted.

A common political game is to make other cities or agencies pay more than their share of the cost of projects or products, power or water for instance. It is still is largely impossible to expose these schemes in the new age of journalism because of shrinking news outlets and fewer reporters.

Our "friend inside" was Assemblyman Bill Bagley, working with Senator Bill Keene and Governor Ronald Reagan. Bagley was a father figure in Freedom of Information matters in California. Bagley was honored by the Society of Professional Journalists for his place in history, pushing the Open Records Act. The other half of openness had begun with Open Meetings laws, which Bagley improved whenever the media asked the Legislature for help. I flew to Sacramento one morning to testify at a Senate Committee meeting. While looking for the Committee meeting, I ran into Bagley. He asked what I was doing, and I said I was there for the Senate committee hearing. He said, "Oh, I told the chairman this morning what we want, he agreed, and it is all taken care of." That was Assemblyman Bagley, a real friend.

Bagley was appointed by President Reagan to chair the Commodity Futures Trading Commission. One of his first public acts was to stand with some helpers on a bridge across the Potomoc and toss to the drink some proposed CFTC confidentiality rules.

A Digest of Unfinished Business

In the four decades after World War II which are covered in this memoir, protecting the First Amendment was a war that grew as new causes multiplied. The war had a name, Freedom of Information (FOI). It isn't over yet. It was directly linked to a parallel concept, the Public's Right to Know.

The main antagonists were news people, lawyers and judges. The battle grounds were mainly courthouses. Prisoners were taken and jailed. Most were reporters.

The U.S. Supreme Court was called upon to decide many battles. Some of its decisions were a great help, such as "Sullivan" in 1964 which kept touchy politicians at bay when they wanted to sue newspaper critics for libel. Bald attempts at censorship were killed.

Open Meetings

California led the nation in some of these sub-battles. An early move in support of the Public's Right to Know was the Brown Act of 1953. California Assemblyman Ralph M. Brown's bill, which was approved by the legislature, said that public agencies were doing public business, and it ought to be done in meetings that were --- open to the public.

There was not a lot of opposition, but another law, Bagley-Keene, was passed later to make sure the Brown Act applied to the Legislature itself. Until then it was not uncommon to see a legislative committee consider a budget in closed session.

Inquisitive folks in the news media collided with closed-door tradition at a University of California Regents meeting at UCLA. UC was a State Constitution creation, and the Legislature could not change that. We encouraged the Legislature to put an Amendment to the State Constitition on the ballot. It passed easily.

An early open meetings worker, Dick Fogel, Executive Editor of the Oakland Tribune, looked into another example: meetings of the State Bar Association Board of Directors. A high official there, I believe then-current president of the Bar, said he would never live to see open meetings of the State Bar Board. Soon after that, SBA meetings were opened to the public. Sensitive personnel matters, a big issue, are normally exempted at any agency.

Cameras

In matters involving cameras in courts, SCOTUS has made decisions based on old and undocumented generalizations. Contrary evidence, if examined at all, was brushed off. Which mattered most? Free Press or Fair Trial? The Press was accused of convicting innocent (until convicted) persons. The battles could fill law books.   One is fully covered here in a chapter of its own, the Sirhan trial. It was new territory, and after our success it was rapidly put to use elsewhere. That was a change in which I was deeply involved. (See Sirhan)

The Right to Counsel

Miranda has become a well-known decision which any crime story reader knows says that a person held as a suspect, or not yet a suspect, has to be informed of his right to call a lawyer. Confessions sometimes were wrung out of suspects in long interrogations. I witnessed one – from an adjoining room -- of a multiple killer suspect in Orange County -- that seemed to go all night, but got nothing from the suspect. Another case dealt with a Beverly Hills merchant who was questioned by an officer, and the officer said the suspect admitted his guilt. The suspect denied he said anything to indicate he was guilty. In those days the jury might hear from both and decide who to believe.

Gag Rules and Protecting Sources

The media got into another war in the 1960s when lawyers tried to keep "prejudicial" information from reaching the public. Censorship by the court was attempted. The news media protested Gag Rules, which the courts referred to as "Protective Orders."

These rules generally were not successfully challenged, and they became ubiquitous. Unpleasantness occurred when someone talked to a reporter anyway and the reporter went to jail rather than disclose his source.

Bill Farr went to jail. I visited him there, as did several others from news outlets. Not even the visitors' room is a place to hang about willingly. It was a prolonged and messy case legally and financially for Farr personally.

Section 1070 of the Evidence Code says a newsperson can't be found in contempt for protecting a source. New ways were tried to make a reporter disclose his source. The judge who first put Farr in jail did know about 1070, but ruled that Farr, a reporter when he first got information, had lost such protection when he – Farr – left journalism and became a public relations man. His 1070 protection no longer applied. That was appealed and Farr lost and went to jail. News people were aghast.

I talked to the KNXT News Director, Bill Eames, and Bill Whitsett in Legal, and we sent a request to New York CBS Legal Department. CBS produced an impressive printed brief containing statements from Network news people supporting Farr. from Walter Cronkite, Eric Sevareid, Mike Wallace, Dan Rather and Marvin Kalb. CBS Legal was producer. It may have helped then, but the struggle goes on.

Hughes and Secrecy

Lawyers may seem to have problems with confidentiality. Howard Hughes didn't. His name became a synonym for "secrecy." His Glomar Explorer was about as secret as the anything the CIA ever did, recovering a sunken Russian submarine. The story got out. So did his marriage to an actress, Jean Peters, a legitimate news item if only because of his vast business holdings.

I was a reporter on the Mirror when City Editor Hank Osborne came to my desk and handed me a page from that morning's Examiner. An item was circled in pencil. It was a column by their Hollywood columnist, Louella Parsons, which said something close to this:

"I have reason to believe that Howard Hughes and Jean Peters are married."

That was it. Osborne said to check it out.

I called the Hughes publicists at Carl Byoir and got one I knew. He listened and said, "I'll get back to you." I waited a while and called again. His secretary said he was out. After another half hour I called again. She said he was still out. Where was he? She didn't know, she would tell him when he called in that I wanted him. I never heard back. The PR man was hiding.

In the afternoon I called a friend who had a way to get the information. He called back soon to report he had not found his source, but would get back to me.

About nine that night my fone rang at home. It was my source, and his source could only say -- it's true. At the Mirror the next morning I wrote a story about that late night call at home with the breathless report: "It's true." No one asked about my source. My source is long dead, so are the principals, but in the Hughes tradition I will disclose only that the source was a person who never worked for Hughes. Wedding details were absent until Osborne called our Las Vegas stringer (part-time correspondent) on a hunch. That reporter chased down the story to a small town in Nevada. A local office holder or preacher had performed the brief ceremony. It was easy to keep a secret in Nevada, briefly.

Even outside and long after my journalist life, Hughes was around – but invisible. Hughes was everywhere. Hughes and Peters divorced. Peters lived in Franklin Canyon, in Beverly Hills or LA. North of Beverly Hills. Some streets ran through both cities. A friend who lived in Beverly Hills said she saw Peters out walking sometimes, and the two neighbor ladies would say hello. Then my friend said Peters disappeared. While working on this report I found out that Peters had died in 2000, of leukemia, a few miles away in Carlsbad, CA. a town that borders on Vista. For 21 years, until 2010, I represented Vista on the Palomar Airport Advisory Committee, which the Board of Supervisors appoints to, effectively, run the airport, which is in Carlsbad. Until 9-11, Palomar was often the busiest single runway, non-commercial airport in the nation.

Hughes' death in April, 1976, was a secret, of course. He supposedly died on a flight with his caretakers from Mexico to Texas. Did he die in

Texas or a hospital in Mexico? Or in Acapulco? Did it matter to the lawyers or Hughes employees? News people did not know he was enroute to the USA, so they were not waiting to greet him. Who was waiting? PR people, and they helped prepare a story about his death.

Who decided what to disclose? Who besides those anonymous male nurses knew anything?

I knew the two Hughes PR people who released the official word. One of them told me so, but offered no details, except that getting the story together had been difficult.

KNXT (CBS Channel 2, Hollywood) had been an exciting world of editorials and politicians, judges and movie stars, far away from the street scenes of print journalism.

I was in my office at KNXT when a young woman I knew slightly, another CBS employee, walked in.

Did I have time to talk? I told her to have a seat.

This visitor, Sunny, was in the sales department, but she also was involved in operations and programming. It was perhaps dull work, but it was Hollywood and CBS. What did she want?

Sunny said the Hughes nurses wanted to sell their story to CBS News. Huh???

A Surprise from Hughes

It could not be a gag.

Sunny said she knew people who had personal access to Howard Hughes in the final years when he was a complete recluse in a hotel in Las Vegas, until his final trip to Acapulco and recently back to Houston. He had been unseen even by his top executives. Hughes, in recent times, usually communicated with those executives by notes or verbal instructions which were carried to them by his trusted male nurses.

Sunny said she was speaking for three Hughes " nurses." They wanted to sell their inside story to CBS News. The connection was her boyfriend, who was a friend of a "nurse." She was the go-between. Could I contact the right people in CBS?

I didn't think selling would be difficult. I suggested we try Bill Small, Vice President of CBS News, whom I saw or talked with by phone every few weeks, at least, mostly about general broadcasting matters such as cameras in the courts or FOI. We also met at conventions or affiliate parties around the country.

I offered to call the current President of CBS News, whom I knew, but Bill Small was much easier to get and would know what to do.

Sunny said OK. I picked up my telephone and from memory called Small's New York office. His secretary said he was out. I left word. I told my visitor I'd let her know as soon as possible. Sunny went back to her job.

Small called back not much later that day, and I told him this almost unbelievable story of a major news break being dumped in our lap.

He cooled it down immediately. CBS would not be interested, he said. The company had been criticized harshly recently for "buying news." CBS had paid $25,000 to the senior White House staffer under President Nixon, H. R. Haldeman, for an exclusive interview. News execs in all media were incensed (and scooped) because CBS broke the general industry tradition: "We do not pay for news."

I knew that historical background, but thought Small might want to work around the Haldeman problem. Many news outlets had paid news makers in the past, but it was a tightrope walk. A source might want to talk, but could also be brought to CBS News headquarters on Fifty-seventh Street in New York for an interview if that was more practical than sending a reporter and crew to the source's home base. Bringing the source in was not cheap if it involved transportation, hotel, meals, perhaps a traveling parent or companion. It would cost money to send a crew.

Cash payment was something else. CBS News had crossed a line. Small said they had adopted a firm policy not to do it again.

Was there anything he could suggest to keep it in-house? Small said he would talk to Don Hewitt, the producer of "Sixty Minutes," for whom such a story appeared to be a natural. Someone would get back to me.

Sunny said she'd tell the nurses.

Small called back the next day. Hewitt was not interested. Did Small know why? No.

Did he have any suggestions? No, we (CBS) were "out."

Thinking it over decades later, it is less attractive than I thought then. The amount of research that might be necessary to confirm details, difficult even with a very public figure, and production costs, could require a heavy investment of time and people. Such research had already had been done, and I knew a source, but that did not occur to me then.

I gave the Hewitt decision to Sunny the spokeswoman. She was disappointed, but said she would relay it to her boyfriend and the nurses. I hoped they would let me know what came next.

She called again in a very few days and said the nurses had changed their minds. They wanted to write a book. They recognized that this was a special job. Did I know anyone who could help them write it?

That was the first time I thought of Jimmy Phelan in relation to her story. Ann and I had met Phelan in a shipboard restaurant in San Pedro harbor, months before. It was a party hosted by a friend and former Los Angeles Mirror colleague, a fellow USC journalism student, Canoy (Connie) Crawford Mesch, who left journalism and became a company representative, a staff company "lobbyist," for a large aerospace firm. I had heard that she was spectacularly successful. Her husband, Art Mesch, had been successful in the early days of electronics in Southern California. When we met at Connie's party, Phelan came across as a big, noisy, crusty, aging, hale fellow newsman. He had been covering Howard Hughes for the New York Times. I had read his stories. We talk-ed casually at the party, not getting into many specifics beyond describ-ing our backgrounds and relating some news events we thought were interesting. Reporters anywhere do have stories to tell by the hour.

Phelan's byline appeared in the New York Times again after we met. He had been working on the Hughes personal caretaker angle, trying to get behind the Hughes secrecy barrier.

I told Sunny that she or the nurses might want to call Phelan. I had met Phelan, knew someone who could reach him quickly, and could relay a message for Phelan to contact her. She said to have Phelan call, and gave me her home phone number. I called Connie Mesch and she relayed the number to Phelan.

In the book that Phelan wrote, "Howard Hughes: The Hidden Years," on page sixteen, a paragraph at the bottom of the page states:

"Three weeks after the death of Hughes, I received a late-night tele-phone call. The call culminated, after certain ritualistic maneuvers that anything involving Hughes seems to inspire, in a meeting with two men."

That was all he told readers about the sources of his book.

The third nurse must have decided not to participate. I was not in-volved in the negotiations that followed, and did not meet Phelan or even hear from him for a year or so. By then I had resigned from CBS in 1946, after twelve years as Editorial Director, to find something more stable. Five station managers was enough.

The Hughes Book Money

Around the date the book was published, Sunny called. She and her boyfriend were filing a lawsuit against Phelan for a finder's fee. He was paid more than $600,000 for the book and gave them nothing. I guessed that Phelan probably split the $600g with the two nurses. We never got into that. Sunny called because she and her boyfriend wanted my testimony about her effort to sell the story to CBS. After a telephone discussion followed by a meeting with her lawyer, I was called to testify for the plaintiffs.

Phelan called before the trial began. He was curious what I would testify. I told him about the call to Bill Small. He made happy talk before hanging up. I told him I wanted a copy of the book. You'll get one, he said. Autographed, I said. Yes, he said. I never got it. I bought a paperback edition.

Completing the "family scene" for all of this, when I walked into the courtroom I was surprised to see my Northridge neighbor from two blocks away, Nancy Harris, working as the court's reporter. I had worked at the Mirror with her husband and briefly replaced him as Labor Editor when he left the paper for another job. The defense lawyer let me testify, without any objection, about the visit from the go-between, Sunny, and my call to New York. Phelan's lawyer had no cross-examination. That was defense strategy. It left no opening for the plaintiff to ask about why CBS did not make a deal for the Hughes story. I testified that Sunny came to my office at KNXT, and I made a phone call to Bill Small and left a message. I was excused, and the judge called a recess.

In the hallway, I talked with Sunny, met her boyfriend and again saw their lawyer. When the jury came out and had to walk past us, Phelan stepped close to me, shook hands, and stayed in the group, presenting a picture to the walk-around jurors of one happy group. Even seeing juniors walk in the same corridor with trial pricipals, was a new experience to me. It didn't work for Phelan. I heard that the jury awarded Sunny and boyfriend around fifteen thousand. I heard nothing about whether Phelan had to pay the plaintiff's lawyer fees from his fifteen grand, or an addition was made in the award, for lawyer fees. There was no more word from Sunny. Connie Mesch, my connection to Phelan, and husband, Art, remained friends until she died in 2015 in LaJolla. Speaking of family, Art Mesch had worked in an electronics firm in Glendale with my son's father-in-law. The Hughes shadow was everywhere.

Another friend and former USC classmate, Mary Neiswender, a great reporter who knew the murderous Charles Manson better than anyone in journalism, was not part of the "nurses" lawsuit and did not know the story. She did know Phelan, and thought his newspaper career seemed to fade away. Mary said he hung around Long Beach for years.

The nurses, whom I never met, apparently made no more public talk about the late Howard Hughes. That has been a pattern with Hughes. When really secret personal things are published, those who do the talking become silent again. An example was the old friend who once told me he participated in the "difficult" official story of Hughes' death in Houston that was given to news media. A few years later, for this story, I asked him again. He said that he had "nothing to do with it." I didn't pursue it, and the friend died in 2016. Maybe I didn't really ask?

Aggie Underwood's Team

Going to see the legendary Aggie about a job in the fall of 1952 should have been intimidating. Actually, it was easy. Four years after leaving USC to work for United Press in Los Angeles I had been fired in Phoenix. In early 1951 an Associated Press reporter I knew in L.A. had told me that that his boss, Pete Arthur, wondered if I would like to work for them. I said UP had treated me well, and I was content to stay there in the UP bureau. Then came Phoenix. Being fired was not a surprise. The next step was obvious. I called AP.

Agness Underwood became a legend among newspaper people when the Managing Editor of the Herald Express, John B. T. Campbell, a gruff and aging emperor, pointed to a chair and told her:

"You sit there."

That was Aggie's story of how she was told that she was the new City Editor of the Herald Express in 1947, the first woman CE of a big city paper.

The Herald was a noisy Hearst trumpet among four newspapers in downtown Los Angeles. In the post-World War II boom, those newspapers and many small-city papers around the county were the only real source of news. Radio news was there, fifteen fast minutes every night at ten o'clock, but newspapers did most of the coverage. Journalism school taught us nothing about the future. Who knew that TV, at least fifteen years old, a Depression experiment, was ready to roar out of electronics labs after the war? The real world, the place we all got our news, was the newspaper.

Aggie, grammar-school-educated and then self-taught, was a star among scores of excellent reporters. She had covered the Black Dahlia, a gruesome murder. The top reporters were there. Aggie also wrote the killing of Bugsy Siegel, who built an Eastern mob's hotel-Casino in Las Vegas. They were in 1947 just before she became City Editor. (I was still going to USC.) Aggie was a tough competitor, tricky if necessary, but she had a big heart, born of a busted family that died and left her in foster homes until she was kicked out and homeless.

Suddenly, this plain, graying, somewhat chunky grandmother was a nationally famed symbol of change in the news business. She was up there with the big guys in L.A., Jim Richardson, City Editor of the other Hearst paper, the Examiner, Bud Lewis at the Times and Chuck Chappell at the Daily News. Testimonial banquets and speeches were her new diet, but she also had to prove she could handle the job. She did so for five years before we met.

Now, in September, 1952, I called Pete Arthur at AP. Yes, he still wanted to hire me and was expecting one of his crew to leave soon, maybe a couple of months. Meanwhile, he said, Agness Underwood was looking for someone to work general assignment for two months. OK?

The next day Arthur took me to meet Aggie and said: "This is the guy you are looking for." She asked if I understood it was for two months. I agreed and went to work. Weeks later, a Herald reporter left suddenly. I was permanent. Pete Arthur left town to become a newspaper editor in Northern California, and I forgot AP.

The Herald Express building was on Trenton Street, near Pico Boulevard, an area that now includes the Convention Center. The Herald City Room was maybe one hundred feet long, by fifty feet wide, on the second floor of an old building that housed presses and all the related mechanical equipment to feed news to a fleet of delivery trucks. The second floor was a busy City Room, surrounded by executive and other offices, and people were moving around nonstop. The City Room was littered with worn desks just big enough for tired typewriters and copy spikes. Posts which held the building up were covered with clippings, signs and jokes. Voices continually called across the desks. It could be Aggie calling a reporter to come to her for an assignment, or a writer yelling "Copy!" to summon a copyboy.

Aggie sat near one end of what she described as a "T" of three desks. Two desks faced each other, abutting the far side of her desk. They were occupied by two assistant city editors, Bill Pigue and Lew Young. Pigue's nephew, Army Lieutenant Paul Mansfield, was married to Jayne Mansfield, who got a divorce, hired a press agent and became a movie star. Before the divorce, she came to a Herald beach party, an unknown but hard-to-miss wannabe star.

Near was the photo desk, run by Ed Krauch, with a skilled and popular caption writer, Edwin Louie, a native of China. Eddie had gone to USC, wrote fluent English, but had an accent so pronounced that hardly anyone could understand what he said the first time around.

The bullpen, filled with desks of general assignment reporters, was at the opposite end of the room from Aggie. Also over there was the office of Managing Editor Campbell.

An Editor's Style

Aggie wrote in her 1949 autobiography, "Newspaperwoman," that guys and gals worked to help her fit into the new job, and would work extra hard any time she needed it. She fostered a special loyalty which was repaid constantly. Aggie did not have a jovial, talkative relationship with the reporters. There wasn't time. If someone called in and said, "This isn't worth anything," or "We got the story," she would bark "Come in" and hang up. There were no hellos and goodbyes. Her compacted day didn't allow it. But they all knew she respected their judgement and ability. When someone was ill or a family member needed attention, she'd find a way to help or give them time to do what was important at home. Union requirements were not the reason or the standard of care. She looked after them, period. The same applied if money was an urgent problem.

Close to Aggie's right, about four feet walking space away, was the rewrite battery, three desks side by side. These were senior reporters, old and experienced guys who had seen it all, could handle any story, did not have to ask how to spell the names of judges, senior cops, politicians, actors and other newsmakers. Most of the time they worked at their desks. If a reporter working outside could dictate his story from notes, which most could, aggie would transfer the call to anyone available to transcribe it. If it was a big new story which needed rapid coordination of developments and required a veteran's touch, it would go to rewrite. A rewriteman might handle a continuing story for days. As deadlines approached and time was short, rewrite did everything, burglaries or divorces from the beats. It was hurry, hurry and then slow down only a little, until the next deadline which began within a half hour or so.

Directly in front of the lineup of the rewrite threesome was the copyboys' desk, a work bench against a wall where they had tools to cut up stories and paste them onto sheets of blank paper. They would hand the clippings to whomever asked for them, often rewrite people changing portions of stories as editions changed. Rewrite would mark up the stories, write inserts, call out "Copy" and the boy would take it all to Aggie for a final check before it was sent to the copy desk for headline, and to the composing room.

Rewrite in 1952, consisted of three people. Jack Smith had been on the Daily News, a few yards from the United Press Bureau, and had become dissatisfied there and moved out. We had met in the News building and out on stories. At the middle desk was Wally Rawles, a dour, middle-aged veteran of public relations and news who could do anything, but was a specialist in a Hearst favorite, Senator Joseph McCarthy. Rawles handled most of the anti-Communist stories, including public hearings. He despised McCarthy, and was scrupulously fair in his stories. The headlines, by someone on the Copy Desk, were wild and angry. On Rawles right, closest to Aggie, was Richard O'Connor, thirty-seven years old in 1952, who did not talk about himself much but was an extraordinary writer. He was usually busy on personal projects, authoring books, except when interrupted by Aggie or the assistant city editors. Rewritemen got more money under the union contract, a hundred and ten dollars a week compared to one hundred for five-year journeymen.

Pictures the Old Way

An important news element was out sight from the Herald City Room. Located down a corridor beyond the Managing Editor's office was the photo lab. They were the other side of the news coverage team.

In those days they used ungainly but versatile four-by-five-inch Speed Graphics with sheets of film in holders which had to be exchanged for fresh film after each shot. Their disposable flash bulbs were the size of household light bulbs.

It as a surprise to see some of the guys (women were almost unknown in the trade but equally good) using cameras with roll film. Why waste a roll for one pic? I went to Air Corps photo school in Denver in 1943 and our civilian *woman* instructor taught roll film. We also used 3-foot-long aerial cameras. Little roll film "candid cameras" were available before the war. The 4x5 speeded developing, maybe. Photogs could read negatives just like b&w positive and know if the shot was good.

Feature films for movie theaters were made on 35mm film. TV used 16mm film. I did a 16mm film interview with the Sirhan judge in 1969 after that trial. Network TV used two-inch tape.

Competition among the city's newspapers stepped up rapidly after Aggie Underwood became City Editor. In the fall of 1948, the Times Mirror Corporation had completed a new building and they opened a new afternoon newspaper, the Mirror, a "tabloid," referring to small size pages, not lurid headlines. Tabloids like the Post in New York were made for easy reading on a bus or streetcar. It was presumed that the existing commuter-reader traffic in New York and Los Angeles would continue and build after World War II. Instead, television swallowed the world rapidly, as the digital era would do to TV and all news outlets forty years later.

About six months after I joined the Herald, Jack Smith quit and went to a PR job. Aggie moved me to the rewrite battery. I heard that there were complaints by older reporters on the Herald, including beat men, who would have liked the rewrite job and the extra pay. I also heard from O.Connor that Aggie squelched such talk by saying I was a faster and better writer than most. However, I didn't get the raise. I figured it was a tryout. After a few weeks, Aggie explained. Managing

Editor Campbell would not approve rewrite pay because he said I was too young. I was barely twenty-nine. Aggie said to hang on, it would come. After about a year, the raise showed up.

Life On Rewrite

Rewrite, with its pressure to write fast, was easy after UP, where every minute was a deadline. A former UP editor wrote a book entitled "Deadline Every Minute." In a world-wide news service, somewhere a newspaper or radio station had a deadline. At the Herald, we had pauses between the five deadlines a day. Soft life.

I had to adjust to working with copyboys. Others might call them "Boy," but unless I was hurriedly writing a long piece I did not even call "Copy!" at them, which was the request to carry a piece of paper from my desk to Aggie's desk a few feet south. I carried it. I was not motivated by the old saying, "Be nice to the copyboy because someday he will be your managing editor." The fact was that two copyboys usually on duty, Bob Hull and Chuck Riley, were taller, heavier, and looked older than I. Hull became a friend. I worked with him for a year or so at Southern California Edison public relations many years later. When I was hired at KNXT, Channel 2, in Hollywood, in 1964, Riley was working in that News Department.

Aggie's desk was about six feet away from my chair. One afternoon, Aggie began yelling on the telephone. She slammed down the fone and quickly stepped over to my desk. She asked for notes on a Wilshire area drug bust. The notes I had taken from the police beat reporter, probably Jimmy Shambra or Norman Jacoby, were on the carbon spike and amounted to a few lines of typewritten shorthand, single-spaced. Aggie put it on the desk and ran a finger down until she came to a line that said, "booked residing house of prost." "Good," she said, and pushed it back. She said the owner of the apartment house where the drug arrest had taken place, an upscale neighborhood near Wilshire Boulevard and Western, was angry because the Herald Express story called it a "house of prostitution." That was wording used by police when they booked someone who possessed or used drugs in a house or apartment. It separated such incidents from arrests in a car or on the street. Reporters knew that, but the apartment house owner was furious, insisting it was wrong. Aggie, noted for supporting her troops, told the woman to go to Hell and hung up, then looked for my notes.

The job was not entirely in the office. Almost everyone covered the Rose Parade. A couple of years I helped cover the Tournament of Roses in Pasadena, then went down the canyon to the Rose Bowl in the afternoon to help a bit on the game. The Herald hired Los Angeles motorcycle cops for the day to run undeveloped film back to the paper from the parade and the game. First, at about dawn, the motor cops led three or four Herald express reporters and photographers' cars on a sirens-blaring parade through traffic to a parking area near where the parade began. The cops delivered pictures of floats to the office and returned. When the football game began, the photog would shoot pictures and I'd be on the sidelines with him writing captions. The motor cop would come to us on the field and rush the pictures down the freeway to the Herald building.

One year I was upstairs with the sports writers. At the Rose Bowl, sports writers sat in a "press room" that consisted of a row of seats, maybe a dozen, on the southwest side of the Bowl. It was a platform, separated from regular seats below by a simple verticle partition over which we looked toward the football field. A long table held portable typewriters. There was a cover in the unlikely event of rain, and a few dim lights. There were no windows. This was open air, it was January first, and it was cold and dark before the game ended. If there was a breeze, it went through coats of shivering writers. Radio had an enclosed booth, a privilege which was given to all press people years later.

The Coliseum press box, where I had helped our UP sports specialist at some football games, was much more civilized.

Quitting the Herex

In August, 1955, I asked to meet Aggie in the parking lot after work. I told her I was quitting and was going to the Mirror. She seemed to take it without any reaction. I told her I'd be gone in two weeks. On Monday, she was cold and upset. She didn't say why, but surely it was about loyalty. She had hired me as a reporter and soon pushed me ahead of the seniority line to be on her higher-paid rewrite battery. She repeatedly demonstrated trust in my judgment and ability, and counted on me to return the loyalty. Now, I was going to the Herald's main afternoon competitor, which she may have considered an insult.

We didn't talk much for the next two weeks. Aggie did not waste words with her staff, but this was something new. We were both stiffly polite with the few words necessary to talk about stories she assigned me throughout the day. The City Desk seemed quieter, which may have been intentional so that I heard less. There were exceptions.

Near the end of the first frigid day of two weeks notice, in a voice that was intended to reach across two desks to my ears, she told Bill Pigue, one of her Assistant City Editors, "Bill, call Ray Parker." She was going after a Mirror reporter. Several days later as she walked by me she said, "Ray Parker is coming over." She did not wait to get a reaction. Parker was one of the better-known general assignment reporters in Los Angeles, possibly the Mirror's best. We had met many times, starting in my United Press days.

City Editors in Los Angeles had an informal agreement not to raid each other's staff. It could drive salaries up. But, if someone was looking for a job, that was different. At the Press Club, I had told a reporter from the Mirror that

I was looking. In a few weeks he called and said if I was still looking I might want to call Jim Bassett, the City Editor. I called and met Bassett someplace close to the Mirror. He asked what I was paid, I told him a hundred-thirty-five, and he said he could match it, but sorry, no more. I could start in two weeks. Fine.

The trade of Mirror and Herald reporters spurred some light discussion on the papers about who got the best deal. I knew I did. I took the Mirror job to join a vested pension plan. The Herald had none for lower-end staff until they reached normal retirement age, if they did. Another reason to move was that working for a Hearst newspaper was not something most of us bragged about. Reporting on the Herald was professional, but the sensationalist Hearst style did not foster a good image. Headlines, which were designed to promote street sales, were trashy at times and sometimes belied the story beneath.

A big problem was the Newspaper Guild, a vertical union which included almost every kind of non-executive job on the Herald. Reporters thought they were outnumbered by circulation people, mainly truck drivers who seemed to go into every contract negotiation threatening to strike. They had walked out in the past, so the threat was real, and unsettling. Guild membership was required to work at the Herald. Mirror employees did not have the Guild. The Guild wrote to me at the Mirror and demanded that I continue paying dues as a "member of the Mirror unit." I ignored it. A second letter threatened to expel me from the Guild if I did not pay, which they did. I was not anti-union. For about six months on the Mirror I wrote a daily column about unions, factual, impartial, and I made lifelong friends among staff members and executives of unions. It's an interesting business. First of all, it is a business which seeks to grow, sometimes for the union staff's benefit.

A few years later, at a journalism banquet, standing at a bar with two guests, Nick Williams, Editor of the Times, and George Hearst Junior, grandson of WRH, who had become publisher of the Herald-Examiner,

I mentioned that I had once worked for both of their companies, now worked for CBS, and said I liked television better than newspapers. "But you had fun at the Herald, didn't you?" said Hearst. I was noncommittal.

Six years later the Mirror-News and the Examiner were shut down. Ray parker complained to me that if he had declined Aggie's offer he would have received thirteen years severance pay from the Times-Mirror Corporation. He got less than half that from the Herald, having been there only six years. He blamed me. I had the same loss moving the other way, but could blame only myself. Ann and I spent my six years Mirror severance during a month in Europe.

I seldom saw Aggie after leaving the Herald. When John Grover, the Mirror's editorial page editor, was invited to be editor of the 1959 Greater Los Angeles Press Club yearbook, the 8-Ball Final, he decided to run some stories about women of the press, including his boss's wife, Mrs. Norman (Buffy) Chandler. Grover asked me to write a story about Aggie. I was an Assistant City Editor of the Mirror at that time.

Opposite the Aggie story Grover ran a full-page picture of a graying Irish grandmother who was a bit serious, maybe suspicious, or just uncomfortable being dressed for an evening social event. The headline told the story: "Portrait of an Executive." It began:

"You've heard and read the story of Agness Underwood, fighting reporter and City Editor. It's a great story, but it has tended to eclipse another – that of Agness Underwood, newspaper executive."

Aggie, the story said, was a boss who was dedicated to her staff, and they to her. It also noted that the staff could not have carried their friend in a job which was that complex unless she had the executive ability to handle the people and the details of the business:

"The job means a lot more than simply acting as mother hen to a group of fun-loving photogs, sometimes strayful reporters and itinerant prima donnas on the rewrite battery."

Soon after the year book came out, I received a letter from Aggie:

"When someone first told me that there was a story about me, by you, in the Eight Ball, I got goose pimples and cold chills," she wrote. "Considering some of the bad times I must have given you, I'm almost overwhelmed. Please accept my sincere thanks... and if at any time I can be of service to you or yours....I'd be proud."

Aggie never gave me a bad time about anything, until I resigned. The only other time her displeasure showed was when, 26 months after that letter was written, the Mirror and the Examiner folded. Aggie was about to become an Editor of the new Herald-Examiner. Someone had told her that I would be looking for a job, and she called me that Friday afternoon, January second, 1962, at the Mirror. I turned her down, explaining that another offer had surfaced already. Bang went the phone.

The following Monday I walked in the Herald-Examiner City Room. Aggie glanced up, returned to her job handling copy for the first edition of the new combined paper, and when she was through left the room without looking at me. I knew she always went to the rest room after hours of putting out the first edition. She would be back. I could wait. I was on my way to the Mirror to finish closing out that career.

I waited close to her desk. When she returned, she said frostily:

"Yes, sir. What can I do for you?"

"I just wanted to thank you in person for the offer, but no thanks anyway."

"Oh."

She softened immediately and asked me if there were any especially good people on the Mirror that I would recommend?

Jeff Davis as a rewriteman was great. Out of shape, seriously graying, couldn't get around very well, but wrote like an angel. The Labor Editor who had replaced me in that job on the Mirror a few years back, Dan Swinton, was good. She hired both.

The Examiner's Labor Editor, Harry Bernstein, was going to the Times where the long-time Labor Editor, Howard Kennedy, was out. The Times historically had a reputation as being virulently anti-labor. Kennedy disliked labor unions, and made it clear. Bernstein liked unions and was known for that at the Times before they hired him. The Times was indeed becoming a more liberal-looking newspaper.

I had spent three years at the Herald, and the best part was on outside assignments.

Thank You for the Ride Mr. President

In March, 1953, Harry Truman, out of office only two months, was on a train headed for Los Angeles. He was going to Long Beach Navy harbor to visit the Missouri, the battleship where papers were signed to end the war with Japan.

City Editor Aggie Underwood dispatched a reporter and two photographers in two cars to meet the train in Pasadena, where it would stop for about twenty minutes around seven a.m.

All of the press would be waiting at the station in Los Angeles. The train would arrive too late for us to get a picture in our first edition deadline, about nine a.m. Aggie decided to send two photographers to Pasadena, hoping none of the other papers would do so. One photog would rush back with the first picture he could get of Mr. Truman. That picture would be in our first edition. A reporter and second photographer would wait in Pasadena until the train left for Los Angeles.

When our crew of three, in two cars, arrived at the Pasadena station, the train was already there. HST was walking beside the train. There was no Secret Service guard for an ex-President. No aides. Nobody. He was alone. He saw us coming, stopped walking and waited.

He cheerfully greeted the three-man news crew and posed for pictures taken by Photogs Ben White and our other Herald Express photographer whose name or face have departed from my memory. The second photographer took their four-by-five film holders and left for the Herald building downtown.

In a moment a conductor stepped out of the train and told Mr. Truman they had to leave. They would arrive in L.A., slowly, in about twenty minutes. Aggie had anticipated a potential story. I had been told what to say, and I was ready.

"Mr. President, would you mind if my photographer and I ride into L.A. with you?"

"Sure fellas, come on," he said, and he led us into -- I was surprised -- his private car. I thought he'd have a private room, not a whole car, and we would find (and pay for) seats somewhere close to ex-President Truman. He said a friend had loaned him the private car which was made for just a few guests.

(I learned years later in another job that it is easy to rent a railroad car of any type. And, not expensive, depending on the time, the load (corn or cars or oil) and distance. It is like renting a truck with a driver.)

Mr. Truman invited us to sit at a card table with four chairs. He introduced us to Bess and the conductor. Then the four of us, not the conductor who was in charge of the car, sat at the table and talked all the way to Los Angeles.

He was a thoughtful host, asking us about our jobs. And, I was happy to finally have a chance to ask about his job. It was like this:

"Mr. President, when you were elected in 1948, I stayed up all night listening to results to find out who won. I read that you went to bed early. How could you do that? I heard it was because you knew you had won. Is that right?"

And he explained that he knew he had won, though Dewey was ahead in the count at that time, because he (HST) knew where the votes were coming from, he knew his voters had not all been counted yet, and he knew that when all were in he would win. So he went to bed on his normal schedule.

My first lesson in political elections: Know who your voters are.

The second lesson was in how to pose for pictures getting off a train.

When the train stopped in L.A., the four of us waited inside while the conductor removed a flat metal cover which was a part of the floor until it was time to raise it to one side, uncovering the steps so the passengers could go down.

Ben and I waited for Mr. Truman and Bess to go, but he waved us over and said "You fellas get off first." Ben and I stepped over to the stairs and started down.

At the bottom, on the ground, was a crowd of reporters and photographers. When they saw Ben and me get off, they booed! We'd had the President all to ourselves.

I found out decades later why Mr. Truman had Ben and me go first. I described the situation, with the press in L.A. booing, to Herb Klein, Nixon's former Communications Director. Of courses, Herb said, that's routine preparation. "Sweep" your photo location and be sure conductors, staff and anybody else who is incidental to the picture get off first or stay back out of sight.

Mr. Truman didn't want us standing at the top of the stairs, appearing in all of the pictures, and he knew the other photographers wouldn't want us there.

Ben had to get a ride back to Pasadena to get his car, and it was worth it. But the picture we would have treasured was never taken around that small table with Harry and Bess. Digital cameras arrived decades too late. It took a long time to realize what was wrong about riding with Harry Truman and Bess on a train. Looking back at the incident more than half a century later, it is easy to see the problem: No pictures were taken, and that was my call. What happened? I missed a story.

When I got to the City Room, Aggie Underwood asked me if Truman said anything, was there a story? Nothing new, I said. "OK," she said, and the assignment was over. If I had said yes, it was a fun ride, she would have said to write something.

Instead, your reporter, a five-year journeyman accustomed to easy familiarity with Governors and murderers, was overwhelmed and blew the opportunity for a funny story. All I did at the time was give a columnist, Bill Kennedy, a note on what Mr. Truman said. The Secret Service was not a privilege of an ex-President. Later ex-Presidents, yes. Mr. Truman told us on the ride from Pasadena that in the White House he had a normal Secret Service staff of thirty-two, and when he traveled it was twice that, but zero now. Kennedy wrote it.

Later in the day I went to the Missouri in the harbor and got in somebody else's picture. On the deck of the Missouri, I'm in a picture, standing in the back of a group, seeming not to pay much attention, smoking a cigarette (which soon was tossed over the side.) There was a small crowd of press around the ex-President, but I was relaxed. I'd had my private time with HST and just watched the others.

Newspapers still run those "Gee Whiz, look at me doing......." by a reporter who is riding a circus elephant or, if able and lucky, goes up with one of the Blue Angels for a dream flight in a jet fighter.

Actually, that is what this memoir is about – looking at what reporters do, and who they are.

Moose

The Moose was unique among Los Angeles rewritemen. In the loose and forgiving atmosphere of the Herald Express, he brought determined discipline as an author and drinker.

Richard O'Connor apparently acquired the name "Moose," referring to his size, from Tom Caton, who used the name often. Caton was the Herald's top general assignment reporter and a future City Editor. He was as tall as O'Connor, probably around six-three, and usually wore a fedora hat, though most reporters no longer did. Caton was a business-suited, talkative news hunter to whom the expression "coat tails flying" applied naturally. O'Connor, his wide shoulders hunched forward, lumbered into the City Room almost unnoticed. His size might have signified strength, but he never hinted at muscle nor raised his voice. He dressed casually, ready to ease into an interview or slump over a glass on a bar.

O'Connor had blond hair and a handsome, round Irish face with eyes that looked through, not at. He was not likely to engage, Irish style, in a lively, lengthy and friendly conversation. He was not slow, but difficult to interest. Conversely, he enjoyed talking for hours with low-end bartenders. He might silently, with raised eyes, announce to a friend his disdain for someone's trite or simple-minded comment. He sometimes appeared to be rudely silent, his mind pondering another world. It was a fact that his thoughts often were elsewhere. His colleagues saw him, but his life was his own.

O'Connor wrote books. He was a Civil War historian and chronicler of the "Wild West." He did his research wherever the material was available, organized it in notes, then wrote some of the books while on the job. Those who were around him were aware of his writing, but he seldom talked about a work in progress except to indicate it was a project that required his attention.

O'Connor wrote his books between stories on his rewrite desk. He went from one task to the other, shifting gears seamlessly, as the digital generation would say. In the spring of 1953 when I went on rewrite, O'Connor was finishing a biography of General Philip Sheridan, who was noted for stomping on Confederate places like Shenandoah Valley, Virginia. How did O'Connor happen to write that book? He said he was interested in Civil War history and had not been able to find a biography of that particular general. The oversight, if there was one, has been corrected in many publications, and O'Connor wrote a good book about the general. I didn't buy it, but borrowed it, and was impressed by what he had done. It had to have taken extraordinary mental organization to produce as many books as fast as he did, a year or two apart, grinding out narratives and references that made good sense and easy reading. He did all of that while being interrupted frequently in his newspaper job, and suffering not infrequent hangovers. The afternoon newspapers of the Forties and Fifties in Los Angeles had four or five editions a day.

At the Herald Express, during deadline scrambles, new stories or updates were put together in a shouting, cutting, pasting chain that ran from a typewriter to a circulation truck. What came out of a typewriter first went to the City Desk for checking, to the Copy Desk where headlines were added, then to the composing room where each story or change was set in type and pages were matted to make half-cylinder metal plates, and finally the press room where the papers were printed. This could all be done in an hour and a half. A delay in the creative beginning at the keyboard could slow the whole machine.

O'Connor was an octave of calm in that kind of tensely noisy situation. He didn't get excited or shout at copyboys. Writing was just a job of pushing keys and making marks on paper. O'Connor's somewhat indifferent manner did not mean he ignored the need to hurry, but that he was one person in the house who could keep things in perspective. This was demonstrated by a story which I vaguely remember that City Editor Aggie Underwood confirmed. If not, it is believable.

The Herald was owned by William Randolph Hearst. He was flamboyant in his public life, running his newspapers and attempting to bully the world into operating his way, also in courting Hollywood and carrying on openly with a movie star, Marion Davies, which was an enduring embarrassment to his children and grandchildren.

Hearst was alleged to have been involved in the death of a producer/director, Thomas Ince, at a birthday party for Ince aboard Hearst's yacht in San Diego, in 1924. Guests included Charlie Chaplin. The cause of death, and the responsible party or parties, were not disclosed. It remains a mystery, though the suggestion was made and fostered by others in the press that Hearst shot Ince and had it all covered up.

The death of Hearst in 1951 was, even among other newspapers, a major story. At the Herald Express, it was "Stop the presses."

Aggie gave O'Connor enough information to start a story and told him that more would be coming quickly. This was history, and the accomplished historian on rewrite could give it the appropriate bombshell touch.

Aggie would never give anyone a lead and say "go from there" to finish the story. It was her absolute rule. She also would not stand over someone while they wrote. Never. She thought it was destructive to the writer's job. She told O'Connor to write a lead paragraph on Hearst, give it to her, and then write long and fast.

O'Connor heard a few details, put a "book" of paper and carbons in his typewriter and began to write. Aggie kept her distance, watching seconds race past, praying for poetry. The entire building was waiting. O'Connor pulled the book from his typewriter, handed the book to a copyboy who handed it to Aggie a few feet away, put another book in his typewriter and continued writing. Aggie looked at O'Connor's first paragraph of journalistic history and said: "Oooooh no!" The first take said:

"William Randolph Hearst today joined Thomas Ince in Heaven."

I first heard that story a year or so after Hearst died, after Aggie hired me. I believe Aggie confirmed it, and I can hear her saying, again, "Oooooh no!" I don't recall asking O'Connor.

He handed over another book in a few seconds. It said: "William Randolph Hearst is dead."

Of course. That was enough for the lead. Descriptive additions would have been excess.

O'Connor's method of writing books was simple, but amazing in a way. His typewriter was seldom idle. He was an author in the moments when he was not working on a story assigned by Aggie or one of her Assistant City Editors, Bill Pigue or Lew Young. The day started at six a.m., with a flurry of activity taking stories from the police beat or the overnight crew who had a radio car and came to the office, or updating stories that had run late the day before.

After the breakfast break about seven-thirty a.m., O'Connor pulled out his notes, which were handwritten on yellow legal pads. Then he put his personal paper in the typewriter. His "book" consisted of a sheet of yellow paper, a carbon and a sheet of white paper, which was on top. Then, referring to notes, he wrote. When he finished a page, he read it, corrected typos or words he felt needed improvement, and then pulled out an envelope and put the white copy in the envelope to mail it to his editor. He took the yellow copy home. At the end of the day, at three p.m., he had a few pages, two or three or maybe six. It was routine to watch him lick the envelope and seal it, and put it in his pocket to mail. Sometimes, when I drove him home, enroute to my home in the San Fernando Valley, he got out at the Hollywood Post Office to mail his book.

Aggie had three rewritemen, and she did not let O'Connor write his books while the other two worked. O'Connor was on salary and earned it. When Aggie had a story, she might call out, "O'Connor, it's Jake," (Norman Jacoby on the police beat), and his phone would ring. O'Connor would pull his book out of the typewriter, put it in the top right drawer so it didn't fall into the mess like we all had on our desks, and would write whatever Aggie had for him. When it was all clear, which was usually after the deadline for the next edition, he took his white-carbon-yellow pages from the drawer, put them in his typewriter, and continued writing. "Sheridan the Inevitable," the manuscript, eventually became a pile of publisher's page proofs which he brought to work and corrected and put in the mail.

He continued to turn out more books. Next was one about the sinking of the Titanic. He had been assigned to go interview a survivor, a woman, and he came back convinced it was a great story and he would write a book. Then he discovered that Walter Lord had recently written a book which was about to be made into a movie, "A Night to Remember." O'Connor had done a lot of work and decided he had enough for his own book. He sold it to Penguin Press paperbacks, with the title, "Down to Eternity," which came out in 1956.

About the time I was assigned to the rewrite battery, Aggie suggested I drive O'Connor to and from work, since my route took me within a block or so of his apartment, and he did not drive. In a couple of years I came to know O'Connor better than most people in the newspaper business. He did not talk much about his books and almost never about his personal background. He did not carry gossip about the newspaper. It didn't interest him. He did say that Aggie "has the instincts of a barracuda." He did not elaborate. I presumed he meant in the drive to beat our competition,

He did have a number of drinking friends. Two of his favorite people that I knew about were bartenders in the same block as the Herald. Both bars fronted on Pico Boulevard.

Moran's, where Curly was head bartender and maybe owner, was where the Herald people sometimes went when they were off work in mid-afternoon. O'Connor spent many afternoons there or down the street a hundred feet to the other bar in that block, the Continental. I usually went home without him those days. I'd pick him up the next morning, coming down Cahuenga Boulevard into Hollywood, and stop at his apartment house which was a block north of Hollywood boulevard. He would be waiting or would come out within a minute. I met his wife twice, at the apartment when I went to the door to get him. She was tall, dark haired, a little older than he (he was about 38). She worked, but he didn't talk about it. We'd drive maybe twenty minutes and be at the Herald by six a.m. He almost always had some home work with him, research for his books. He spent many hours a week at the Hollywood library.

Probably better than Curly at Moran's, O'Connor liked George Banker, bartender at the Continental, which was on the northeast corner of Pico and Georgia Street. Just south of that corner was the Georgia Street receiving hospital, where we reporters often went to check on stories about people experiencing the sudden need for trauma care. O'Connor seemed to enjoy hanging out at the Continental more than anywhere. It was only a step from Moran's, but had a lower class clientele of neighborhood drunks whom Curly did not want to have around Moran's. George, the Continental bartender, was loud and friendly, the opposite of Curly at Moran's, who was friendly but quietly authoritative. "The Banker" was O'Connor's bartender of choice, which meant more and longer visits than to Moran's.

Following these late days, O'Connor was always able to work the next morning, both for the Herald and on his books. One morning he tried to work, but as soon as Aggie called a break for breakfast, about eight, he went to Moran's. A few regulars from the Herald went to a small cafeteria across Pico from the Herald parking lot. It was almost directly below the second-floor apartment occupied by Bell, who used to open the window and call out unintelligible demands or insults to passers by. Bell, sometimes seen on the sidewalk, was toothless and had scraggly gray hair, with clothes to match. She was the oldest (middle seventies) prostitute working in Los Angeles, according to the experts.

O'Connor's breakfast this day at Moran's continued after the others returned from the cafeteria, which was unusual. He was still missing when a reporter and photographer who had been on a special assignment, some-where on the Mexico border, arrived home and came to report to Aggie. They had done some drinking at a bar. In that haze, they were offered and bought a kid, a small, dusty tan goat, the size of a large cat, but with longer legs and small bumps on its head which would become horns.

They saw that O'Connor was out and decided to make a gift of the kid to him. It had a rope leash, and they pushed it under O'Connor's desk where his legs resided when he was writing. They pushed the chair under the desk far enough to hold the goat in place, then moved to a far corner of the City Room. O'Connor came back soon. His audience pretended not to notice him. He didn't talk to anyone, just pulled the chair our and started to sit down. Then he saw the little goat.

He held the rope leash, pondered it briefly, then pulled the goat out, untied the rope, picked up the goat by its midsection, put it under his arm and announced: "I can get ten bucks for this." And, he walked out. He did not return all day. The story heard from Curly was that O'Connor sold the goat to another customer, and O'Connor took a cab home to Hollywood.

After I quit the Herald in August, 1955, stories about O'Connor contin-ued, usually relayed by Tom Caton. Three months later O'Connor wrote a letter to me at the Mirror. It was on New York Journal American stationery, another Hearst newspaper. He said he was "now illuminating the New York scene. I wonder if there's any truth in the legend that anyone who leaves the Herald always betters himself?"

He didn't say what he was doing on the paper, but gave a clue. "It isn't a bad place to work. They have SIXTEEN (his caps) rewritemen here, six of them on the lobster (night) shift."

He was still writing books. His next letter said:

"My agent says she's going to get $1200 out of McCall's for me on the Johnstown Flood piece, and Doubleday sold the paperback rights to the Chickamauga novel for $6000 to Bantam, but I only get half. They want the Civil War novel I'm writing now for next summer, and Bat Masterson for early '57. I don't see how I'm going to be able to leave here with all the money that's lying around."

"All the money," $7200, was about a year's pay in 1955.

The Moose said he had met up with some of his L.A. drinking friends in New York. The tone of his letters indicated he'd prefer to spend the time doing something else, but drinking pals deserved loyalty. A December, 1955, letter said:

"My agent sold the rights to an English edition of the Titanic book, which is coming out in this country January 31 (1956). I still think it's the best thing I've done and the best idea I've had, and should have got wealthy off it. I suppose I'll have to endure poverty for another few years." That letter closed with "regards to Ann."

O'Connor finished a book, "Bat Masterson," published in 1957, which he dedicated to "Ruby and Tom Caton for native guide work in western Kansas." The Catons were in "Dodge" briefly and Caton said they tracked down some minor information for O'Connor. That book was named for a famous gunslinger/lawman, and was nicely timed with production of a television series. The producers paid O'Connor a consultant's fee of $300 a week, according to Caton, about the same as Aggie's salary. The opening of the "Bat Masterson" TV programs carried, on-screen and enlarged behind the title of the show, the cover of O'Connor's book. It was a break for the author, boosting sales and his name. The money O'Connor got for "consulting" and use of the cover of his book would discourage any other writers who might have tried to claim "Bat Masterson" was their story. Meanwhile, O'Connor produced another book, "Wild Bill Hickok," published in 1959, about a late 1800s gunfighter.

O'Connor finally moved back to his home grounds, Maine. During the Herald Express days he occasionally mentioned Bar Harbor or Ellsworth. Caton reported that O'Connor had dropped anchor at a local bar in Ellsworth. When Ann and I visited that state for the first time, in 1989, we drove through Ellsworth. O'Connor had died years earlier, I believe at age 60. I considered stopping at any bar that looked like one he would accept, and inquire if he was known there. But, I could not think of anyone at home, still living, who would be interested in an update.

Atomic Dawn

Soon after World War II ended with an atomic flash, the United States began experimenting with modified nuclear devices in the Nevada desert. The momentary light of those pre-dawn explosions could be seen in Los Angeles, almost 300 miles away.

The tests were announced in advance. Gamblers in Nevada knew when to pick up their chips and step outside to watch the sky turn from black to white and black again. It was part of the excitement in the desert resort, although some people complained that tourists might stay away rather than radiate.

At least one newspaper ran a picture of the Los Angeles City Hall tower silhouetted by the Atomic Dawn sixty-five miles northwest of Las Vegas. That made atoms a personal experience.

Agness Underwood had a better idea. She decided to put a reporter and photographer up there in the sky. The newsmen would carry Herald readers to a front-row seat with words and pictures.

In those days, there was a Glendale Airport, Grand Central it was called, located in what is now an industrial area West of downtown Glendale, near the future home of the Los Angeles Zoo.

Photographer Ben White and his reporter went to the Glendale airport about three a.m. Our pilot, Kit Carson, had a four-seater, single-engine, high-wing monoplane, ready for an unusual mission, a first for any newspaper as far as we knew.

Carson briefed us. We'd be flying straight at the test bomb, but far enough away so we would not be tossed around. He made sure we were strapped into our seats. There were no parachutes. With Ben up front beside him, Carson took off and flew northeast over the Tehachapi Mountains to the desert towns of Victorville and Barstow. He checked in by radio with the Civil Aeronautics Administration (FAA now) controller in Daggett. The "bomb" was still scheduled to go off at five-twenty a.m. Not *about* then, exactly then, to the second. They were precise in such details. Carson turned north toward Yucca Flats, Nevada.

The story in the Herald-Express that afternoon said we circled over Daggett until shortly before the atomic device was scheduled to go off, and that we were sixty miles away from the test site. That was a mild cover-up, written to appease the Civil Air Administration. We didn't circle or even slow down near Daggett. The CAA did not want any copycats following our trail in their own planes when future tests were scheduled. Pilots were always warned to stay away. If someone got too close, a test might have to be delayed or canceled. These events required a great many people and cost millions, which midway into the Twentieth Century was a lot of money. However, we were going to get as close as was allowed, in Nevada, not California.

About five a.m. our little plane was purring into the darkness north of Mount Charleston, a resort west of Las Vegas. We could not continue much farther toward Yucca Flats. Carson began to circle over the desert at twelve-thousand feet. We wanted to be pointed toward Ground Zero at the right moment. He kept checking by radio to be sure his watch was correct and the test countdown was proceeding on schedule. He wanted to know the blast time so Ben White could take his pictures, but also he did not want to be staring into the darkness when the flash occurred right in front of him. He was flying on instruments and did not want to chance being temporarily blinded.

The countdown proceeded, with Carson repeating to us what he heard by radio on his earphones. A couple of seconds before blast time, the pilot put his head down. His passengers stared straight ahead.

Imagine a black velvet night, with nothing visible except stars. The desert at night can be very dark and lonesome. Far away on the ground were two or three tiny white spots, separated by miles. They might be automobiles on remote desert roads.

Then a flashbulb went off in our faces.

The sun rose instantly. It was daylight everywhere. My eyes squinted at what looked like a noontime sun that displayed hills and sage out to the horizon. Carson, head down, saw the floor of a suddenly visible cockpit. From that altitude Ben and I could see about fifty miles of desert, in full daylight, but it slowly grew darker as the mushroom cloud faded.

The public was accustomed to seeing photographs of witnesses to the blasts wearing dark glasses. We didn't have any. Carson would not have worn them while flying, in case another aircraft was in the vicinity, visible only if we could see blinking wing lights. But, Daggett would have cautioned us if anyone else flew into the area. Carson's chin was on his chest and he continued to look at the floor. Ben and I looked ahead trying to absorb it all.

"Jesus Christ," said White.

The pilot asked if it was safe to look up, and we said yes, don't miss this.

We were flying toward a huge fire, a spreading mushroom straight ahead at about our altitude and rising. It was big and it was wild. Being up there gave us a new insight. It was not a cloud. Countless pictures showed the mushroom. But, this was a boiling doughnut of fire and smoke. The lower flaming surface rolled up the outside of the doughnut and over the top of the doughnut and down into the middle, then up again on the outside, roiling over and down inside the doughnut hole. It was a continuous churning rainbow. Brilliant purples and reds, yellows, blues mixed with black streaks of smoke, occupied the middle half of our horizontal horizon.

Ben was busy taking pictures with his Speed Graphic, flipping film holders over, shooting again, removing holders and replacing them with others, and shooting more.

As we flew closer, the doughnut seemed to expand outward and move upward. Slowly, the bright perimeter of the atomic cauldron moved toward center, and a slim dark cloud moved up, drifting in the wind. The fires faded until it was dark all around again.

We hadn't felt any bump from the blast. All we had was light to match the sun.

Dawn, the real one, was coming rapidly. The sun began to brighten the eastern sky, and we began to see a tower of smoke above the doughnut. It started to drift eastward, zig-zagging as winds changed direction at higher altitudes.

Was it frightening? In our business we saw lots of violence: floods, crashes, fires, quakes. The scale of those events ranged from small to gigantic, especially forest fires. The difference here was the light. That was the spectacle, by itself.

Time to go. We had pictures to develop, a story to write, a deadline for both. We turned and started back. The sand and brush were easy to see now in the natural dawn. Carson checked with the CAA in Daggett and later landed at Glendale. We rushed to the Herald-Express, and did our black and white pictures and story, which were permanent memories of a new world.

After more than 50 years, it's no doubt a clear memory also for the thousands of Marines and Navy personnel who were involved in those dozens of tests, soldiers who were in trenches a few miles from ground zero on some, and those technicians and members of the public who were invited to observe from bunkers, safe places on the desert, with dark glasses.

Not many years later, over San Joaquin Valley, while flying in a commercial airliner from Sacramento to Los Angeles shortly before dawn, there was a flash in the eastern sky beyond the Sierra Nevada Mountains. I was looking for it: another publicly announced nuclear test in Nevada. From that far away the burst of light was still impressive. The instant dawn in the east silhouetted the north to south Sierra peaks, beyond which was Nevada. It faded in seconds, and the flaming doughnut was never visible.

The Other Pilot

Ben White and I, and our pilot, thought we were alone for our bomb burst.

Decades later, members of the Board of Directors of the San Diego County Water Authority were having lunch at the agency headquarters in San Diego At a table of six Directors, one talked about a recent adventure. He described it as the thrill of a lifetime. I don't remember his "Thrill," but eclipsed it easily with a memory that was still vivid after half a century. I told of going to Nevada to watch an "A-bomb" explode while flying toward ground zero in a small airplane. It was an assignment for a newspaper. The light and the fire were unforgettable. Wow, they agreed that had to have been exciting.

Another Director, Capt. Bill Knutson (USN Ret.), asked, "When was that?" I gave him a rough date. Knutson said he may have been there, flying near the bomb for the Navy. I checked my newspaper clipping at home, and he checked his pilot's log.

At the next Board meeting a month later, we exchanged information. Knutson, a Navy test pilot who went to Vietnam later, was in Nevada on that day I could not forget, the seventh of March, 1955, piloting a jet fighter, a Navy version of the Lockheed F80, out of the Navy base at China Lake, California. He made several such flights during those early atomic tests. He flew closely around the radioactive fire in the sky.

His mission was to learn what effect the "bomb" had on his plane. The explosion we witnessed gave his plane a solid kick in the butt, he said, bumping him upward a few thousand feet. Those of us out there for the Herald Express were far enough away not to feel anything, though we saw a lot. Knutson said he flew within two miles of the cloud. My smiling friend Bill pointed at me and said:

"I did that while you were forty miles away."

Twenty!! Or less. Much less by the time we turned away from the mushroom.

People have asked both of us about radiation. Was it not a danger to us? I told Knutson my answer:

"I don't really I know yet. We will have to wait and see. I was 32 years old then. I'm just 92 now and Bill is only in his late 80s."(We were young even then).

The Girls You Meet Dowtown

Beverly

Beverly was getting married. We weren't going to miss that story. However, she was having trouble finding someone to perform the ceremony.

Beverly and her husband-to- be had arrived at the Hall of Records, got their license, and then looked for a judge. Not easy to do.

Someone often called the Press Room when an unusual couple showed up at the Marriage License counter, like a movie actor.

Beverly had a history. This was Number Fifteen.

The license had to be issued. But, no judge could be found who would join the fun. It did not take much imagination to guess what colleagues or the clergy might say. Some judges did not like to "do" weddings. It was a chore that interrupted serious legal business. One who had become known as "The Marrying Judge" and appreciated voluntary gratuities was not on the bench that day.

For the beat reporters, this was a story. To give it a happy ending, they would help. First, they made sure of the facts. Number Fifteen was a normal-looking guy of middle age, dressed neatly for a wedding. He watched and listened attentively while Beverly, middle aged and blondish and dressed happily in bright colors, was asked, and confirmed, this was Mr. Fifteen. That was enough to resume a search for a judge.

No, thanks, one reporter was told, have your silly game recorded with someone else's name as the presiding dummy. It was late in the day and that judge just wanted to get out and go home.

Rudy Villasenor, the Times courthouse chronicler for decades, promised not to make it a circus story with the judge as ringmaster. It would be serious, if skeptical. Beverly was not sleeping around, she married her guys. The judge agreed, but would make a firm statement that marriage was a no nonsense decision. Deal.

This was the last for Beverly. I have a hazy memory of a short story a few years later that said Beverly (last name du jour) had died, still married to 15.

Marital Musings

In the Twenty-first Century, in California, the couple could choose a relative or almost anyone to marry them. Even I did one at request of the couple. The law was stricter half a century earlier. Presiders had to meet qualifications or have authority in something, which in fine print might include performing weddings. The ceremony could be as brief as, "Do you take Bev to be your wife?" But, filling out the Certificate of Marriage was not simple, and it had to be done correctly before the marriage was recorded and official. That might take days. A judge told me that twice bridegrooms had called him the day after and asked the judge to tear up the certificate. Request denied. A judge knew better than to participate in a fraud.

There were other questions not asked. How did Beverly get a divorce in those difficult times? Liz Taylor had to go through a court hearing to get a divorce. Did not Beverly do the same? Or did she go to Nevada?

We did not go deeply there. In fact, I believe a couple of the reporters signed the marriage papers as witnesses. Anything for love.

Mommy

It was a routine call from the Police Beat. Someone was sick. An ambulance had been dispatched from Georgia Street Receiving Hospital.

Maybe it was just a drunk, or drugs. Probably, there would be no story. However, the address was in the middle of Skid Row. That was only a few blocks from City Hall and the Los Angeles Times. The Times could get there first. If it was a story, the Herald-Express City Editor would not let the Times have an exclusive. A reporter and photographer were sent to check it out.

The Police Beat reporter had said a woman called for help. She said her son was ill. She didn't know what was wrong with him. He did not want her to call an ambulance, but the woman said he really needed help. What were the symptoms? She couldn't answer, he was just sick.

A police car and a Los Angeles City ambulance had arrived before the Herald-Express crew. We parked near them on a dirt lot outside a door on the first floor of an old two-story wood-sided building. It may have been a large home decades before, but now the paint that may have been light gray was faded, off-white, streaked with dirty water runoff from many rains. At this early hour, not long after a cloudy dawn, there was no hint of human activity. Two doors, ten yards apart, looked like something cut into a wall to enter two one-room apartments. One door was open a few inches. The reporter and photographer walked in just as a listless and scrawny young man in T-shirt and white boxer shorts, was being lifted off a bed and put on a gurney.

A policeman stood near the woman who called, apparently the ill man's mother. She studied the reporter and photog. The policeman ignored them, so she did, too.

Eyes had to get accustomed to the darkness. A pull-down shade over the one window let in a little bit of light. "Home" was a single room. The walls were dark, probably from age. There were stains on the wallpaper, which had no discernible pattern, it was just light brown, mainly. Central to the room was a bed, a sheet pulled back to extract a man. An electric hot plate sat on a shakey old table against one wall, and a door beside the table led into a bathroom. There were dirty white dishes stacked on the table waiting to be washed in the bathroom sink.

One bare lightbulb hung from a cord that fell from the center of the low ceiling. Its dim yellowish light did little to improve the shadowy gloom in which furniture and people blended. The room seemed smaller than it was, because little piles of clothing, grocery bags, boxes and paper covered almost any open space not frequently traveled.

When the ambulance crew had loaded the son, one of them came back and closed the door. That darkened the room more. The officer made notes on a pad, and in another minute turned toward the door. The reporter asked the cop what happened. He said he didn't know, the kid was just sick. Drugs? Maybe. When he was gone, the reporter and photographer could take over. It was their time to question Mommy.

Mommy was thin, maybe five feet tall, elderly, all gray, with stringy hair down her back, not combed or brushed in this week, or month. The small face was gaunt, her eyes roaming, not recognizing or stopping anywhere for long. She wore dirty grayish house shoes and a tired, once-white nightgown, mostly covered by a whitish robe which was thin and hung loosely on her.

What could the mother tell about the son's condition, the young man she worried about so much? Had he been ill? She didn't appear to understand the questions, and just looked at the large camera with a flashbulb which the photog held lightly by his side, ready to be lifted for a shot.

Mommy mumbled and walked around the room aimlessly, pausing, walking again, sometimes looking at but not really paying attention to the visitors. They didn't take their eyes off her.

At first, in the dark room, the most unusual thing about her was the white bird. It was sitting on her shoulder, a mid-size parrot, less than a foot high, plus dirty white tail feathers. The parrot balanced easily as if it were part of her clothing, which it was. When Mommy moved, the bird barely stirred, and it, too, became a silent element of a picture lost in shadows.

When she walked away from the visitors, the view of her back was puzzling. Then it made sense, in a way. From her left shoulder and down the back of the robe she wore, down to her waist and farther down to the bottom of the robe, was a dull white and yellow and brown streak, two to three inches wide. It was parrot excrement, dried and crusted, built up for a week, to judge from its thickness. Maybe a month.

The parrot obviously spent days on her shoulder, and its creamy expulsions had become part of her clothing. It was natural to wonder if she took the robe off to lie down or go to the toilet. She would not go outside in her nightgown. Did the sick man bring food to her and the parrot?

A five-foot coat rack near the window showed signs of excrement on its horizontal bar, and more had dried in a saucer-sized pile on the floor below. A high-backed, ragged overstuffed chair also had parrot "mud" on its top ridge and probably there was more on the floor behind. A long look at the bed, with time for eyes to adjust to the low light, disclosed that the bed from which her son had been removed, had been used by Mommy, too. She slept there with the robe on, and dried chunks of parrot crap had fallen onto the sheets. The room did not smell of manure. It was simply musty.

The reporter looked at the photographer and tilted his head toward the door. There would be no more questions, no point in wasting a flash bulb.

The cop was still outside by his car, making the required notes about his call. The photographer waved and drove away with his reporter passenger. There was no sign of the L.A. Times, but it was their exclusive if they wanted it.

Joining the Mirror

On my first day at the Mirror, I learned that the desk next to mine belonged to Otis Chandler, who was a reporter.

That and the relatively new steel furniture throughout the room, gave the place some polish that was absent from the Herald Express. In fact, it was another world. Not that it was clean. Newspaper city rooms were inherently dirty. The printers' ink that rubbed onto hands and clothes of subscribers at home was pervasive in city rooms. Fortunately, ink was soon developed that we who worked there said did not threaten reporters with "Black Lung," the coal miners' disease.

The Times and Mirror were a class above the rest. The Herald was a place to earn a paycheck. The Times and Mirror gave journalists a reason to call their job a profession. It was an attitude, a bit of style that separated groups of people doing the same job at the same level. Location, location also gave TM a power base in the middle of Civic Center. City Hall and the State Building, Board of Supervisors, Police and Sheriff Headquarters, Hall of Records, Courthouses, County Jail, the County Morgue and the Federal Building all were within a block or two. Sheriff Gene Biscailuz, winding down half a century in that job, had his hair cut in the barbershop on the first floor of the Times.

The Redwood Room, a bar/restaurant on the first floor, was home for City and County officials, lawyers and clients. Times and Mirror reporters and editors and press agents were there on business or after work. Next to the Redwood's cashier was a phone, an extension from the Times switchboard.

Skid Row was a few blocks away, but it was invisible, unlike at the Herald which was in a neighborhood of cheap saloons.

With all that uptown coziness at the Mirror, it looked like the Times owned Los Angeles. Not completely, yet. For years the Times, a dignified local newspaper, had been fighting the Hearst empire's boastful morning Examiner for political power. As a pre-high school teen-ager growing up in Glendale during the Depression I was aware of the competition.

After World War II, the Times was winning the morning-paper circulation war, but something was missing: Hearst also owned an afternoon daily, the Herald Express, with a big circulation. The Herald's competition was the independently owned Daily News, a dedicated arm of the Democratic Party.

Correctly anticipating a population boom after the war, Norman Chandler, publisher of the Times, decided to start his own afternoon daily. A new building was added on the southeast corner of the block, at Second and Spring. It housed the new afternoon paper, the Mirror, which started publishing in October, 1948, three years after the surprise atomic peace with Japan. The addition of new newspaper jobs likely created the UP vacancy which I was hired to fill: I did meet one UP staffer nipresser who moved to TM.

It was an open walk-through from the Mirror to the Times, passing among clattering linotype machines and make-up tables in a large room which the papers shared to assemble the pages that would become curved metal molds to fit on the presses.

Big Red Cars traveling on rails from Glendale area suburbs had their own subway entrance to downtown, ending at the underground Hill Street

Station. Yellow streetcars covered city streets. The Mirror was supposed to attract a growing flood of commuters on both.

Norman (it was a company thing to call everyone by his/her first name) started the Mirror with the best of everything: money, a new building and an excellent staff. Norman made Virgil Pinkley, United Press Vice President in charge of Europe coverage during World War II, the Mirror's first publisher. Pinkley brought in another Unipresser, J. Edward Murray, as Managing Editor. Casey Shawhan, an experienced L.A. newspaperman and Hollywood publicist was City Editor.

Shawhan later quit to become head of NBC's West Coast publicity office in Burbank. He was replaced as Mirror CE by Jim Bassett, Admiral Halsey's public relations chief during World War II and later a Times political writer, usually credited with helping Richard Nixon move up in politics. It was Bassett who hired me in 1955.

A Competitive Life

The Mirror had to play catch-up with the Herald Express, building circulation with promotion stunts, colorful entertainment writers, top sports writers adept at cliché-free English, and serious political reporting without the ideological headlines that scarred the Hearst newspapers. A gimmicky sideways tabloid format on the Mirror's front page didn't fit a serious approach to news, and it was confusing, so it was dropped, and the paper looked more like the "broadsheet" Times.

One promotion stunt that had to be dropped was the MirrorPhone interview, which was supposed to be a special report on a key topic or person of the day.

It died in one of the most embarrassing mistakes a paper could make, being caught stealing the opposition's papers out of the press room and calling (Mirrorphony?) the Mirror office uptown to report what was in the Herald.

The thefts were discovered and the next day a Herald photographer was waiting. The Mirror reporter was photographed going into the Herald press room, picking up a copy of the paper, walking a block or two to a payphone, calling his office and reading things from the Herald, then getting on a streetcar back to the Mirror. The reporter didn't even try to run or go someplace else like a café or a bar. He was followed by the Herald photog all the way to the Mirror. It made a hilarious string of pictures for the Herald. Confession: The Mirror did something like that later, and I was involved. (see Lana Turner chapter).

The Mirror "bullpen," as the City Room full of reporters was called, had maybe 25 people who covered special areas such as aviation and smog control while also working general assignment. Sports and Financial crews had separate areas in that room. "Women" stories and Hollywood were covered by reporters elsewhere in the building. Art and Photo departments were separate from the Times. The Mirror's Chief Editorial Writer and Political Editor had no connection with their Times counterparts.

Outside beats included courts, City Hall, Board of Supervisors, Police Department, Sheriff, District Attorney, Grand Jury and the Federal Building. At first, the beats were all staffed by Times and Mirror reporters.

By the time the Mirror and Examiner were "merged," some beats had been consolidated or abandoned. The Federal Building, which at one time had four or five reporters in a press room, was deserted unless a good story was going on at the District Courts and the United States Attorney's office.

There was even a hotel beat, with a press room in the Biltmore. Their job was to report what occurred at conventions, of which there were usually two or three at the downtown hotels, from plumbing fixture manufacturers to bankers to physicians. The idea was that convention goers would buy papers. That beat faded away.

While on the Herald, covering a downtown auto accident, I had met Otis Chandler, a reporter on the Mirror. His father, Norman, was preparing him to become Publisher of the Times, and Otis had even worked in the press room, a two-story palace of noisy and amazingly complicated machinery shedding grease from rollers, dust from newsprint speeding over them, and soot from black ink.

I heard that Otis never bothered to cash his Mirror paychecks, a beginner's salary of about sixty-five dollars a week. He just dumped them in his desk drawer. Maybe it wasn't true. I never looked. A few years later, when Times Mirror Corp. went public, and stock holdings of corporate owners were listed, I calculated he made a million a year just in dividends from company stock. He soon moved to the Times, first as a reporter, then to the business side, becoming a friend of staffers everywhere he went.

Times reporters people quoted Otis: "Reporters don't get paid enough." They loved him.

At the Mirror, we hoped his idea would spread. However, the "low" pay scale continued a few years until the Times payroll numbers became public after a movie critic was hired at New York rates. In shame, perhaps, salaries were raised, though I did not know how deeply in the ranks. The Mirror no longer existed then.

Colorful personalities had gathered at the Mirror. The religion writer for years was an expert in the field and eloquently cynical. His beat was a diverse world of the robed and collared, plus fiery Pied Pipers who elbowed one another for press coverage. It was said that California attracted an unusually large number of them. His successor as religion writer was a closet atheist.

California was a world center of airplane development. The aviation editor, Don Dwiggins, who came from the Daily News, ground out flight stores at top speed with little apparent effort while also working general assignment. He quit to write books. His successor, Lee Pitt, quit to do publicity for Howard Hughes and Hughes Air West, where he worked with Arelo Sederberg, a former Mirror financial reporter. A writer in the Women department, Dorothy Coleman, told Ann and me years later that she had been married to Don Coryell, coach of the San Diego Chargers. I said that Coryell's arched eyebrows made him look mean, and she said, "He *was* mean." Kendis Rochlen, a tall, pretty and enthusiastic blonde, might have been a movie star instead of a reporter covering the Stompanato inquest.

Chester Washington was an outgoing, talented beatman in Civic Center who consistently produced more stories than the City Desk wanted – and was criticized for it, but I thought it was our job to screen them and spike what we didn't need. On the other side, I told friends that the City Desk was "Like being buried in a mountain of garbage," but that referred to the stacks of "news" releases we got every day from publicists. Real news did not often arrive in the mail. Chet was a world class speed typist, over 100 wpm. His charming, pretty wife, Alma, objected years later to the post-Watts-riots movement to call Negroes "Blacks." "I'm not black, I'm a Negro," she said. She lost that argument.

Moving around on the Mirror meant learn all the beats. When Don Harris quit the post of Labor Writer, I took over writing a daily column on unions.

Covering strikes was unpleasant because of its tension and the deliberately fostered hatred toward the company and management which was part of a scenario to keep union members picketing. Union brass was interesting with its politics and large expense accounts. The rationale for high living and fancy offices was that the union leader should be on a par with the corporate boss. The Teamsters Union leadership in Los Angeles included questionable characters, so I was not shocked to see one at La Costa, a San Diego County resort rumored to be a Detroit Mob hangout in those days. However, a Teamster public relations man, Jim Peck, and the editor of the Joint Council newspaper, Jim Shourt, became friends for life.

Newspapers were the victim of TV, which took advertising dollars on to airways. I was told that the early management of the Mirror made the situation even worse. A Mirror editor got into an argument with one of the area's largest department stores, Robinsons, and the store never again bought any advertising space in the Mirror, though they did advertise in the Times. Robinsons opened a new store in San Fernando Valley. It was a legitimate news item, and the Mirror carried a story, but we didn't get a line of advertising. The other papers did.

Another management slip involved two headlines in the Mirror. The headline across the top of page one of a day's final edition said:

LIZ TAYLOR IN MENTAL HOSPITAL

The headline across the top of page one in the in first edition the following day said:

LIZ TAYLOR NOT IN MENTAL HOSPITAL

It began with a discussion about whether to run a story which someone had received from an old and reliable source. The report could not be verified. Part of the task of confirmation consisted of calling the hospital in the Midwest, a well-known treatment center for famous people. A hospital spokesman said he could not confirm or deny our report on Liz Taylor. There was serious discussion around the City Desk by several people, including Managing Editor Ed Murray. Was the hospital's refusal to confirm or deny a confirmation in itself? Otherwise, why would they not deny she was there? The final decision by Murray was to run the story. As soon as it hit the street, a press agent called to deny the report. The press did not normally go with unconfirmed reports. But the public sometimes believed it was common.

I left the Labor Beat after several months to become the Mirror's Chief Editorial Writer, a job which at other newspapers in future decades became known as Editor of the Editorial Page.

John Grover, who had that duty, was given a column, humor mainly, by our latest new Publisher, Arthur Laro. Grover often operated out of bars in the downtown area. When he told me about the column, I asked about the editorial job. He didn't know who might movein. I told him I'd be interested, had a background in city, county and state government coverage, and had been an International Relations major in graduate school at USC when I quit to work for United Press, planning to become a foreign correspondent. Our new publisher, Arthur Laro, gave me the job, and it was a path which led to the CBS station in Hollywood in 1964, doing the same thing.

The Mirror think tank was a room about twelve by twelve feet, with glass windows on three sides from desk-top level to the ceiling, separating it from the City Room. It contained four desks, two pairs facing each other. The room was on a path from the elevators to the composing room and the Times City Room. People coming from the parking lot or special offices inside the building often stopped by our hideaway. John Grover and Political Editor Dick Bergholz had desks facing each other. On the other side, Matt Weinstock and I looked at each other. Matt usually arrived in mid-afternoon to sort his notes and type his column. He had been columning for a generation, starting on the Daily News, and was likeable and unassuming. Bergholz had a cranky side, but it was reserved for politicians.

Weinstock would accept items from his colleagues on the paper --- my pre-teen son's bright sayings, for instance. One afternoon I told Weinstock about visiting Paramount Studios to see a writer, James Poe. I had an appointment and walked into his office. A young woman was sitting on a couch crying. She quickly rose, fumbling a pencil and shorthand pad, and said, "I'm sorry, the scene he was dictating was so sad I couldn't help it." She left rapidly. Weinstock called Poe to find out the name of the movie he was dictating to the secretary, and did an item on that sad scene. I talked to Poe again a few days later and he said Weinstock's column caused more than one funny friend to accuse Poe of telling his secretary it was over between them. That was life in Hollywood.

Editorial Policy

Editorial policy on the Mirror was strictly up to the publisher. During the last year or so of the Mirror's existence, Norman attended an Editorial Board meeting, the only one I witnessed. He was just visiting, not contributing. He did say three words. I had gone through a short list of editorial ideas for the Board, which included Publisher Laro, ME Jack Donahue and a couple of other editors, including a copy editor. Someone mentioned that the John Birch Society, a right wing political favorite of some unseen Chandler family members, had gone off the edge of rationality again. I said I knew about it, but we had rapped the Birch Society the previous week, and maybe that was enough for a while. Norman, whose reporters had done investigative reporting on the Birch Society, had criticized it editorially in the Times, creating some family friction. Norman told us: "Hit 'em again." OK. We did.

As related here in the JFK RFK chapter. there was no Editorial Board discussion about supporting Richard Nixon for President in 1960. The Mirror did not reflect the Times editorially. We paid little attention, though I did talk occasionally with the Times chief editorial writer, the aging and humorous Kirby Ramsdell, but not about topics or policy. I wrote about Ramsdell in an L.A. Press Club yearbook, giving his description of research on editorials. Ramsdell had told me:

"You arrive at work sometime before 9:30 and spend half an hour or so skimming the papers. Then you go into the editorial conference and start shooting from the hip. You hope you can make your well-considered opinions stand up against the asinine objections of the other guys, who haven't given the subject as much deep thought as you have."

Ramsdell had been around many years, and there were few new topics that he had not studied deeply. The future of rapid transit in Los Angeles was one topic where we differed.

The early post-war suburban Red Cars had disappeared, replaced by buses. The city itself had both buses and yellow streetcars. Other large American cities had speedy subways. Compared with the Paris Metro and London subway, the Los Angeles system was slow, fragmented and antiquated. The Mirror editorial page clamored for rapid transit, while the Times, which was more influential, opposed spending money on subways when we had a bus system that supplied "everyone's needs." "Everyone" meant Ramsdell who, I was told, lived a block or so from the bus line through Pasadena that took him to the corner of the Times Building at First and Hill.

The chief of the Los Angeles Rapid Transit support group pleaded for help. He asked to meet with both editorial boards, the Times and the Mirror. Otis was the Times publisher then. He agreed to invite the Mirror, but when we gathered in a conference room Otis told the transit boss that this was a unique gathering. He said the Times had its Editorial Board and the Mirror had its own, and there was no connection.

Mr. Transit said that was the problem. He had an important job, which was to speak for the traveling public and advise City and County leaders how to improve the system. He pleaded:

"Mr. Chandler, it would help if you and the Mirror both wanted the same thing. Can't you both, whether you are for me or against me, at least stick together?"

Otis said "No." He said the Times board made their decision and the Mirror board made their decision, and no one was going to tell them they had to be together.

Exasperated, the transit director pleaded, as if in considerable pain:

"Mr. Chandler, what am I supposed to do? If we come out with a proposal, and the Times says one thing, how will we know what the Mirror will do?"

Otis said, seriously, "I guess you'll have to go buy a paper."

The meeting broke up.

The Times Mirror Corp bought other newspapers, but I never heard how their editorial decisions were made. Perhaps it didn't matter. Newspapers were a slowly fading institution nationwide.

Getting to Know Sammy Davis Jr

Covering Hollywood for a newspaper was like covering any other group of experts in a trade or business. They were better known to the public, but the spotlight shines on stages or in governmental institutions or sports. Stars get there by skills and luck. A big part of the story is how he or she got there. That applies to all, even serial killers. And yes, some are special.

Sammy Jr. was friendly, energetic, talented. He got to you. Sinatra became his friend way back, soon after WWII. Sinatra could name one big reason: "I can't stop laughing when he imitates me, he is so good." Impersonations were just part of what Sammy did, and he had learned how the same way he learned to dance or croon in his own voice. He watched and listened and practiced.

Sammy learned to dance as a near toddler, imitating his dad and uncle in vaudeville. He didn't go to school much. He learned to sing instead. He was a 1950s phenomenon, one of a nationwide chorus of singers, big band musicians, dancers and comedians who became famous, or more famous, after World War II.

When we met, Junior and Sammy Sr., and "uncle" Will Matson, had become rockets over the Sunset strip. One-night changed everything for them. It was Oscar Night: The motion picture Academy Awards were handed out at Pantage's theater in downtown Hollywood. It was not a forever midnight television show in those days. When the awards were over, the stars went to parties at night clubs to be seen. Win or lose, their names would appear in newspaper and trade paper columns.

Ciro's was their favorite show-face location. It was a party place, and this was the biggest party of the year. Table hopping was in, jokes and laughter were in.

There are times and places when a singer, who normally should get a polite audience, can't crash a wine and bourbon dinner. The timing, even for a brief song, is wrong.

Janis Paige, a big name singer who had made several movies, was the name on the Ciro's billboard above traffic on Sunset. She was the star. She had the bad luck to follow a jazzy song and dance act that captured the spotlight of an Oscar night with brilliance and energy. Sinatra was quoted later as saying he would not have followed Sammy Jr, that night "If they gave me forty percent of the joint."

When the Davis segment ended, the stars in the audience went backstage to tell Sammy Davis Junior how great he was: Jack Benny, Jeff Chandler, Dan Dailey -- nobody kept track, but Hollywood welcomed a new star. Stardom included a contract in Las Vegas.

It was not automatically a terrific new life for Junior. Friends wondered if he could take instant fame. Sammy wondered how to have a real home with a wife and kids. He didn't like to fly. He had a bad auto crash driving home to his Sunset Strip hillside house from Nevada, and lost an eye. That was when I was given a special assignment: Who was this guy?

During the final years of World War II, Sammy Junior was in uniform, a solo performer in the Army's entertainment groups. After the war he rejoined his family on the road. Frank Sinatra hired the Trio to be part of his show at a theater in New York in 1946

Sammy Junior acknowledged that many people helped him, but he credited Herman Hover for giving them that really big break. How did that begin? Ciro's owner Herman Hover had competition but stayed in the lead by always looking for something new. I talked to some principals. I had met Eddie Cantor elsewhere on another story. Cantor said he saw and liked the Trio, and recommended them to Hover.

After the Ciro's success, Cantor put them on his national television show. With that boost, the Trio got a Las Vegas casino contract. Money was no longer a worry. Sammy Junior bought a house above the Strip, a view lot that once belonged to Judy Garland. His dad and Uncle Will and other family members lived with him, including Peewee, Junior's grandmother. Sammy Senior was taller than Junior. Junior's looks came from his mother. Junior showed me a photo of her in the house.

When I showed up at the house on Evanview Drive, per arrangements I made with his public relations man and good friend Jess Rand, Sammy was preparing for a trip to New York to renew his career, and the atmosphere around the house was like a hurricane. That afternoon Rod Steiger, the movie star, dropped in just to hang out a while. Sammy introduced us, but Steiger was not excited about meeting a reporter. Within half an hour the Hi-Los arrived. They were an acapella group, college type guys. They came to talk with Sammy Jr. about a promotion for an album they made.

In the living room not far from the front door a record player provided music. Sammy put on one by the Hi-Los, and came back, straddled a chair facing the Hi-Los and led them in a sing-along. I sat with Steiger on a small couch behind Sammy. Sammy began to rock and bounce, waving his forearms up and down, snapping his fingers in time with the music, directing the Hi-Los. He had it memorized, knew the parts and pointed to a live singer when he knew that one would do a solo on the record. It was a private show for two guests on the couch. We applauded.

Another day we went to his eye doctor's office in downtown L.A. This was an important visit. Sammy said he had a "mortal fear" of losing his other eye. He was in the office of his doctor to be sure the glass eye was fit correctly and a few days of wearing it had not hurt the tissue that held it in place. The doctor took it out, which was a bit difficult. It was not round like a golf ball, but more like a one-eighth slice of apple, a curved piece, thicker in the middle. It was tricky putting the eye back in the socket. The doctor dropped it on the artificial tile floor. It bounced. Quickly, Sammy began to move around, furiously stomping on the floor with one foot as though crushing a bug, and wailing, "My eye! My eye. You dropped my eye."

The doctor laughed and picked it up. He cleaned it with a cloth and fluid from a small bottle. He tried again and got it right. Sammy would look good on stage, though the eye could not move.

The doctor told Sammy he could have special eyes made. Some people have imaginative ideas about how they should look. He had a sample, an eye with an American flag where the pupil normally would be built into the glass. He said another patient had one with a small figure in the center, a nude woman. Sammy wasn't interested, saying that in show business a camera might zoom in on his face. Sammy didn't know how the artificial eye would, in time, affect his career. (The glass eye was still working when Sammy got cancer and died in 1990.)

I did not see Sammy again, except briefly one afternoon in Hollywood a year or two later. Mirror City Editor Hank Osborne said that the Chicago Daily News was interested in Sammy's romance with Actress Kim Novak.

Jess Rand, Sammy's great press agent, said he had no comment but he would call Sammy in Vegas and get back to me. The callback came from Sammy himself. He said he would be back in town in a couple of days and asked if we could meet. My memory of it is that we met in the lobby of the Earl Carroll theater on Sunset, a long block from Columbia Pictures, which was across the street from the Art Deco building of CBS, Columbia Square, home of KNX radio and KNXT Channel Two where I would work a few years later.

Jess Rand was with Sammy, but walked away and let us talk. It was off the record. Sammy mentioned our days at his house, and said it sure was a different world for him now. He was doing great in Las Vegas, but still wanted a wife and family. He wanted to clarify something about his life. He and Kim were in love and wanted to marry, but it was out of the question. Harry Cohn, the strong (some called him tyrannical) boss of Columbia Studios had told Kim to forget Sammy. If they married she would be finished in Hollywood, she'd never make another movie. For Kim's good they decided to call off the romance. He was unhappy about it, but said he had to agree with Kim that it was safer for her to forget him. I never saw him again. The Rat Pack which came later was not what his friends wished for him.

Slim parallels in our lives began in the Army in World War II -- being there and doing nothing combative. While sorting old files for this report I found a picture of Sammy in the White House Yellow Oval Room with Richard Nixon. I have a picture of me with President Johnson in the Yellow Oval Room. My days in Mickey Cohen's apartment and the letters mess with Lana Turner and Johnny Stompanato in Beverly Hills began with a birthday party for Sammy Davis Junior, a party that I knew nothing about until it was over.

Half a century later, a stage play was done about Sammy. Something was missing. I always think of him singing "Hey there, you with the stars in your eyes....." The real Sammy.

Chessman and Wein: They Didn't Hurt Anybody

Caryl Chessman was convicted of kidnap-rape and sentenced to death. Edward Simon Wein traveled the same kidnap-rape road to death row. Chessman was executed. Wein eventually went free.

Both were charged with violating the Little Lindberg Law, which allowed a death sentence if a kidnap victim was injured. The same law allowed that moving the victims from one place to another could be kidnapping. The prosecutor on both trials convinced juries that kidnapping occurred even though they were moved just a few feet.

Chessman was said to be brilliant, not a stereotypical criminal at all according to fans who did not see him personally. He had been fighting a death sentence for rape and robbery for almost a decade before Wein was arrested late in 1956.

Chessman was convicted of accosting couples in "lovers lane" locations, and removing women from cars to rape them while their boy friends remained in the cars.

Wein, in his early thirties, had a bland round face, almost cherubic, and a soft look in his eyes that convinced the women who let him into their homes that he was not a threat, until he pulled a knife and raped them.

Wein was convicted, but the death penalty was halted by a court decision. Governor Pat Brown said Wein had not actually hurt anyone and reduced his sentence, and that led to Wein walking out of prison. Wein returned to his old rapist ways, killed a woman for the first time, and he died in prison.

Wein originally was charged with raping eight women. It was no credit to the press that they covered Wein's story fully and accurately after he was caught. He got at least some of his leads to victims from want ads in newspapers. Wein would look for an ad, such as fur coat for sale, go to the home and say he was a potential buyer. If circumstances looked favorable for him, meaning no one else was at home, he would pull a knife and rape the woman. When he was caught, the press referred to him as the "watch stem" rapist because he pretended to lose the stem from his wrist watch, got on the floor to find it, and if the woman knelt to help, he pulled out his knife. Calling him the "want ad rapist" might have alerted women to be wary of purchasers.

Wein was identified as the rapist after bumping into a former victim on a dance floor in Long Beach. She recognized him, called police, and they arrested him. He was close to being caught anyway. Los Angeles detectives, during many hours of questioning victims and neighbors, had learned that, while Wein was raping someone, children playing on the sidewalk had noticed a parked car on the street that was not usually around that neighborhood. The young boy and girl who saw it could not provide much detail. However, the girl remembered some letters that were on the license plate. That gave the cops a long list of possible cars and owners. The detectives, Bud Schottmiller and James Close, (investigators in the Mickey Cohen waiter beating case later), got permission to have the boy hypnotized to see if that would help him remember the make of car. It worked, and the much shorter list of possible suspect's cars included one owned by Wein. They were that close when a victim saw Wein at a dance.

Wein could face a death penalty, and he cried for help. It was a bad dream, he said, he was innocent and could prove it if someone could help him. He called the Mirror from jail and I was sent to hear his story. Interviewing the prisoner was easy. We could talk privately across a wood table. Wein denied he was a rapist. He said that when one victim claimed he raped her he was somewhere else. He gave considerable detail about a restaurant near downtown Los Angeles. He had been there. If someone would take his picture there and ask around, maybe someone would remember. He begged me to please help. I said my editor would decide. I thought he was lying and the editor agreed. Soon, the number of stories by victims, fingerprints and other identifications made it obvious he was guilty.

Not Now Leavy!!

The prosecutor, Deputy District Attorney J. Miller Leavy, was a stocky, handsome guy with a voice that resonated like an organ pipe. When he laid out facts before a jury, he was as convincing as thunder bouncing off the courtroom walls. He had prosecuted Chessman, and won a death penalty. Wein provided the same drama.

From the press standpoint, Leavy was easy to work with. He understood our role and our needs in covering stories. In a preliminary hearing, a judge would decide whether there was enough evidence to try the case. Wein took the stand to deny the charges. I was sitting inside the rail, to the right of the judge, facing Leavy from about 10 feet away as the prosecutor outlined the circumstances of a want-ad rape. It didn't take long, and apparently it didn't sound serious to Wein. Perhaps he thought he could stop the prosecution here.

In the witness box, Wein stated that he was innocent, the police had the wrong person, and it was a terrible mistake. He was not the person Leavy had described.

Leavy's cross examination was brief and memorable. He started slowly, getting Wein to restate what he had testified. Leavy said to Wein: You never answered an ad? No, said Wein firmly. You did not go to that house and say you wanted to buy what was offered in the ad? No, said Wein. Did you ever do that anywhere? No, said Wein. You would never do that? No, said Wein.

Leavy paused. He had been facing the judge on the bench and Wein in the witness chair. He turned to his left, to face me across the room, then pointed to the back of the courtroom. The "Leavy voice" was turned on now, decibels mounting.

"Your Honor," he said, "I would like the bailiff to please bring in Mrs ...." He gave her name.

The bailiff, having been told what to expect, opened the door. In walked a woman, middle-aged, petite, well-dressed. Leavy raised a hand

and she stopped by the gate that separated participants from the public. Leavy turned to Wein:

"Have you ever seen this woman before?" demanded Leavy, in full thunder.

Never, said Wein.

Leavy turned my way and said, "Your Honor, I am going to bring this woman back after recess....."

I caught his eye and locked on. He paused.

Please, Miller, it's mid-afternoon. She's a want ad victim, right? If you bring her back today, it will be too late for my paper, the Mirror. The Times isn't here, but they can call to find out what she said, and this will be their story this evening. Radio and TV will have it tonight. I won't be able to get it in until tomorrow morning.

None of those words were uttered. I just moved my head a fraction of a degree left, then right, eyes still on his. He saw it, understood instantly, and resumed talking:

"..tomorrow, your Honor. I will bring her back tomorrow morning, and she will testify."

My eyes were on his again as I nodded, my head barely moving.

The judge said all right, he was going to close court a bit early this day, and see you all tomorrow morning at nine.

After Leavy talked briefly with the woman and she left, I said "Thanks" to him. We did not discuss the timing. Newspaper reporters constantly worked that way if they could, arranging to have a story happen on their time, not the opposition's. Lawyers, public officials of many kinds and press agents writing releases all had reasons to time a release or a press conference. As the business changed, more and more such things were arranged in advance of television stations' schedules. Some were timed to fit national TV network time-zones. In the digital world, timing is still a consideration, and can have world- wide significance when newsmakers ponder the best place and time to talk.

The woman in the Wein case came in the next day and described how Wein had arrived at her house in answer to her ad to sell a fur coat, or stole, and had raped her.

Wein was convicted and got the death penalty in five cases.

The Newsman's Jail Key

Caryl Chessman was on death row for many years after his arrest in 1948 and trial. Close to a decade later he was granted a review of the trial transcript, which had been used by the State Supreme Court's review of his trial and sentence, automatic in capital cases. The court reporter who made the shorthand record died before he could transcribe it and produce a complete formal transcript. A final transcript was put together by others. Chessman said the transcript given to the Supreme Court was fraudulent, full of errors caused by those who had a chance to examine and approve it, including Leavy, before it was sent to the Supreme Court.

This was Chessman's "last chance." He represented himself, and had to convince Superior Judge Charles Fricke, the trial judge, that the transcript seen by the State Supreme Court was faulty. To prepare his case, Chessman was moved from Death Row in a Northern California prison to the Los Angeles County Jail.

In a book written while he was struggling to avoid execution, Chessman referred to Death Row as "an ultrahigh security unit bristling with elaborate custodial safeguards, sealed off from the rest of the California state prison at San Quentin." He referred to Death Row itself as a line of cells behind "a double-gated, multi-locked entrance called the Bird Cage."

It was quite different in L.A. County Jail. He was given an "office" which was one of a few cells along one side of a corridor that led out of the central part of the jail on the ninth floor. The other cells, maybe two or three in that special wing, were empty. His office cell had the usual bars for a wall, a "door" made of bars and a lock. Beside his cot was a table to work on his papers and law books.

The Press Room for the Hall of Records was on the sixth floor, just outside the lobby receptionist desk and the entry to the District Attorney's offices where deputies and investigators worked. Municipal Courts were up a floor, Superior Courts two floors up. Three floors above the press room was an office used only by Lloyd Emerson, the Examiner's tall, gangly, weathered and graying beat reporter. His open office, 9th floor, was a clean desk, probably holding nothing, and a telephone.

Public elevators served the courtroom floors, seven and eight. Emmy walked up a nearby flight of stairs to his office on 9, the same stairs we sometimes used from the Press Room from the sixth floor to courts on 7 and 8.

Emmy did not work out of the press room, but he was part of the syndicate, sharing all with everyone. The Press Room was crowded and had a lot of visitors. Distractions. Emmy liked to be alone, and he was not in any one place for long. He walked and walked. He prowled the corridors and knew everything that was going on. He would drop by the Press Room to share something the others had not found. He had the building wired, he knew everybody, they knew him, and he had everyone's absolute respect and trust.

One day I asked one of the veteran reporters on the beat, Pat Foley, of the Herald Express, about the special treatment Chessman was getting, with a specially guarded cell. Foley said to ask Emmy.

I went up the stairs to Emmy's lonely desk and was lucky to find him there. I asked about the super secure place where they let Chessman work when he was not in the courtroom.

Emmy told me to follow him. We left his office, and I remember we went up a flight of stairs, which would be to the 10th floor, a jail floor if it was in the jail part of the building, otherwise a public area but seldom used. In other words I had just walked up open stairways from 6th floor to 10th – jail or public – floor. Then Emmy and I walked maybe ten feet down a public corridor.

He stopped in front of a door. It was an ordinary wood office door like innumerable others in the building. He pulled out a key and opened the door. In front of us was a hallway. Along the left side were cells with steel-rod walls facing the corridor, with steel rod gates and large locks built into the gates. The other side of the hallway was a wall.

Maybe thirty feet down that hallway, sitting in an ordinary office chair outside one cell, was a Deputy Sheriff. He turned and glanced at us, then he relaxed again in his chair. The cell by the deputy was empty, as were the two or three empty cells we had just walked past.

Emmy knew the deputy, and asked, "Where is he?"

"Gone to lunch," the deputy said. "He'll be back in a little while."

We could see a small table covered with papers inside the cell. The deputy was there to make sure no one bothered Chessman's files. We didn't wait.

We walked back out the door through which we had entered. Emmy's key locked the door. I asked if that deputy was all that was between Chessman and Emmy's office and the stairway. Emmy said yes, except Chessman reached his "office" from the other end of the corridor we used. He came from the main part of the jail on that floor. His "home" cell was watched by a deputy at all hours. I could imagine Chessman breaking away from his deputy guard, dashing maybe thirty feet to the door that Emmy's key had opened, and in another second being on the stairway downstairs to mingle with normal courthouse stair users, if any were around. Foot traffic usually stayed on the eighth floor or below. Strange escapes had happened, or had been tried, in that building. Emmy had a key to the jail. Emmy was trusted. So was anybody with him. The prisoner who left the "bird cage" surveillance of Death Row could be visited here by Emmy, who had a key to the jail in a remote wing.

I asked Art Alarcon, the judge and former prosecutor, about Emmy's jail entre. Alarcon had worked on floors six through nine in another part of the Hall of Justice. He never heard of Emmy's door to the jail. Jurors on eighth-floor criminal courts, the courtroom of Judge Walker and the Sirhan trial, for instance, had a private room for resting at recess, or when deliberating. It was on the ninth floor above their courtroom. (The Sirhan auxiliary courtroom would be on the fourth floor).

Chessman had a large fan base, even abroad. They wrote letters to the courts, to newspapers and to legislators demanding justice and freedom for the convicted rapist who had never killed anyone. During that final phase of Chessman's lifetime, I was assigned to go to Hollywood and talk to a psychiatrist who had called the Mirrror City Desk and said he was certain that Chessman was innocent.

It did not go well. The doctor had not examined Chessman, had never met him. He was associated with a group that did not believe in capital punishment, but said that had nothing to do with this matter, Chessman was innocent. His brilliant mind was not that of a criminal, he could not have committed the crimes he was accused of. The doctor's experience told him that. Chessman possibly had acted erratically, but not like the prosecution said.

I suggested that the jury had heard it all and said he was guilty. The doctor said Chessman should not be executed because, he repeated, Chessman had a brilliant mind. He could be rehabilitated, and it was important to the public that medical science should have an opportunity to study Chessman's mind and "find out why he did it."

"But, you said he was innocent," I replied.

The doctor reacted angrily and said I was wasting his time. I left.

Superior Judge Charles Fricke presided over the hearing on the transcript. Trials are often dull. This was excruciatingly slow to mere watchers with nothing personal at stake. It was shorthand experts reading sentences, explaining the meaning of curved lines on paper. Chessman was trying desperately to pull the transcript apart, but was getting nowhere. It was a search for error, with minor, meaningless differences or mistakes turned into "gotchas." It seemed to have no end, as the relentless search for a major blunder went on.

One day while walking the corridor with Lloyd Emerson, we met the Distritct Attorney's staff electronics expert coming out of Judge Fricke's court, which was not in session at that moment. Emmy asked the electronics man what he was doing in there. This was Emmy asking, which meant speak frankly. The graying veteran of the DA's investigative staff replied that he had a setup in the Fricke courtroom to record on tape the entire proceedings of Chessman's transcript hearing. He said Fricke was not taking a chance on getting into another fight over the accuracy of the transcript of this hearing.

I don't know if Chessman knew. Emmy was entrusted with the secrets of the beat. Maybe this was one.

In the trial of Senator Robert Kennedy's assassin, Sirhan Sirhan, in 1969, Judge Herbert Walker had his own tape recording made of the entire proceedings. I knew that. The judge told me. He said he was going to keep the recording and would not turn it over to the county, but I don't know what finally happened. I did not ask his family after he died. It was easy to record that trial because the judge and each witness wore a "lavalier" microphone on a cord around the neck, and that transmitted the sound live to another courtroom for overflow reporters, while our hidden camera transmitted a live picture. Jurors also wore the microphone when questioned before a final jury was selected -- voir dire in legalese. None of that was recorded, except by Judge Walker who had an audio recorder out of sight under his bench.

The Blondes of Hollywood: Marilyn Monroe Faced Jail, Perhaps

No one in Beverly Hills Municipal Court that day really believed Marilyn Monroe would go to jail as a scofflaw. The offense was minor and common. She ignored parking tickets.

Marilyn had no place in her busy mind for such trivia. People took care of details for her. However, one day the court system pulled a bunch of unanswered tickets together, and the movie princess was ordered to appear. She was an ordinary citizen.

The enormity of her transgressions was cranked up a few levels in the press, portraying potential punishment as jail or at least a public lashing. Monroe had done what lots of other people did, but the court could not let a star go free. It would be a bad example.

Movie Star Monroe, blonde curls and wearing a tight-fit dress, arrived at the courtroom with time to spare. She would not be late for this. She was serious and contrite, as all could tell by looking at her serious expression. There was no idle talk with reporters. Later, please. The press and TV reporters were as restless as she, while we waited for the judge walk in and take his seat up there on the decision-maker's bench. He was in his chambers, presumably reviewing the facts.

Few reporters, even those covering Hollywood full time, would have noticed the man who had arrived early and was standing in the back when Monroe and legal help arrived. They ignored him. He was middle-aged, dark hair with a bit of gray, slender, serious, wearing his usual inconspicuous gray suit. I had seen him only a few times. We had never talked. His job would be difficult to define. He was not seen at news events.

His job was to move around in Hollywood quietly building connections. That would include making political campaign contributions from the studio, plus keeping track of campaign donations made by others who had direct ties to the studio. He could get an audience when and where necessary, even in Beverly Hills Municipal Court. It could classify as a courtesy call, not at all tied to the next judicial election.

Miss Monroe had probably never seen him, but his anonymous presence in court that day signaled major studio interest. The publicity that would accompany a superstar going to jail could be damaging, and that would not be all of it. The press would cover everything Marilyn did while she resided inside a jail cell, and they'd be waiting when she was released, asking what it was like to be a jail bird. It would demean her, it might affect her box office appeal. It might interfere with plans for her next movie. A new movie would probably not be ready for release for about a year, but the studio would not want to take a chance that she would be an embarrassment. Any project she might be working on, now or later, could be affected. Therefore, the studio sent Fixit Man. That was my name for him. I never talked to him, nor about him with anybody else, just saw him around the courts.

Mr. Fixit was not seen at purely publicity engagements, where PR people shepherded and protected the valuable studio contract properties. I had first seen him hanging around a courtroom in downtown L.A. maybe a year earlier. He did not fit the lawyer mold. I asked the court clerk who he was and what he did, and the clerk knew.

On Monroe's day, there may have been a press agent in the Beverly Hills courtroom, but this was lawyer time, and Marilyn stayed close to hers. Mr. Fixit waited in a back corner of the courtroom until the clerk came in. The judge must be ready. Mr. Fixit quickly straightened up in his corner and walked to the clerk's desk, going through the gate and into the territory reserved for lawyers, witnesses and other trial participants. He and the clerk knew each other. The clerk went away, passing through a door to an out-of-sight office. He returned in a moment, nodding for Mr. Fixit to go in. If Marilyn noticed, it did not show. Her lawyer had to know. He gave no sign.

Fixit's speech would be brief and humble. He was there to determine whether the judge was much upset with Marilyn for ignoring traffic citations. The question was whether he was upset enough to jail her, whether he felt he had to make an example to show he was impartial. Mr. Fixit would assure him that Miss Monroe wanted to apologize. She was genuinely sorry. It was not a truly criminal matter, she hadn't hurt anyone. She did not mean to ignore the minor tickets. She thought the studio had done whatever was necessary. She was just soooo busy that she had to trust that the studio and lawyers were looking after it. The judge was a veteran in that courtroom. He would make no promises, but he would scold and admonish and make sure Miss Monroe paid her fines and penalties.

A crowd of court employees on coffee breaks, press and TV cameramen waited. They would not have thought anything about it when Fixit, a stranger, took the short walk to the door that led to the judge's chambers. Fixit was gone only a few minutes. He came back to the courtroom, and stayed on the sidelines. No obvious nod or other acknowledgement of each other had passed between the lawyer and Mr. Fixit, but each had to know what the other was doing.

The judge came out very soon. The charges were explained to Monroe. Her lawyer said it was a misunderstanding on her part and it wouldn't happen again. Monroe was chastised, warned, lectured and otherwise treated like a mere public person, then was sent on her way, properly admonished to pay the fines and obey the law or else.

Outside the courthouse, on the sidewalk, she met the news people. Cameramen waited while the lawyer delivered her to their care.

Television needed something special to illustrate the story because they could not photograph Marilyn during the courtroom session. They took film of her walking out of the courthouse. She posed with her lawyer. A small crowd gathered to watch. When they all were finished with the parts they would play, and it was time to go on with life, a cameraman, a Watson

Brother, took charge. The Watson brothers (there were four or five in news jobs in Los Angeles) were famous for their hard work, their good pictures, and their sometimes unique approaches to news photos. This one was probably Harry, who worked for a television station. He persuaded Marilyn to take a walk, away from the crowd, and he showed her what to do. She understood and was ready.

What the movie camera saw was Marilyn, one hand on hip, the other hand reaching high over her head, walking away from the crowd, her up-reaching arm swinging like an upsidedown pendulum from side to side while she turned her head to look back at the cameras. The result was a view of her backside, hips swinging wildly with each step and arm wave. It was a show-stopper, a victory march for a young woman who just escaped a jail term.

In old notes found in files, I mentioned seeing Marilyn three times.

Only one other incident emerges from memory, not connected to the courthouse, and it may put the Monroe stardom in perspective.

A reception was held at Warner Brothers, and Marilyn was to be there to chat about her latest movie, which was being released with a big, big publicity buildup. For someone who didn't know her, it was to be a handshake and nice to meet you. It was the same with Jack Warner. The publicist introduced me. Warner didn't know me, didn't care. Someone at the Mirror had asked me to find out, at this affair, if Monroe was going to get a role in a new movie that was getting a lot of early publicity and speculation about casting before shooting began. This was the kind of pre-production gossip that bounced off trade paper columns in Hollywood constantly, possibly in hopes an actor would be considered, or to build up contract dollars. I asked Warner if Marilyn would get that part. He looked pained. He did not respond with a useable quote. A different movie, now being released, was the reason for this party.

"I'm putting a major production in theaters and you ask me about umbrellas," he said, with intended contempt.

"I hadn't thought of her as an umbrella," I said. He didn't answer. I was dismissed.

The umbrella line was used again, I know not why. My friend Jim Bacon, who covered Hollywood full time for Associated Press, picked up the umbrella line in another context. I wondered how often it would be repeated. This was Hollywood at its upper level. Umbrella was today's word.

Barely into retirement, when I was *barely* seventy years old, an invitation came to talk with a group of seniors in San Marcos about covering Hollywood. My Monroe file had little to talk about. There was a clipping, a story which I wrote. I said I didn't remember talking to her, but must have if I did the story. Someone in the audience challenged such an unbelievable lack of memory about so famous a movie star.

How to explain the humdrum of Hollywood? I named a City Councilman in nearby city. Yes, the audience knew him. Well, in the news business one may deal with movie stars every day. A lot of it is routine, forgettable. On the other hand, I had been to Paris four times in my life and could remember each visit clearly. Now, this friend, the Councilman, was an airline pilot. He flew as a passenger most Thursdays from San Diego to Dallas. Once there, he did not leave the Dallas airport except perhaps to rest. Airlines keep nearby hotel rooms for crews passing through. Then he took command of a plane and flew it to Paris, and he flew another one back to Dallas a day or so later. Did he remember every visit to Paris?

It was the same with movie stars. News people might see them often, but they were just people we bumped into. Live around L.A. for a lifetime and you see a lot of them, up close. Smile and they are happy, but don't stop and try to talk. They, too, are running errands.

The Blondes of Hollywood: Marie Mc Donald, Kidnap Victim

Marie McDonald had everything. She had been a show girl in the big nightclubs of New York, came to Hollywood, got a major studio build-up and was a movie "star." She had a millionaire husband and a growing young family.

She was a loser.

The star system invented her. It built upon a name she had acquired earlier, "The Body." She made some movies, most were forgettable. The body itself was not unusual for a starlet or showgirl, but the head was flakey.

Her kidnaping was a crazy story, true but so goofy it ruined her life. A tragedy that was not her fault.

Before that happened, a separation from her husband, Harry Karl, was followed by a newspaper story in which Marie said she was pregnant, and Harry had hit her. He said he didn't. That was the first time I saw her, when a photographer and I went to a large west-side home, a mansion that she and Karl had occupied. She showed bruises – on her arms as I remember, and the photographer took pictures.

Marie pursued the press. She was a frequent name in Harrison Carroll's Herald Express column. Soon after we saw her she began calling the Mirror News. They gave her to me. Marie was a fun gab, as movie people went. Some actors are trees. Wooden. Marie was lively, and it was non-stop talk, usually half an hour or more. Movie stars get lonely like mortals. I took notes on my typewriter. She said Harry cheated on income taxes. It went into the notes. She had a daughter. She was lucky, I said, because Ann and I were trying to have a family, with no success yet.

During one of those long calls, I told her I had work to do, and suggested we could continue if I stopped at her home in Encino, which was on the way to my home in Reseda, an L.A. neighborhood about five miles North of the somewhat rich area where she lived.

The house that Harry provided after the divorce was one-story, ranch-style in white stucco with a wood shake roof. It was on the North side of Magnolia Boulevard, a couple of blocks North of Ventura Boulevard, in West San Fernando Valley. It had a large living room and dining area and kitchen all in one big, mostly open room. Outside, there was a yard mostly filled with trees and bushes. It was at least half an acre. From Magnolia on the South side of the house, a long looping driveway went by the front door. In that area, most of the land near Balboa Boulevard sloped downward to the North.

On the first visit, her mother helped Marie serve me a drink and then disappeared. Her mother lived in elsewhere in San Fernando Valley, but was always around. Marie was living with her infant daughter, two other children and a housekeeper. I never saw them. Just grandma.

Marie may have associated with newspaper people more than just for the publicity she thought they might give her. She had wanted to be a reporter. Her mama, who had been in New York show business, thought journalism was a waste and told Marie to try Broadway. So, Marie started acting and singing in New York. In post WW II, Hollywood was the big deal, and she went there. Universal Studios put her on contract and gave her the starlet build-up. She made a string of films.

After Marie got her divorce from Harry Karl, her headline days waned, but she continued to call the Mirror. I made maybe four visits to the house. It was better than talking forty-five minutes on the fone at a busy office. I usually went there after she had called the newspaper to air a peeve about the press reports on her and Harry Karl.

Personal things came up. Marie had rid herself of a kitchen range. She bought a stainless steel electric barbecue in which she could roast a turkey or bake a cake. The idea sounded good. I told my wife, Ann, and she agreed to try it, though she never saw Marie's setup. It worked fine, but Ann decided she didn't like it as well as a normal range. When we moved into a new house in Northridge in 1964, Ann got a new range.

Marie talked about her problems in having a baby. I told Marie that Ann and I, after ten years marriage, applied to the county adoption service, and that was not promising.

Ann became pregnant. Marie was one of those I called to report the news. The following summer our son was born.

Marie's kidnap story was not just surprising, it was at times a continuation of her word battle with Harry Karl. The kidnaping occurred late at night. I didn't know until the next morning when I reported to work downtown. I was sent back out to the Valley, to the house in Encino, to report on what was happening there. It meant standing around outside by the hour, speculating with other reporters.

We knew little. The kidnapers left her baby in the house. We wanted more detail, but cops weren't sharing all they had. They did their examination of the scene before most reporters showed up.

Friends came by, including Michael Wilding, a former husband of Liz Taylor whom I had been trying to contact about a new husband, Mike Todd (see the Todd chapter).

Lieutenant Herman Zander, from the homicide division, was in charge of the case. He wanted any tip anybody had, and I gave him my notes from Marie's long calls. LAPD didn't have Xerox machines then, and he kept my originals. It turned out that the subjects we talked about were unhelpful.

Marie reported that two guys came to the house, showed a shotgun, and took her away in the night clothes and robe she was wearing.

The first "contact" from anyone was a telephone call early the next morning by Marie to Harrison Carroll at his home. She told him she was being held in a house, she had no idea where, and she was in a bedroom, alone for the first time. She had found a telephone. There was no number on the phone, though that was standard in those days. Instead of dialing O for Operator and asking for police, she called Carroll. Carroll said she ended the conversation quickly, telling him that someone was coming. There were several versions of that and possibly other calls, with "reports" that the kidnapers made her call. Stories that were printed later in fan magazines contained speculation about many calls. Perhaps they were true. Nothing more was heard that day.

That night she was released by the kidnapers on a highway east of Palm Springs, close to Desert Center, a wide spot on what is now Interstate 10. She flagged down a truck, and the driver took her to a phone to call police. From there she was taken to a hospital in Indio to be examined.

Marie came home unannounced. The misdirected press was not waiting in the driveway. I learned at the Mirror that she was home. It was time to visit her and get some details. Before starting home from the Mirror in the afternoon, I called. Marie said she was being interviewed by a detective, but it was okay to drop by.

Her mother let me in and disappeared as she always did. Marie introduced Detective Sergeant Al Ortiz, Los Angeles Police Department, who was seated at the opposite end of a couch where Marie sat. I sat on another couch a few feet away facing them. Ortiz worked for Lieutenant Zander. I knew Ortiz by name only, having seen his name in other stories before the kidnaping. He was an experienced cop, my size, average, but heavier, and somewhat older. He was friendly, barely, not a guy who trusted people a lot.

Ortiz was about through with his interview. They had been going over all the story of the kidnapping, again. It occurred to me later that Marie told him I was on my way, and he had waited for me to arrive before end-ing his session with Marie. He probably wanted to meet anyone associated with Marie, even a reporter.

Ortiz also likely wanted a witness. He was finished with questions. He shifted around, preparing to stand up, but first reached into a side coat pocket and pulled out something in white paper, like tissue. He reached out to Marie and said:

"Miss McDonald, I am returning this ring to you. We have had the dia-mond appraised, and it is worth about eight-thousand dollars."

She took it from him without saying anything. There hadn't been any talk about jewelry in the kidnap story, not that I heard.

"What's that?" I asked Marie.

"It's mine," she said.

I wondered how Ortiz got it? He wasn't saying anything.

"Were you wearing it when you were kidnaped?" I asked.

"Yes," she said, without explaining.

"The kidnapers didn't take it?"

"No," she said. "I hid it."

She was wearing a night gown and a robe when she was kidnaped. The robe probably had pockets.

Ortiz got up from the couch and left. I waited until she closed the front door and came back.

While Marie was in custody of the kidnapers, she telephoned Harrison Carroll. When I worked at the Herald Express, Carroll was seldom seen in the City Room of the Herald Express. He was just an elderly guy who some-times brought in a column and quietly departed. He occasionally wrote a short, friendly item about Marie in his columns.

Sitting in her living room after Detective Ortiz had gone, I asked:

"Why didn't you call me?" My paper competed with the Herald, but I didn't say so.

Her answer was that it was nighttime, she called Carroll frequently and she could emember his phone number. It made sense. There was no 911 fone number then, just an O for operator, who wouldn't know where Marie was calling from to get help.

I could have asked her about what people were saying, that she had behaved oddly and it must be a fake kidnaping. There was a lot of sneering and laughing about her. I didn't want to make it any worse. She was going to the Grand Jury the next day to tell them about the kidnaping. She would go with her lawyer, Jerry Giesler. I would see her there.

The chatter about a phony kidnaping picked up overnight in news reports, based mostly on the fone calls she made. Lieutenant Zander, the dapper cop in charge of the case, did not comment.

The complete police report probably had not been disclosed, but the District Attorney decided that the Los Angeles County Grand Jury should investigate. They would interview the police and anybody who had anything to do with the case. It was possible they would indict her for making a false report. Nothing they did would surprise those of us who had covered Grand Juries in the past. I had first worked that beat nine years earlier for United Press. One zealous Grand Jury, with less than serious regard for facts, and fueled by a flawless imagination, went on an amateur's unicycle ride for months. They indicted the Los Angeles Police Chief, for instance. Case dismissed.

Marie's date was at the Hall of Justice about two p.m. During the morning, the Grand Jury heard mainly from the police. Sgt. Ortiz was openly skeptical. Things didn't fit, he said when the two of us talked in the Hall of Justice after his turn with the Grand Jury. The phone call to Harrison Carroll was suspicious, he said. How she could have gotten out on the desert? A friend must have been helping her. She wasn't raped, she wasn't touched.

Ortiz asked whether I knew how to tell if it was a real kidnaping, or not?

"The ring is the key," he said.
Why? He didn't explain.

Grand Jury Secrets

Grand Jury testimony is supposed to be secret. If an indictment was re-turned, the testimony would usually become public, so the secrecy rule did not apply at all times. Police and prosecutors had learned to work with the press, providing factual information to prevent incorrect stories from being printed. Other times, keeping the press informed was insurance. If a number of police, guys whom we reporters recognized, began to show up at the District Attorney's office, or went the Grand Jury room, it was easy for the press to recognize that something was going on. If the police were seeking secret indictments in a drug ring, it could involve many cops pre-senting evidence, and as many as a hundred suspects who would be named in secret indictments. Reporters could easily find out what was going on just by calling around, but they did not want to compromise police work. Even a published rumor that "something big" was about to happen could send suspects fleeing. So the reporters in the Press Room, and their editors, were advised, in confidence, usually by a Deputy District Attorney, what was happening. That was routine. In other cases, Grand Jury testimony that could cause no harm to a prosecution was often disclosed to the press and was printed without mentioning the source.

A reverse of this tradition of trust could work as well. Pat Foley and Olive Foley were a Herald Express team on the D.A.'s beat. Pat was the aging know-all in the sixth floor of the Hall of Justice. His wife was known on the beat for having developed a source in that runaway Grand Jury that willy-nilly indicted an LAPD chief. Pat noticed one morning that the Grand Jury was in session. He saw a well-known Los Angeles city department manager going in a room. He didn't know why, but found out from a staff person that the GJ would be around all morning. Foley asked to see the Chairman of the Grand Jury at the next break. He got the call and told me to go with him. He introduced us to this new Chairman and asked what the GJ was investigating. New Chairman said he could not say. Pat patiently explained to new Chairman how and why the press was part of the justice system. Chairman was not going to talk, proceedings were secret, period. Standoff. Pat finally said, all right, he would find out what they were doing, write a story, it would run in the paper's next edition which would be on the street in – a little under two hours, and would bring New Chairman a copy when GJ broke after lunch. Let's go, Pat told me, back to the press room. You call xxx at City Hall, he said, and find out what potential legal problems had been discussed lately. Foley called another City Hall official. Within a few minutes we had leads, rapidly found out why City Official had to be at GJ, we called our City Editors, Pat planted a story for his next edition, my Mirror CE could wait. When first paper of Herald came off press, a copy was rushed to Hall of Justice, handed to Pat, we went to lobby outside GJ meeting room and Pat handed it to Chairman when they emerged. Chairman did not comment. GJ was through for the day, and Pat and I waited for GJ members to leave, then huddled with the usual staff and confirmed our story. Not a big story, but something was not right at City Hall and would be fixed.

Marie McDonald was not a press victim. Circumstances were beyond control of any principals except the never-caught kidnapers.

Before Marie's visit, the press knew most of the story. Sergeant Ortiz or someone had told about the ring. Reporters were told that the detective thought the kidnap story was a fake.

The McDonald Grand Jury took an early break for lunch. A witness came out, a somewhat distinguished middle-aged man in a business suit. He was surrounded by reporters. He gave his name and said he was a physician. He had examined Marie shortly after she was freed, to find out if she had been sexually abused. He said that he couldn't discuss his testimony.

Reporters and photographers were waiting shortly before two p.m. when Jerry Giesler and Marie came out of the elevator in the Hall of Justice. Marie didn't look at me. She didn't talk to anybody. Marie went into the Grand Jury room. She was there for over three hours, then left with Giesler, still saying nothing.

When all the witnesses were gone and the Grand jury had discussed the situation and departed, the press got a routine briefing. A Deputy District Attorney emerged from the Grand Jury room. Reporters gathered around the Deputy, whose name would not be used. He was tall, rugged, a bit slouched and looked tired, as always. He calmly recited facts, without opinion, giving us a solid report on the daylong sessions. Within his ten-minute briefing was the ring story. He said that Marie had been taken to a hospital to be examined for possible sexual abuse. The gynecologist had probed, touched something hard, pulled out what he saw was a ring, handed it to a nurse who put it in a tissue, and completed his exam. The doctor did not ask her about the ring.

Marie had given the cops a description of the kidnapers. A drawing was made of the suspects. The kidnapers were hungry and stopped at an isolated grocery store outside Beaumont. They had no money. They had a ball-point pen, a new and expensive toy then. They traded it for a loaf of bread. The cops showed the drawings to the store clerk, and he identified one. The cops got the pen, one of about two-hundred given away by a private investigator, not the well known Fred Otash. The cops traced most of them to dead ends, but could never find who had the remainder.

The story died, but Marie became angry at Harry Karl and accused him of arranging the kidnaping. Then she recanted. It added to the doubts some people had. Marie didn't help herself.

A year later, for an anniversary story, Lieutenant Zander agreed to talk to me. Was it a real kidnaping? He said he was sure that it was. Zander, immaculate in appearance, also precise in words, summed it up briefly. He said he was convinced because they had checked her story out thoroughly and it fit. The craziness, the call to Harrison Carroll the movie columnist on the Herald Express, didn't make sense, but that was Marie. She was scared. It was weird, but Zander said he knew of no rule book for kidnapings.

It was possibly a year or two or more years before I saw Marie again. She was launching a singing career. She had done an album. Her publicist called a news conference late one afternoon at the Earl Carroll Theater, a night club and theater on Sunset Blvd. near Columbia Square, home of KNX radio and KNXT television. I had known the press agent for years, and he invited me to Marie's new career sendoff.

There were lots of press in the theater lobby. The bar was open. The press agent greeted me and we talked about his current project with Marie. He asked if I'd like to meet Marie. I said yes.

He led me to the bar where Marie was talking to someone, her back to us. He said, "Marie, I'd like you to meet Howard Williams." She started to turn our way. As she turned, but before she had turned enough to see us, we could hear her say, calmly, "I know Howard." She completed her turn, looked at me expressionless and held out her hand, which I shook. The press agent left us and went to went to see a new arrival.

I told her I wondered if she would speak to me.

Marie said, "I think I understand. If I were in your place, I probably would have done the same thing."

I wished her luck and did not stay long. I was in no position to help, having left the Mirror's cityside Hollywood specialist duties for other tasks.

The singing career went nowhere. The fight with Harry Karl went on. Strange people claimed to know a lot about the kidnaping, but they didn't really, as far as we could discover.

A few years later at most, in 1965, she committed suicide. An overdose of something. She was forty-two. My newspaper had folded by then and I was working at KNXT.

Not long after Marie died, probably within the year, I saw Lieutenant Zander at the Sportsman's Lodge on Ventura Boulevard, Studio City, at a meeting of a police social club, the Footprinters, which I had just been invited to join.

The McDonald story came to life again when I saw the smooth cop. We covered the "that was when I saw you" stuff in a minute, and I asked Zander, again, was it real? He said he was still convinced it was a real kidnaping.

I said thought if we had been more emphatic in public about that, she might still be alive. Not a nice thing to say.

His answer made sense. The kidnapers were dumb and disorganized. If they thought he was skeptical and disinterested the kidnapers might get careless and talk, so he did not become her champion in public. The kidnapers were never caught.

In this computer search engine era, I looked up Marie's kidnaping and found it said the Kidnaping was possibly fake. Wrong. I tried to correct that story, got nowhere.

The Blondes of Hollywood: Jayne Mansfield

Any mention of the death of Jayne Mansfield in 1967 stirs a sharp visual memory of a damaged car on a road from Biloxi to New Orleans. It is dark, and a flash-bulb news photo shows a white spot on the hood which was said to be a blonde wig, removed somehow in a collision with a truck. Unlike almost any other story about stars I met, this was one I took personally because of a silly a rainy day ten years earlier when I drove Jayne and Mickey Hargitay to her new home on Sunset Boulevard.

Jayne had crossed my newsmaker horizon only a few times. The first was at a Herald Express beach party in 1954. She was the wife of an Army lieutenant, Paul Mansfield, nephew of Bill Pigue, an Assistant City Editor of the Herald Express.

Jayne, twenty-one years old and married since she was sixteen, was already working to become a star and would play her first small bit on TV before the year was out. She was a unique presence at the beach party in a one piece red bathing suit. She strutted a bit awkwardly through the deep sand of Redondo Beach, hands on her waist. She rubbed her hands downward on the suit as if tugging it to fit tighter, while she pulled her shoulders back to help emphasize her breasts. She was there to be noticed.

When we met again three years later she was a much publicized starlet under contract to publicists, agents and studios. I asked:

"Do you remember the Herald beach party?"

"Riiiight, the grunion hunt. With my aunt Mary and uncle Bill (Pigue.)"

"We never dreamed then we'd be doing this," I said, a reporter interviewing a star.

"I dreamed of it," she said. "Maybe you didn't. I've always had only one ambition, to be a successful motion picture star."

She sat for a two-hour interview, accompanied by her studio press agent, John Campbell, son of the former Herald Managing Editor. One reason for the interview was to confirm exactly how she happened to walk into a swimming pool in Florida and, according to various witnesses and others, out-bosom several women from Hollywood, including Jane Russell.

One story about her trip to Florida was that Jim Bacon of Associated Press had suggested to her personal press agent, Jim Byron, that she go to Florida with the group for whatever publicity it might bring. Everybody else in the pool was superfluous, it turned out. Another incident to be confirmed or not was her photo with Sophia Loren, in which Sophia's eyes were drawn to Jayne's boob which almost flopped out of her dress. The Loren picture was purely accidental. They were not friends. As for Florida, Jayne said she didn't want to go there, but her agent and press agent insisted. That checked out, too.

Jayne was a smart woman, aware of her figure but not crude. Actually, she was more like a good mother, which I believed after watching her with her daughter and her daughter's friends chasing in and out of the house on Beverly Glen during the interview while Mickey Hargitay, second husband to be, was roaring around the neighborhood testing his Jaguar.

Hargitay came along after her marriage to Mansfield was over, if not ended yet by court action. Jayne recalled that Paul Mansfield was willing to move to Van Nuys after his Army tour, but Hollywood was not a fit for him. Jayne's movie career was not his idea of their future. At one point in such discussions Mansfield didn't want Jayne, who had light brown hair, to be a blonde, she said. "I changed anyway," she said.

We also talked about her relationship with Press Agent Jim Byron. When he met Jayne and she told him she wanted to be a big star, he said he could do that. He would make her a star, and would be her personal press agent, in return for five percent of her earnings. Jayne acknowledged what Byron did for her, but said he had made a lot of money off her, more than enough. She didn't like the deal any more. He had a contract.

The last time we talked was when she bought a big old mansion on Sunset Boulevard. Jayne had inherited money from her grandmother, and wanted that house, which had around ten bedrooms, I had heard. I went there, but did not count. It cost more than a hundred thousand, she said. Likely a million plus in 2016 bucks, I thought. On moving day in November, 1957, Jayne and Mickey flew home from Las Vegas, where they were making big money. We met at her old place in Benedict Canyon. A photographer, Gib Brush I believe, met me there.

The moving van was being loaded, and Jayne and Mickey were busy watching, directing, making sure everything was handled gently. When they were close to leaving for the new home a few miles away Jayne made a final check of the house to be sure nothing was missed. I went with her. The bed was still in the master bedroom. I asked why, and she said the guy who was buying the house wanted it and paid for it. I had an idea:

"Why don't you leave a lock of your hair? Pin it to the headboard."

"Yes!" she said, enthusiastically.

She got her purse, took out some small nail scissors and, reaching under the long hair on the back of her head where a missing lock would not show because she was still performing in Las Vegas with Mickey, she cut a pencil-width patch of platinum hair maybe two inches long. She pulled a hair pin from her purse, paused and asked:

"Should I leave a note?"

No, I said, he'll know whose it is. We laughed while she pinned the hair to the padded head board.

When the final house check was done, we joined Gib Brush and Mickey and the movers outside. It was raining a little. The movers left, and Jayne and Mickey hurriedly got in my red Studebaker V-eight two-door with the twin mufflers that had a lovely muffled boom boom sound, better than Mickey's Jag noise. It was a tight fit with Mickey in the middle and Jayne against the right door, but we didn't have far to go. The photographer got there first and took some pictures around the house. One that had to be done was Mickey carrying Jayne over the threshold.

I never saw either of them again. It was just another day on the job, Hollywood for a change, and was nothing to be especially remembered until a few years later when I was working at Channel Two in Hollywood and heard how she had died. That newspaper picture of the blonde hair on the hood of the car spoiled memories of a goofy day.

The Mirror Folds

The end of a newspaper could be compared to the final shoot for a motion picture or a television series. The people who supplied the news and entertainment had shared excitement and stress for a long time. Their photographs and words recorded most of the emotions that humans feel. That record would exist for generations. But, "Fade to black" means the same in print or on television. The show is over. With luck, the search for a new paycheck will not take long.

Reality was on a slow track in 1961. A small recession was ending. That was the story we read in our paper, or thought we did. A lot of people had been let go at the Mirror, fired because advertising did not support the size staff we had since 1948. But the paper was solid, we thought. I cannot recall talking with anyone in 1959 or 1960 who thought the Mirror was in potential trouble.

Not even in 1961.

Berlin Just in Time

Late in the Spring of 1961, Publisher Laro's secretary buzzed me and asked me to join him in Managing Editor Donahue's office. After our "good mornings," Laro said. "We'd like to ask you to do something."

"OK," I said.

"Don't you want to know what it is before you say yes?" he asked.

"Nope."

"We'd like to send you to Germany for three weeks."

The details were brief, so far. It would be a tour of the country, completely arranged by their government but taking me to places and people I would select. The only requirement was that I had to visit Berlin, all of it, east and west. It was safe. Bonn would provide a guide. If JFK could go to Berlin, which he did, I could, too.

The Russians were making angry noises. It was a city as big as Los Angeles, parts of it under control of post-war allies, the East part controlled by whatever the Russians allowed in all of East Germany. I would not go there. The Airlift, ended a dozen years earlier, defeated Russian attempts to shut down the city which their part of Germany surrounded. East Germans were still a flood into West Berlin. Russia wanted that leaky boundary closed.

I met with the German Consul in L.A. I would go to SFO, then Lufthansa to Frankfurt. After a night there I would follow the itinerary. Upon airplane arrival in a new city, I would hear my name announced, with word where to meet my new interpreter-guide, with car and driver. The trip would take me to Munich, Stuttgart, Bonn, Berlin east and west, Vienna and Hitler's mountain retreat (a concrete cave), Hamburg, Frankfurt and home. I spent at least forty hours studying German. There were few brief talks with the Consulate staff in L.A. to complete the itinerary.

First stop, a Frankfurt hotel. Dinner alone in the hotel dining room. There was a party-dressed lone woman at another table. Another lone man walked in. There were four waiters, in tuxes, for three separate guests. The man was at a table next to the classy middle-aged woman. He talked, English. She ignored his first remark, responded to the next verbal approach, but after that would not agree to his suggestion that she let him join her at her table, or that she move to his. This pickup effort continued, got him nowhere. He left, she stayed and was there when I left. I started a trip diary when I got to my room.

I left out the part about the woman and the friendly man. Who else but a reporter from L.A. would have recognized the man at dinner, the chief of a government bureau headquartered in L.A.? He didn't know me. I never saw him at home to ask why he was in Frankfurt.

A guide/interpreter was at the Frankfurt airport the next morning to be sure I was on schedule before my plane left for Munich. I was met in Munich by another guide, with car and driver. This detailed care continued at all stops. There were visits with a civil service chief, the U.S. Consul in Berlin, and a chance to see and hear interviewers screen refugees from The East before the refugees were taken to Templehof and a plane to West Germany. No criminals could flee to West countries.

The tour was thorough, educational, exciting at times such as walking past (ignoring) tommy-gun guards when going through the Brandenburg Gate. Berlin was a busy, thriving place, but the tense feeling was alive everywhere, every day. More than once my guide and I boarded a streetcar in East Berlin, saw a young couple with a child and one suitcase settle warily into seats until the streetcar stopped in the West, then saw them get off to begin a new, free life. It was that easy, but scary even for a visiting American, though East Germans and Russians seemed unable to stop the trraffic.

I returned home, after a diplomatic stop in Brussels arranged by the Belgian Consul in L.A. It was enough time, overnight, to meet their press relations expert and get his personal view on Berlin, and hear some WWII history. There was time to call Art Buchwald in Paris. The hotel telephone operator tracked him -- to Monaco. Next trip, maybe.

On return home I wrote a think piece in the Mirror.

Two weeks later the wall went up. I was in Los Angeles. Missed the big story. Wrote it from L.A.

By the end of November, 1961 the Mirror was rumored to be closing.

We found out later that the Hearst company and Times Mirror Corp. each agreed to drop one of their newspapers in Los Angeles, leaving two downtown instead of four. Rumors jabbed our hearts. Everything looked the same. Bosses did their jobs, assignments were given, we wrote stories about the city. The publisher okayed editorials.

There was no one to ask. The Hollywood trade papers were our information source. Their reporters dug, asked questions, got blank stares, pried into things as good reporters knew how to do. The movie reporters got hints, enough to make a story. We who were on the inside didn't do what we were trained to do.

When it was no longer a cloud without shape, and lightning had struck, Eddie Louie invited me to write a story about the end of the Mirror for the 8-Ball, the Greater Los Angeles Press Club monthly which he edited. In our paralyzed community it was hard to imagine not going to the Times, if the Mirror was closed. The 8-Ball story relates how rumors bounced and rebounded like errant electrons.

I, like others, had no direct contact with Norman Chandler, for instance. I did not ask my publisher, Arthur Laro until two days before the end, and it was I who called Laro.

As Chief Editorial Writer, a common title nationwide which later became known as "Editor of the Editorial Pages," I had direct contact daily with Publisher Laro. He was my only boss. In his absence, I decided whatever questions came up. I might choose to ask Managing Editor Jack Donahue about something, but could ignore his advice. Jack once advised me to do something, I said no, he called me a crazy SOB or something similar, but friendly, and we laughed.

We were all looking for signs, but nothing materialized. On Wednesday night I called Laro at home about six o'clock.

A neighbor, Ernest (Bud) Portenstein, was assistant manager of the Beverly Hills Hotel. He was the handsome and charming host at the hotel, and met many of the people of note that I dealt with in the newspaper world. Bud personally welcomed heavyweight hotel guests, put them in their suites and made sure the staff had everything properly prepared. At home I had talked with Bud about the rumored closure of Hearst's Examiner and the Chandlers' Mirror News.

Wednesday night, when Portenstein got home, he called with information that he knew I would want. William Randolph Hearst, Junior, had checked into the Beverly Hills Hotel earlier that evening. Bud escorted Hearst to his cottage, and while walking across the hotel grounds Bud said he asked, "What's this about the Mirror and the Examiner closing?" And Hearst unhesitatingly responded, "Yes, everybody knows about it."

None of the other brass, or owners, had been quoted so far. This was The First Word.

Arthur Laro's reaction on hearing what my neighbor found out was surprising:

"I don't believe it," he said.

I was not prepared for that. We talked only a short time, with me saying my friend and neighbor could not have made up that statement by Hearst, and Laro again saying Portenstein was mistaken.

Two days later, post Norman's farewell, Arthur and I were saying goodbye, and I didn't bring up that conversation. He might have known a long time, but could not admit anything. Otis Chandler was quoted much later as being bound, reluctantly, to secrecy in corporate matters because of Security Exchange Commission rules regarding information released by publicly held companies. Insider information is dangerous if repeated. Otis himself could not confirm or deny. Laro may have been trying to silence me without telling me it was a secret and to keep quiet. I did not repeat our conversation, and I did not tell anyone else what my neighbor Bud had reported.

In my old age, knowing the value of numbers, I realize I should have inquired about circulation and income, would have seen what was inevitable and would have been job hunting at the Times, which would experience a circulation increase and also would increase its staff. That resort to logical conclusions did not occur to me. Like the others, I waited. Surely, I would be moved to the Times.

On Friday, a microphone was set up in the City Room of the Mirror. It was tested, sounds came out, and the mike stood there like a skeleton, prepared to announce the end of our world. Norman came in and went straight to the microphone. I'm sure he felt the loss in a family sense, way beyond the corporate and financial struggles which had been his to bear because of his mistaken belief in a strong future for newspapers after World War II. He hadn't known that television would decimate our advertising foundation. Financial planning has its blind spots. Now he was standing in a buzzard roost, a thirteen-year-old building designed to house a newspaper staff and print the paper that would be exciting but was terminal at birth. Now, the building would find other uses. Maybe we would, too.

Four of us shared an office across the room from the City Desk. One of us in the room was not going to move over to the Times, and I was that one. John Grover had been the Chief Editorial Writer, and when he was assigned to write a column, I asked for and got the editorial job. The Times could take one editorial writer, and the decision was to take Grover. I couldn't argue with that. I did not know that the Times City Editor, Smoke Hale, would have hired me as a reporter if I had asked. It was a year or so before we talked about the changes and he told me. The others who shared the four-man office at the Mirror and went to the Times were Richard Bergholz, the Mirror's political editor, and the much loved veteran Columnist Matt Weinstock.

Almost as soon as it was over, Jack Donahue hastened to find me and said, "You and I aren't going anywhere."

Bergholz was taking calls from Sacramento and others, non-stop, that Friday afternoon. One was from Jesse Unruh, my classmate at the University of Southern California. Unruh majored in Journalism and Political Science. Unruh and Bergholz talked about who was in and out.

According to Bergholz, when he told Unruh I was not going to the Times, Unruh said, "Howie doesn't have to worry. We'll take care of him." That was good news. Unruh had been elected Speaker of the California State Assembly a few months earlier. I had seen mutual friends go to Sacramento after past elections.

Later in the afternoon, Aggie Underwood, my former boss at the Herald Express, called. She heard I was out. I said yes. She asked if I'd like to go to work for her again on Monday. I said I was extremely grateful for the offer, but could not accept, I had something else cooking and hoped it jelled soon. She ended the call abruptly hanging up. She always did that.

It had been a more-than-busy six years at the Mirror, and the change did not turn out badly. I worked at L.A. Medical Assn. I told Ann that if I went to work quickly, we were going on a trip. In July, 1963, I took my reluctant wife on much the same tour of Germany I had, and was her driver, in a rented Volkswagon, driving through Checkpoint Charlie into East Berlin. And back.

We toured the wall, which still was incomplete, just a flimsy wire fence in one place, or an imaginary line in water between East and West river banks. Occupants of tall guard towers watched with binoculars when we stopped, got out of our car, and Ann, doing what I asked her to do, waved at them. It was a different Berlin after two years.

Years later I was working for CBS and had an opportunity to tell Jesse Unruh why I had turned down a chance to go back to the Herald Express in 1962, which would have been a lousy career move. I thanked Unruh for telling Bergholz that he, Jesse, would take care of me. Jesse was puzzled, and said he would not have said that. He guessed that he probably meant that I would get something good, based on my record. I told him that the misunderstanding was, in itself, a fortunate thing, because it caused me to turn down Aggie's offer. A few years later he told me to go F myself, but that was about something else, a job he wanted. Governor. (See KNXT editorials). No grudges. Such things were forgotten when we attended a funeral for another classmate who had been well placed in a state service after working on an election for Governor Pat Brown. Unruh also died young, a giant in CA politics without ever becoming Governor.

Meanwhile, employees of the Mirror had scattered. The lucky ones, a combined Times and Mirror mid-level leadership, elbowed for Times positions. The Times side lost key battles to a quiet shiv, and Otis convinced himself he had discovered hidden greatness among his staff. The ship sank. It would have died anyway, with a boost from the digital world. The Chandlers sold the place to someone who wanted the Times but got a shell.

Columnists and Ordinary News People

An institution consisting of newspaper personalities, invented by newspapers, also died with their papers. All five of the downtown Los Angeles newspapers in the Post-War boom had "entertainment" columnists. The purpose of the columns was to capture loyal readers and turn them into addicts. Thousands of curious minds would hunger for a daily fix that was stronger than nicotine. These print personalites were as real as famous book authors, and they knew how to get public attention in other areas, such as making speeches to community organizations.

Some of that reader loyalty survived the television hurricane, but advertisers moved to TV. The famous old newspaper Hollywood columnists who were both idolized and feared by movie studios, lived in a decaying kingdom. Some of the best, Jim Bacon and Bob Thomas at Associated Press, and Ginny MacPherson, Vernon Scott and Aline Mosby at UPI reached a huge audience, but it was based on newspapers with dwindling circulation.

Eric Sevareid on CBS News was a popular opinion maker on TV for decades, but the public's punditry interest also faded. CBS's news feature, Sixty Minutes, tried a humorist. That got old. Radio disk jockeys, spinning records and chatter, disappeared. They were replaced by talk show pundits who found a gold mine with cult followings. At the same time, editorials on television, my trade for twelve years, slowly vanished by the '90s. Newspaper sports columnists were a genuine circulation draw, even in the bad times, but their readership could not pay for general news coverage on other pages.

A giant wave of computers and search engines, plus the emerging email and picture blockbusters which ran ads, finished the newspapers. The story was the same almost everywhere in the country. Columns were for fame and fun, but the throne was built on sand.

Before newspapers became rudderless ghosts, it seemed as though every special interest had a fan base to be courted. Movies and TV and sports were basic. I took over a daily column on labor unions for a few months, then ran the Mirror's Editorial Page. Looking back after years away from journalism, the daily chore of filling the Mirror editorial page with columns from Washington, D.C. habitues was a waste. The columns arrived by wire or mail, and cost about $10 each day. Each author was supposed to be important. I picked out two or three a day and had them set in type for the opinion pages, and dumped the rest. Often, our own Mirror editorials were about the same world issues or tax plans. The big difference was that Washington pundits were syndicated, selling to hundreds of newspapers, which was 18k gold as long as they got column space. Most have disappeared. Those who hit the lecture lecture circuit could do well, if they could grab an occasional headline.

There wasn't any straight, clear path to being a columnist. Luck helped. Bob Hull at the Herald Express went from copy boy to TV columnist. The Managing Editor didn't want to spend a journeyman reporter's salary on TV. Hull did a good job, but the paper did not.

Bill Kennedy at the Herald Express reached for the little guy. So did Matt Weinstock, with whom I shared office space at the Mirror. They always used cute family tales we gave them. They, too, drifted away when papers died.

Jack Smith worked on three L.A. papers. He began doing columns when reporters at the Times were invited to submit stuff of their choice. He wrote about his family, their L.A. neighborhood, friends and about his Baja home builder, Mr. Gomez. It became a regular column. The company tried to "syndicate" him, but it was too local. He did make extra money by selling books based mainly on his columns. My wife, Ann, saw that Smith would sign books at the Northridge Mall near our house. She took a friend to meet him, then they took him to lunch. When it was time to leave, Jack, typically, could not find his car.

In Paris, Art Buchwald knew what he wanted to do and talked his way into a night life/ humor column for the English language International New York Herald Tribune. He was an international phenomenon. Even so, he told me that he gained sixty-five new papers when he moved his dateline from Paris to Washington. We kept in touch as long as he worked in Paris. A lot of single-space letters flew across the ocean, keeping up with USC friends in both countries until he returned to the States.

He, too, sold books of old columns. We were walking in Beverly Hills when Art saw a stack of his latest book of columns on display in a bookstore window. We walked in. Art went to the back of the store, talked to a man for a couple of minutes, and returned. He picked up a book, opened it, pulled out a big black pen and wrote on a blank leaf:

"Ten percent of the price of this book goes to --

Art Buchwald"

And then he signed another, and .... maybe a dozen before we left.

Jack Smith was a bleeder. Every word had to be perfect. Jim Murray, the sports columnist, was the same. The day Murray's first Times column ran he stopped by the glass cage where the Mirror's pundits resided, just off the elevator, and asked, "How was the column?" We assured him he would succeed. He had proven that already as a magazine writer.

Buchwald and Smith began to share column space in the Times. Each wrote three columns a week, and the columns were rotated so that each guy had the top-left column of the WOMEN section's first page, three times a week.

They had never met. Buchwald was coming to L.A. so I asked him to talk at a Press Club dinner. Buchwald agreed. He wanted a minimum of publicity because his speaker's bureau back East did not like for him to talk without getting a fee, which the bureau would normally arrange for him and share. Buchwald did not drive, claimed he never had, and said he hired a car and driver when traveling. I was to pick him up at the Beverly Wilshire.

I went by the Press Club to check the head table setup. Jack Smith arrived early. I suggested that he go with me to pick up Buchwald, and they could finally meet.

Art was on the sidewalk waiting. I put them both in back so they could talk – twenty minutes to the Press Club in traffic.

When columnists talked privately, they usually complained about how hard they work, grinding out columns day after day. These two humor writers were no different. They also agreed that answering mail from readers was a big job.

Buchwald said his secretary had difficulty keeping up with it.

"You have a secretary?" asked Smith.

"Of course," said Buchwald, don't you?"

Smith answered with a memorable negative:

"Not only do I not have a secretary, I work forty hours a week on general assignment and write my column on the side."

They did not pursue the subject.

One of the last times I saw Buchwald was while dining at the Bistro in Georgetown with the station manager and the news director of KNXT, Ray Beindorf and Bill Eames. Buchwald took a booth, obviously "his booth," near the entrance. I went over to say Hi, and took him to meet my CBS people. Art did not stay. He said he was "Waiting for Kissinger."

Kissinger did arrive soon. Washington pundits lived in a whirl of Cabinet Secretaries, Congressmen and Senators. While newspapers collapsed, Buchwald became a high-paid speaker, supplying a change from the routine business-expert speeches of large conventions. How high? Several grand, subject to negotiation. Not nearly as high as Kissinger. Current headlines added zeroes to speaker fees..

Buchwald got an honorary degree from USC later. I don't know if he paid. He had joked earlier that a mega-gift by him might get a building name or an honorary degree.

I never discussed speaking fees with Jack Smith. Once I asked if he enjoyed the recognition he got from strangers on the street, and he said, "Don't knock it."

What to Say When You Meet a Prince

Paparazzi do not set the rules of engagement for contacts between celebrities and the rest of the journalistic world. Paparazzi are the street urchins of journalism, freelancers looking for a money shot.

At other times, gratefully, it is different. Reporters, those with pens and paper, and their genteel photographers or cameramen, both in proper attire for a tasteful occasion, not a forest fire, greet the famous, who may even be Royalty.

There are rules to be learned and obeyed for Royalty, whether elected or inherited. The rules are prescribed by specialists and are conveyed to the press before the encounter. Security is often a factor, so rules are taken seriously.

Lieutenant Daniel Cooke, the legendary public relations man for the Los Angeles Police Department who retired in the 1970s, saw all forms of royalty and was a frequent guide. When Queen Elizabeth was in Los Angeles, the State Department and federal agents were also part of security. Lieutenant Cooke looked after more personal things, such as advising the press that except for a possible handshake it was "forbidden to touch the Queen's bod." No friendly pushes or pats on the shoulder. The Mayor's office also was involved in important visits. The City's protocol advisor for Mayor Tom Bradley was Bea Canterbury Lavery, a journalism grad. It was a world in which an error in a table place card could be a slight, always to be avoided.

Instructions might include a precise ritual. When Prince Bernhardt of the Netherlands was at the Ambassador hotel, he wanted to make a Royal impression simply by being there. He was enjoying a visit to California. He would say nothing of significance regarding his nation's international relations posture. The Ambassador's handsome, graying, smoothly courteous woman public relations manager explained that the reporters would line up facing His Highness, who would step up to one reporter, shake hands, release grip, step aside to another reporter, shake hands and move on. (You see this often in the White House, of course.) When it was his turn, a reporter would face the Prince, take a step forward, extend his or her hand, shake hands with the Prince, and tell him who you were, such as: "Williams from United Press, your Highness." Then the reporter would step back, the Prince would move on and another reporter would take his turn. The Prince would not relax and shoot the breeze. That was not expected. Was he stuffy? Oh, yes. He was Royalty.

It was somewhat less formal for Sir Anthony Eden when he came to Los Angeles. The Prime Minister, earl, viscount, knight was not quite there. He strode among the news people shaking hands. He was a goodwill ambassador. Dignified, of course.

Prince Michael Romanoff fit nicely into the royal mold. He was at least as remote and lordly.

At a general membership meeting of the Greater Los Angeles Press Club one evening, he spent a while discussing the joys of living in Hollywood, and of opening a new restaurant on Wilshire Boulevard in Beverly Hills.

There had been a steady flow of publicity about Mike, er... Prince Michael, for months. He was becoming a Hollywood fixture, a name that could at least cause heads to turn and see what he looked like. He was not pretty. His head was average size, the body, too, and hair was gray, as was a disciplined, short gray moustache. He dressed well, and carried his suit as though it had cost a princely sum at an "in" tailor shop. His posture was stiff, his comfort level in a dignified role was high, and he had a broadcaster's deep and resonant voice. He looked and sounded princely, like someone accustomed to being listened to.

There was a definite publicity tinge to his visit to the Press Club. He expected it to pay off in business. But that was normal. He didn't have to be a Prince to do that. Press agentry was necessary, even for a real prince if one had a be-seen-at restaurant.

In an evening Press Club meeting at the lower-case Case Hotel across the street from the Examiner building, it would have been natural for reporters to ask some penetrating questions about his pedigree. The questions might start with, was he really Harry .... from Brooklyn? Was he really a phony? A poser?

Surprisingly, just one question hit the subject hard that night. It was polite but pointed:

"Are you really a prince?"

His answer was, of course, prepared in advance, and had been wherever he lived. The answer had, in fact, been refined and burnished over years of having to respond. In giving it, he carried the role of prince as he should, with the same polite aplomb as stars of Hollywood. They knew an actor, knew a good one, and knew he belonged, so they were glad to visit his restaurant and be seen with him.

His answer at the Press Club was interesting in its subtle and unstated invitation to the members of the press to become what he was, if they wished.

"Anyone can be a prince," he said.

Oh? A bit of a surprise. Was he confessing? But he kept talking, and his explanation was inspiring. It was not original. Picture a football coach urging his team to assume the role of champions, and do what was needed. It isn't easy to be a champion. You have to work, work. That philosophy is poured into the brains of young people everywhere to encourage their dedication to sports. Many take the vow and go to Olympic Games. Others decide there's a less demanding, more pleasant way to live. Many try and don't make it, but trying has to be the first decision.

It is not easy being a Prince, Mike – Michael --said. One must commit his entire being, every day of his life, to the mantle of Royalty. One must prepare for it. Royalty does take preparation. After that comes a lifetime of being there. One must stay with it and, in every awake moment, do all that is expected of a Romanoff prince.

To be a real prince, a person had to perform perfectly in the role, leave no gaps, no soft spots, no pieces of a skeleton sticking out that shows there is something unexplained beneath the suit. It is, he repeated several times, a total commitment to every detail. Given that, he said, it can be done, if you really want it enough.

His message was common not only for coaches, but also advertising sales managers and car dealers. The message was heard in convention halls from inspirational speakers and politicians. Aspire, work, don't let up. It was never delivered with more sincerity than was heard from Prince Mike.

Could Prince Bernhardt have said it better? Did House of Orange blood make a Prince's appearance among us any more meaningful? What was the difference? Well, Prince Bernhardt was appropriately, Royally bored and unemotional. Prince Mike, if he wasn't Royalty, had that air, but it was different, or so it seemed. Perhaps it was the suspense, waiting to see the screen lifted.

Michael spoke with an air that added silver to every word. Bernhardt of the Netherlands bore a proven European kingdom's name with the same dignity. Was he more real?

All around, on points, Mike won.

I should know better.

Journalism on Hold

Many reporters left journalism public for public relations jobs in business or government. Often it was for more money. Sometimes it was to escape what appeared to be a dead-end job. In January, 1962, they left news because the Examiner and the Mirror News ceased publication.

It was not a massive upset of news gathering and distribution like the changes which occurred decades later in the Digital Age. In 1962 ex-reporters could find jobs. The Los Angeles Press Club's 8-Ball Welfare Foundation existed to help people in trouble. Many requests for financial aid were expected when half of the downtown newspapers folded. A fund raiser was quickly organized. However, the Foundation received very few calls, less than a dozen.

On Friday I had turned down the Herald Express and was expecting an offer, possibly from Sacramento. The first weekend was barely over when my neighbor Bob Dingilian called Monday morning. His boss, Duke Wales, PR chief for the Motion Picture Association, would like me to do some writing until I found another job. I would have an office and phone at the Association.

The writing began a very few days later – a series of features sent to newspapers and other outlets about the "Shurlock Office."

Geoffrey Shurlock, a soft-spoken, kind old man, had the job of acting as the "censor" of the movies. There were no "Sixteen years and over" or X-ratings then. Every movie had to meet certain standards or be denied show dates in most American theaters. Shurlock had a smart crew from a variety of backgrounds helping examine scripts and view the film versions when completed. Producers often tried to slip in something risqué into a movie that was not in the script, hoping to get a bit of industry buzz. It was a constant push and pull to stretch the rules. The big money guys, tough people, winners in a competitive universe, obeyed the law that they created.

After a few weeks there, writing and mailing features to a big mailing list, a call came from Carl Dyster, the former Mirror Medical Editor. He was leaving the Los Angeles County Medical Association. They needed an editor for their monthly magazine. The pay was at least as good as the Mirror. I was hired by the LACMA General Manager, Rueben Dalbec, a month older than I, a veteran of Medical Associations, a jovial, interesting talker who spent many hours teaching me the medical business. We became good friends for life.

The LACMA magazine, distributed to thousands of physicians, soon became a side job. The Association's Board joined medical associations across the country in a giant program to wipe out polio.

About ten years earlier, the Salk vaccine had promised freedom from the summers of fear in which polio maimed and killed. However, taking vaccine with a needle in the arm was a difficult hurdle, according to some people. It was a mental block that still frightened people in the new millennium. Scientists developed a vaccine to be taken orally, a drop on a sugar cube. It was an "attenuated" virus, not dead but weakened enough to immunize against polio. Either vaccine worked.

In a few months, doctors in medical associations around the country organized to finish the job of eliminating that still frightening disease. In L.A. County they enlisted thousands of volunteers to staff 600 clinics. Every clinic had to have a doctor on site for six Sundays early in 1963, two million patients, plus nurses, vaccine servers and money collectors at 25 cents per dose, if you wished to give. A record had to be made of each person who ate the vaccine, because this was medical care, medical research on a huge scale.

An outside public relations agency was hired. All of the news media joined the campaign. Clinics were held in schools, churches, meeting halls. There were probably nine polio-like paralyzing viruses. We would have vaccine for the three most worrisome types, one the first two

Sundays, the others on the following Sundays. The county population was about six million in 4000 square miles. Our experts thought the goal of eliminating polio could be achieved if two-million men, women and children showed up to take each kind of vaccine. We had to be sure the public knew which days. One of our PR experts, Sparky Saldana, and I went to see the Times editor, Nick Williams, whom we both knew well. We begged for a box on Page one for each of the six Sundays, advising that this was a Sabin Sunday. He agreed.

The PR guys talked to the Los Angeles Rams' team physician (this was 1963) and set up a Rams vaccination at their pre-season practice field. The first guy in line would take a cube, swallow it, and run out the door to the field, and the whole team would follow his lead and do the same.

The first guy in line balked.

How did he know it was safe? "Your own team doctor said so," we told him. He was stubborn. Desperate, I told him: "I took one of these doses last week at a dry run for clinics. I'll take another dose." He watched me, then reluctantly took a cube, downed it, and the team followed.

Our training sessions included a lot of background information from an epidemiologist. What would happen if somebody took two doses? Bravado was easy. I knew the worst side effect might be mild diarrhea. It did not happen.

We had a hot line for questions the first Sunday. A male caller asked, can this intestinal virus (the vaccine) be transmitted to other family members by a child's feces from a dirty diaper if the child has taken the vaccine? Without hesitating I told him, yes it can be spread that way. It would be a desirable side benefit if the child was the only one in the family who took the vaccine. The other family members could be vaccinated by contact.

The man asked, "Are you a physician?"

"No," I said, are you? "Yes," he said.

A careful doctor. I told him that our physician experts agreed with him.

There was a flurry of sorts when it was a reported that a relatively young woman died a couple of days after taking the vaccine, and there was no apparent reason. A newspaper writer called. He was doing a story.

I asked, "Why don't you wait until we get a report on what she died of? Doing it now will scare people away. We'll know by tomorrow?" No," he said. I knew the guy. He was a bit self-impresssed. I said: "If you go with it now, not knowing what you're talking about, I'm going to your editor. I know him better than you do."

He agreed to wait. We learned the next day the woman died of a brain tumor she didn't know she had.

After the polio clinics ended, I returned to work on the medical association's business.

Late that year the death of President Kennedy brought journalism into the television age faster than newspapers could have foreseen. A few months later, I got a call.

Television 101

The guy on the phone said his name was Roy Heatly, and he was the News Director of KNXT. I presumed he was somebody who worked for Jerry Dunphy, the news anchorman on Channel Two. I had a lot to learn about television. (Dunphy worked for Heatly.) Heatly would probably want something on the Sabin polio vaccine program which the County Medical Association finished earlier in the year.

"What can I do for you?"

Heatly said the station was looking for an editorial writer. He wondered if I knew anyone who might be interested.

I laughed.

"Does that mean you are interested?" Heatly asked.

I said there was only one person in L.A., far as I knew, who had local experience as an editorial writer and was not currently employed in that position.

Heatly said he had heard that. If I was interested, I might want to call the station manager, Robert D. Wood, who did the station editorials on the air. They had not done many, I had seen none of them, but did not tell Heatly that. Heatly said he was not involved, not beyond making this call. He gave me a number.

That was how it was on a newspaper. Editorial departments were a different world than news. I heard later that when Pete Noyes, who was working in KNXT's News Department, found out the station needed a new editorial writer, he suggested that Heatly call me. Heatly was helping Wood find a qualified person. I had met Noyes a few years before when working news stories downtown, and he knew my editorial writing background at the Mirror.

Bob Wood was a fun interview. We went to USC at the same time, but never met. He was a man about campus. He studied sales and advertising. I was married and working almost full time. I told him I was a CBS fan, so had become a stockholder and had bought fifty shares a few months earlier. I had worked the town for years, knew the politicians and other community leaders and knew the issues they faced. And, I knew how to write for broadcasting, a different style than newspaper writing. He said he'd let me know.

We talked on the phone a couple of weeks later. Wood said if I could pass a physical I was hired. My vital signs were tested and approved by the Television City medical department, and we set a start date in June, 1964. I told Rueben Dalbec at LACMA, and he was pleased. Rube and I remained personal friends until he died about twenty-five years later.

It was time for a crash course in television. Wood told me to take a few weeks and learn the business before we started doing editorials. First

I learned that the anchorman, Jerry Dunphy, worked for Heatly. The News Director hired the reporters and news writers, cameramen, producers -- a staff of 200. The General Manager was directly involved only in hiring an Anchorman, the station's public face. Dunphy was paid twice as much as Wood, plus a new Rolls Royce convertible, but vice president/managers got bonuses. The anchor did not assign reporters, did not select which stories to cover, nor did he write or produce the news. He read the script that was prepared for him.

The other stations were the same. Dunphy was the best. He did have a news background in the Midwest, and it showed in his easy familiarity with news subjects. An anchor who doesn't know the community loses something in his delivery. We brought a woman reporter, Connie Chung, in from CBS News New York to be a co-anchor, maybe. She flew in, and was brought to the station about dark, in a limo. The management did not want to start rumors, so she was let out of her ride at the "back" entrance to the station, a glass door, almost never used, that opened between Wood's office and mine directly onto Sunset Blvd. It could be opened from the outside only with a key. We didn't have cell phones in those days, but we knew her ETA and I was waiting to let her in.

A day or two later I watched a replay of one of her secretly re-corded "anchor tryout" sessions. I could compare it to me reading a baseball game wrapup carefully prepared by an expert. What's a"flied out"? Something would sound unfamiliar. It can be learned quickly if there's gray matter behind the eyes. In this case, I remember hearing her read a local story, and I thought, "She doesn't know what a 'Board of Supervisors' is." She came to work at KNXT, and did learn. But the other network stations, for years smothered by our ratings, were ex-perimenting and gaining. Connie was young, learned fast, went back east later and anchored for all network outlets, it seemed. A Board of Supervisors is not a good measure of smarts.

One big change was disclosed early at a small dinner hosted by our station's Business Manager, Alberta Hackett, to welcome a new News Director. Ann and I were there and Berte's sister. This new boy told us he was going to dump Jerry Dunphy. because "people are tired of gray-haired old men." Yup. He did. Dunphy went to KABC-TV and took a chunk of his KNXT audience with him. An earlier KNXT News Director said it wasn't fair that KNXT "owned" the evening news with Dunphy by so large an audience. But, Anchors flew by often, and the others caught up. It was constant change.

Behind the camera, the real world continued. This was the era of sixteen-millimeter film and two-inch magnetic tape. In engineering, a 2-inch tape recorder was the size of a kitchen range, with oven. There were specialists who prepared visuals that the news needed, including charts, maps, names of people on slides, teleprompter scripts and film.. News also shared some people with programming and other areas that needed the same people, like makeup and engineering and stage crews. Editorials used some of them, too, including the (unseen) booth announcer who was voice-over all day and at night to read copy which might introduce the news, or an editorial replier, or a guest on a local program.

There was so much involved that it required about 15 people just to tape a one or two-minute editorial, from the writer to the booth engineers with the director, to the lighting technician and stage hands who moved the set out. There wasn't time for it to become a ho-hum routine.

Many years later a movie was made about TV news, and it opened with a person running along a hall to deliver some film to engineering only seconds before the station's news program began. It was a panic moment in a mad, speeding production. Friends asked if it was really like that. I said absolutely, almost every day. Film editors put together pieces of stories that were filmed by reporter/cameraman crews during the day, and the various film segments were on a projector, ready to go on the air in sequence over a half-hour news segment. Often there were separate "B" reels carrying sound effects that the "A" camera showing the story participants might not pick up.

Many times I took people into the studio to watch a director coordinate these pieces so it looked like the smooth proceeding in one's own living room. I would deliberately stop in the hallway near engineering and caution the visitor to wait, and to stand against the wall, because if he or she was out in the middle of the hallway, he might be knocked down by a stampeding messenger carrying the reel of film. It seldom failed to unfold as predicted. A runner would race down the corridor past us. The film would be handed to an engineer who put it on a projector. It was ready in a few seconds before the start of the Big News. Later, the Electronic Age of editing tape replaced this thrilling sprint.

Starting at KNXT was almost a homecoming. Noyes was in News, writing and producing, and so was Chuck Riley, who had been a copyboy when I started on the Herald Express in 1952. Neither was "on camera." One of our cameramen had been among those who went to March Field in Riverside and shot film for a newsreel company, which ran in movie theaters, when I was at UP and my brother's B-29 bomb group left for Korea in 1950. I had met most of the other cameramen and reporters when I was out covering stories for the Mirror. Others were met at the Press Club dinners, at the meetings of the Society of Professional Journalists or the USC Journalism Awards.

In the Mirror days, an advantage of being the editorial writer was that it came with an open door to the office of the publisher. For the next twelve years at KNXT the editorial office was separated from the (five in 12 years) manager's office by the desks for our secretaries, who covered each other, staying there while station managers changed and changed again.

The Editorial office had its own department budget, but had almost no staff, only a secretary most years, and required help from other departments. More and more I was involved in non-editorial activities that involved much travel. It was a unique executive-level opportunity to see what was involved in running the hottest TV station in the Western U.S. and a network. We saw CBS employees in network operations. It also allowed considerable freedom for me to work for television and for all news media when a growing group of would-be censors appeared in government from the White House and the highest courts down to City Councils, state legislators and local activists. Talks before journalism groups, service clubs, lawyers, students and other crowds were frequent diversions.

Editorials on TV were somewhat like those on a newspaper. They were not a crowd pleaser. It was a part of being active in the community. Bob Wood had done a few editorials.

The first ever KNXT editorial was done by Reporter Bill Stout in 1958, encouraging a Congressional exemption from the Equal Time law for Presidential Debates. That bill, when passed, let the stations provide time for the debates between the leading candidates for President. Otherwise, stations which carried the network feed of the debates, from wherever they took place, would have to provide the same amount of time to each of the other candidates, which often numbered up to about twenty, mostly unknown outside their home towns or states, usually local "leaders" from fringe parties or self-professed public interest groups with little if any national recognition.

Todd Hunter, the original editorial writer, decided to leave the business, and I stepped in. I talked with him. He thought the job was not interesting. Senators and Governors and a battalion of candidates or bearers of causes were regular callers. Presidents didn't call the house on weekends, but the others did.

CBS, meaning Bill Paley, the CBS Chairman and founder, and Dr. Frank Stanton, the President of CBS, decided to let stations do editorials as a function of free speech. They had approval from the Federal Communications Commission, which laid down some rules about providing time for other viewpoints.

CBS made it absolutely clear that the station manager was in charge and would decide the subject matter, and the policy for editorials. New York did not know Los Angeles problems. It was like being the publisher of a newspaper.

Station managers were not supposed to do the editorials on the air. The on-air person was supposed to be the Editorial Director, but that was an unstated policy which some ignored. In New York at WCBS-TV, the home of CBS, Peter Kohler, the Editorial Director, did them on the air.

Wood decided he would do them. Wood also decided to have an editorial board. It consisted of the two of us plus one old-timer who had worked around the company a long time and retired, also the Progam Director, Leon Drew, and the Community Relations director. I had an Editorial Board on the Mirror, and adapted the same format of issue discussions easily at KNXT.

The Chairman is Not Pleased

In the summer of 1964, with no prior alert, I was told to go to New York the next day and join Bob Wood, who was already there. We would meet with Dr. Frank Stanton, the President of CBS. This was a stratospheric trip for a guy on the job at KNXT for barely two months.

I spent the night at a hotel which Wood's secretary arranged, had breakfast and walked a couple of blocks to meet Bob at the St. Regis.

Wood came down, and the doorman waved up a cab. Bob realized he didn't have any change and asked me for some. I fished a quarter out and gave it to him. Bob waved fingers at me, meaning "More, More!" I took the change from my pocket and held it out to him in my palm. He took out a couple of fifty-cent pieces and said:

"Howie, you work for CBS now."

I got the idea. The CBS image was First Class.

Two-bits was not first class? It was money in 1964. That was the last year quarters were made out of silver.

Bob said we were joining the General Managers of the other four CBS VHF television stations and their Editorial Directors, who came from WBBM TV in Chicago, WCAU TV Philadelphia, KMOX TV St. Louis and WCBS TV New York.

We got in the cab and reached our destination rapidly. The new CBS building, Black Rock, would not open for months. This meeting was in one of several CBS locations in New York City. We took an elevator to the small conference room.

We walked in about five minutes before the meeting was to begin. We were late.

Dr. Stanton (Ph.D), was not a stand-around and chat guy. He was supremely well organized and did not waste minutes. He told Wood that we had only missed the introductions, and ....now ... as he was saying...

.... editorials by CBS stations were expected to be the best. Chairman William S. Paley wanted to set an example for all stations in the country, not just those owned by CBS. Editorial subject matter and opinions might differ among the stations, but factual accuracy was a presumed starting point at CBS. It was a must. We should set the standard for all. TV editorials were new, and we were showing the industry how to do it. I felt pretty good about that, being the only Editorial Director in the company, or anywhere as far as we heard, in any radio or TV station in the country, who had done this job on a metropolitan newspaper. Experience helps.

Dr. Stanton asked how our communities reacted to editorials. Did we have any problems? Did we need anything special to achieve the Chairman's goal of excellence? Were politicians aware of our efforts? Did they understand what we were doing?

There was no hint of direction from Stanton other than what he said at the start, CBS was going to be the best. CBS executives did not tell the network News Department how to operate (see Schorr), and the same applied to local editorials.

Dr. Stanton had met the day before with the General Managers and News Directors of the CBS-owned and operated television stations, known in the business as O&Os. In the cab going to this meeting, Bob Wood told me about going to that meeting with Roy Heatly. The message was the same: Be the best. Somewhere a slogan was born, CBS was the "Tiffany" of broadcasting. Everything had class. The famous eye logo, even the letterheads on which we corresponded were designed to send a message: Tiffany.

About three-hundred and fifty stations carried CBS network news and programming. Nearly all were "affiliates," owned by individuals or corporations. The owners of those stations did what they wished about editorials and local news. CBS was slow to start full-time broadcasting in color, an embarrassment, but it would start soon.

This meeting with Dr. Stanton was held just days before the Republican National Convention in San Francisco, where Barry Goldwater was expected to win against Nelson Rockefeller.

It may not have been coincidental that Dr. Stanton told us about a CBS News problem, in case we had not heard before.

We had, indeed, heard the news, it was "wow" gossip among news people across the country, though not aired in any network news program.

Daniel Schorr, a veteran CBS News reporter, had clumsily hinted on the air that Senator Goldwater was going to link up with right-wing think-alikes in Germany, basing that conclusion on the fact that after the San Francisco convention Goldwater would be vacationing at an American military installation which was, coincidentally, located in the former Nazi stronghold of Bavaria.

Schorr later said he did not mean to suggest "a conscious effort" would be made by Goldwater to connect with the German Right. Dr. Stanton said that not only was the "story" sloppily worded, it was false.

Dr. Stanton said Chairman Paley had tried to call Senator Goldwater to apologize, and Goldwater refused to take the call.

Chairman Paley was upset.

Our little group speculated, after Stanton left us, that Schorr would not be with CBS long. However, Paley really did not tell CBS News what to do. An apology was aired by CBS News. Schorr was still with CBS three years later when managers and editorialists attended a CBS meeting in Washington.

Three decades later I told this Schorr story to Herb Klein, who had been President Nixon's Communications Director when CBS and the White House collided again over Watergate, and asked if he knew whether it was correct. I had known Klein since his early days as an L.A. area newspaper-man and had visited him in the White House, but had never mentioned Schorr. Many years later, Klein and I had moved to San Diego. Klein was not in Washington in 1964, but White House press spokesmen are life members of an informal club. These people have had a common experience, dealing with news men and women, and they talk to each other. Time and political party become irrelevant. I wanted to check the accuracy of my memory of the Schorr report. Klein said he knew the story. After hearing my report on Dr. Stanton's report to us in New York about Schorr, Klein said that was "exactly what happened."

Endorsements on TV

About a year into my editorial job, CBS decided to let the stations endorse candidates. The rule of absolute station independence was unchanged, but we were told not to endorse anyone for President. We endorsed candidates for Congress, U.S. Senate, Governor and anyone else we wished, except President or Vice President. The President appointed the members of the Federal Communications Commission, which gave us a license to broadcast and renewed it every three years. We might have legal reasons to deal with the FCC and ask for impartial treatment.

As on the newspaper, the Mirror, it was my job to bring in ideas, propose positions to the Editorial Board, defend them if necessary, and write editorials once the manager said OK. Actually, we both proposed ideas.

We invited candidates to come in for interviews. Most did. My job was to tell the losers and invite them to send us a person, a non-candidate, to tape a reply. Governor (Pat) Brown insisted he would do his own. I said no. Putting Brown on the air would launch an equal time sequence. We would have to provide reply time to every candidate for the office, including some whom the public at large never heard of. I think he sent Gregory Peck to reply. We endorsed an actor, Ronald Regan. An actor replied.

An Actor for Governor ??

Bob Wood was looking out for lightning bolts when he decided to go along with his Editorial Board and endorse a candidate for Governor. He hadn't joined a hunt for Big Game before. The City Council and School Board races that we had sidled into gently were quiet. However, even those contests for local glory awakened people who were not heard from earlier when our Editorials dealt sternly with political patronage in Sacramento. Local politicians and their friends took those KNXT endorsements personally. Some got unfriendly. The Governor's race could be really big.

Governor Edmund G. (Pat) Brown had been a happy Sacramento warrior for over a decade, which included an earlier stretch as Attorney General. He was so comfortable and popular in the Capitol that he decided to run for a third term as Governor in 1966. That revived 30-year-old memories of FDR's fight in Washington. Roosevelt won a much-argued third term as President in 1940, because WWII was blazing across Europe. FDR was also elected to a fourth term in 1944, but the war would end someday and Roosevelt would go away. He died early in 1945 and Truman became President, finishing FDR's term. Truman ran on his own in 1948, and that was enough by the "old rules." All of this was current history in 1966. Members of Congress and the Senate could run and run, gathering "valuable" seniority, but an Executive Office was too full of temptation to trust it on anyone for long, even a Governor. Or, so Bob Wood's Editorial Board said. They were unanimous. We should endorse Ronald Reagan for Governor. Lieutenant Governors seldom gathered much support to run for the Governor's job.

A movie actor? In Hollywood, actors were real people, not screen roles. Wood did not want any flap, and was uncomfortable when a Hollywood trade paper wondered, in print, whom KNXT might endorse. KNXT was the only network-owned station in L.A. that endorsed in any race.

Pat Brown was a pothole, not a mountain. Also, Bob Wood appointed people to run things and let them do it. His editorial board said Reagan. Wood did not openly hesitate. He told his boss, the President of CBS Television Stations division, who simply said, "I hope you know what you are doing." Wood was nervous. I was the experienced old timer who had done it in a newspaper, and assured Bob he would survive.

There was background noise. Bob had not told us, but he had to know that in a month or two he would go to NY. He would replace his retiring boss as President of TV stations.

At KNXT, some older veterans who had grown up in television's early years thought that Bob would soon become President of CBS Television Network, the entertainment boss of the world. He did, but his KNXT fans overlooked a corporate fact. He first had to get used to the New York sphere of President Stanton and Chairman Paley. Those two would decide if he could run the TV Stations Division. Bob had told me how some others from West of NY, including an heir-apparent to the top corporate job, had stumbled. We saw others from our era fall short in New York CBS jobs. New York was tough, but Wood's KNXT gang thought he would would be a winner. Some KNXT people hoped they could ride along to the network, at its Hollywood area production facili-ties. That was not likely. I was an unusual one who got an offer.

Bob called and said the corporate public relations post in New York was opening, a one-man operation, and he thought I could do it. It was not entertainment or news publicity, and he could recommend me. Wood reminded me that I'd want to find a good place to live, which would require a train ride to work in Manhattan. He said, "You won't have a limo pick you up at home and take you to work like I do." A deal breaker without equal.

At the time, the move raised big questions. Our son was on the verge of we did not know what. He liked Bob, but would not see him in NY. All of our families were here around L.A., or at most a couple of hours north of Vegas – Idaho. Son Darin was high IQ. While in high school, he was hanging out at the Cal State U Northridge campus a mile away. We got a letter from someone at Cal State Admin. saying they would let Darin take classes there although he was still in high school. He had asked without telling his parents. He knew how. His HS counselor said Darin could graduate a year early at 16. We decided not to try the N.Y. move. If we moved, would he go to Harvard? It would have been interesting, but my job at KNXT provided him excitement at times, including trips to NY and DC. Darin finished high school at 16, and we told him he could choose a university (USC??) He decided to go to UC Irvine. He kept his car and motorcycle on campus, carried a double load of classes, sometimes worked in a fast food place, came home most weekends to see friends, and got his degree in two years at age 18. He immediately got a good job in a new computer company in Texas, and was married six months later at 19.

However, this chapter is about endorsing Ronald Reagan. Many years later I wrote a short piece for Emmy Magazine about the endorsement. On taping day, Wood, the cheerful VP, was stiff, silent, not the "Hi ya" Bob who always greeted everyone on the set. I think we all felt the tension. Wood rehearsed the teleprompter for taping, then did one take and went quietly back to his office, probably sweating a lot. He could not have heard the crusty old stage hand say the endorsement was "BS."

We got about 1,000 phone calls, starting seconds after the editorial ran. We took calls for an hour or more before telling the telephone operators to keep track of the numbers. The calls continued for days. Most were negative. About 350 letters were 2 to 1 against us, typical of any editorial on any subject. Friendly people seldom call or write.

Pat Brown insisted on doing the rebuttal to our endorsement of Reagan. I talked to him and told him he could pick any spokesman who was not a candidate for anything.

The station's own News Department got into this. A reporter interviewed Brown, who said we (KNXT management) should not be allowed to endorse a candidate for Governor. News was exempt from Equal Time law. I agreed with that. A Free Press, print or Broadcast, should be free of censorship, which Equal Time was in the broadest sense…. censorship by penalizing free speech.

I missed news item but saved a transcript of KNXT's news segment in which Governor Brown commented on the Reagan endorsement. Brown said it was a "very dangerous precedent," and letting a Federal licensee use a 'monopoly" wave length that way "will be one of the most dangerous things that has ever happened here in the United States."

Exact dates exist in calendars filed somewhere, but generally it took a while to know the new Governor. We also had a new station manager, Ray Beindorf. The Reagan endorsement as Bob Wood's decision.

Months after the election, after Wood had moved to New York, I called Lyn Nofziger, Reagan's press boss, and suggested, "Why don't you bring Ron down for lunch at the station?" Lyn called back with some dates and we set one when Ray Beindorf was clear. I notified the News Director and a couple of others, and confirmed with our master chef for our private KNXT dining room, Thelma, a tiny gray magician. Reagan came with Lyn and possibly another of his staff. It was pleasant, enlightening, and we agreed to do lunch again, which we did. And again.

Reagan was soon being talked about in news reports concerning a campaign for President. It took a few years before he made it (1980). Our last station lunch was early 1970s.

Ann and I were on vacation at the in-laws Idaho home when I finished a fast round on the 9-hole local golf course. There was a message. Call home NOW. Ann said the office called, we had to cut the vacation short and leave the next day. The following day after that I would join the station manager and News Director at the Capitol in Sacramento for lunch with Gov. Reagan in his office.

Reagan was always "on," but in a friendly way, keeping conversation lively. He gave us a souvenier in his office, a pen in a box. It had his name embossed on it. Thinking of the beginning of talk about him running for President, I studied the pen carefully and asked, "What's this 1976 for?" The date was being mentioned nationally as a possible start for a Presidential campaign. Reagan looked at Nofziger like "somebody goofed." Usually, Reagan would have laughed." There was no date on the pen. My joke. Sorry Lyn.

I never saw Reagan in Washington, but we saw other Presidents, and we visited CA Congressmen on The Hill regularly, once or twice a year. We preferred to avoid New York. CBS had a lobbyist in Washington. We got to know FCC and national broadcaster groups.

Bob Wood moved up to Network President. On trips home he would grab me to tour station offices and prevent people from tying him up for long talks. Keep moving. A staff lunch with Directors was the place to tell his plans – Skelton was out, "All In The Family" was going to lead the ratings. Wood ran the network nine years, a record. How did he like New York? Wood said only that Paley was "tough."

TV City Briefing By Desmond

Much later, a new station manager invited about a dozen people from Television City (the Network) to his office and told them how we did editorials. It was a CBS women's group. TV City people were part of CBS and in a way we, station KNXT, were speaking for their company, although the station manager was the final decider on editorials, even by fone if he was traveling.

Someone asked "How much research do you do on editorials?" I said, "About twenty years." That was how long I had been reporting. Writing editorials is very much a reporting job. Knowing background helps. Not many new ideas are launched in a year to solve local or world problems. Every few years someone announces he knowns where Amelia Earhart's plane went down in the Pacific. All he needs is someone else's money to take a search party wherever the (always confidential) site waits for him and his financial backer. It was the same with political ideas. Most were old.

Another visitor asked, "If the manager differs, how can you write something you don't agree with?"

I hadn't thought about it, because it almost never happened. I looked at the questioner, and said:

"Instead of writing this way...," and I put both hands in front of me, as though over a keyboard and wiggled my fingers pretending to type, "I write this way," and I moved my forearms to form a horizontal X, and wiggled my fingers as though I were typing in reverse, or his way. Backward.. There were some laughs. I finished by telling them:

"I'm paid to write what the Manager says, and if we differ I have to consider the slim possibility that he may be right." Even the manager laughed at that.

Wood Himself

Bob Wood started doing editorials as a station leader, and became well known, but it didn't change him. He was a regular guy, not a big manager stereotype. Everybody loved him. Driving back to the station from a speech-lunch, he pointed to the HOLLYWOOD sign on the hill above us and said that was "us." But, he added, "I just see myself as another guy with a wife and a couple of kids and a job." Not long before he left for New York and soon became Network President, I was in a San Fernando Valley freeway crash, two dead, two hurt, I was in an MGA and "okay," he was told. What's OK? He drove out from home in Beverly Hills to see for himself. That was our Bob.

We were required by the FCC to present differing opinions. Some stations called them "rebuttals." Somebody suggested they be called "Replies" because "Rebuttal" sounded like there was a strong and more legitimate opposition viewpoint. Non-CBS stations used either.

If we were criticizing something, I always called the target person, or someone associated with the subject, before the editorial aired, and I usually invited a reply which we would tape as soon as it was convenient. Such calls sometimes prevented errors or eliminated that most embarrassing of replies, the one that began, "If the manager of this station had bothered to talk to me and get the facts....."

I never had one like that.

Editorial writers sometimes feel that the editorials are hardly worth the effort, because nobody pays attention. KNXT's private audience surveys said our editorials were not an audience magnet. Most letters to editors of almost any newspaper are about matters in the news, not about editorials on the subject. At the Mirror, with maybe 350,000 circulation, we'd get only a few letters. Barely enough to put in the letters-to-editor column. It was same on television with an audience of perhaps a million in several counties.

Two subjects always brought the most angry protests from one side or the other – public transportation and fluoridation of water. The most prominent and outspoken foe of fluoridation was also outspoken on another subject he knew nothing about, treatment of cancer, and he supported proven quack remedies.

Opponents of expansion of LAX raged about noise. Lawyers were attracted to the free air time for replies and campaigned against airplane noise. Publicity doesn't hurt. In the San Fernando Valley, the same person was complaining in rebuttals decades later.

Most repliers had never been in front of a TV camera. We welcomed them, advised and rehearsed them and tried to make them glad we took our "mistaken" position so they could come in. Out of many hundreds, we "lost" only one to stage fright, a young man, maybe thirty years old, who could not finish reading his script without shaking and stopping. He came back a day later and did just fine.

We had movie and TV stars. Charlton Heston, Gregory Peck, Eddie Albert, Rod Sterling the TV writer. Albert was answering an editorial on an environment subject, and he had to do it on a Sunday, to fit his busy professional schedule. I brought my wife, Ann, and son, Darin, about 10 years old, because we were on our way to visit family. They watched from the sidelines while Eddie emoted angrily about the wrongs we at KNXT supported. When he finshed, my family applauded. Eddie beamed.

Cameras in the Courts

Only once in my fifty 50 years in and around news have I heard that a President of the United States expressed an opinion in public regarding television in the courts. Bill Clinton said television made the O.J. Simpson trial "a circus." California Governor Pete Wilson said the same thing; surprising viewpoints of lawyers.

Neither knew what he was talking about.

Most people ignored cameras. When you put some clowns in front of a crowd, you have a circus. That was an OJ circus, not the camera. It became a circus when OJ led a slow chase down a freeway before his arrest. My friend Linda Deutsch of Associated Press, who covered big trial trials for several decades, did not blame OJ defense lawyers. The lawyers did not change styles for cameras. Linda talked of technical legal things in the trial, not lawyers acting for a camera.

Of course, lawyers do emote for juries. It may be part of strategy – or maybe not. Lawyers do not imitate robots. The real argument raised by camera opponents is whether juries are influenced by the mere presence of cameras and decide a person is guilty because a camera is there. As if members of a jury don't know they are deciding a "publicity case." Judges who have experience with cameras have been surveyed. Cameras win big.

Cameras began filming trials in Colorado in 1954. The Chief Justice of Colorado's high court believed they belong, as much as print media or citizens. Colorado had no priblems.

There was a hidden camera in the trial of Sirhan Sirhan, the assassin of Sen. Robert F. Kennedy. The principals all knew it was there. Did they perform like clowns? No, those lawyers never did. That was about eight years before OJ.

Then why was the Sirhan camera hidden? CA judges had decided to ban cameras and broadcasts a year or so earlier. Why? A mystery, except it was no secret that CA's Chief Justice Traynor didn't like the press and "experts" kept demanding a ban on cameras.

A few of us, including Bob Wood and I, met with Justice Traynor. He was cool and indifferent to our side. However, later he did let his name be added, as I did mine, to a list of voluntary committee members interested in a McGeorge Law School project in Sacramento, "The

Courtroom of the Future," which made use of cameras in new ways where they could help. For instance, on the counter in front of each experimental juror's seat was a TV screen. An exhibit was not put on an easel or passed around. It was placed on a pedestal below a camera in the ceiling, and a picture of the exhibit appeared on the screen in front of the jurors. The system could be adjusted to the need.

It suited the Sirhan court's needs to let us put a camera in that courtroom, but only with tacit approval from higher up, or so I guessed. After seeing our demo, "higher up" opinion makers remained out of sight, with one exception -- to view a demonstration. The trial judge was in charge. The camera relieved the judge of having to decide which journalists could see and hear the trial. The whole system worked well. It was more years before the camera ban was lifted. We got into Sirhan only because it suited the court's needs to let us put a camera in the courtroom. We did it then only with unspoken, tacit approval from higher levels of California judiciary.

Do Editorials Influence Anyone?

Mail from an audience of a million over several counties was almost always light. Two-thirds of those who wrote told us how wrong we were. Most of the other third who wrote said thanks for agreeing with them, not that we had persuaded them.

Some critics who had a way with words, attacked our "vast wasteland" as an industry certain to make kids delinquent and rouse latent criminals. These people thought that the damage we did with was reversible in the "right" hands. Theirs.

Those of us who had the on-air "power" were humbled by the fact that we did not appear to be changing the world out there. An obvious answer to the critics might be:

"If we in television had all of the influence that people say, we would put it to work full time making the public love everything we do. There would be no flops among our shows. We'd be applauded for everything we did. Our news people and flawless programmers would be cheered every day."

A variation on that theme would be to wonder aloud why people were murdering each other for thousands of years without being influenced by TV?

Of course, it was not that simple. Editorials did have influence. People wrote to say thanks for supporting or opposing something and for giving them helpful background. Most of us appreciate a vote of confidence. Maybe an editorial slowed some of those on the other side, maybe even convinced them to take another look. If they were hurt, dismayed or angered, they might let us know. Anger stirred more people to write than agreement, two to one, but the mail pile was small.

We could not believe editorials made a difference at the polls. Most of our choices won, though we could only take credit for one. In that case, the winner gave us the credit and the loser blamed us. It involved not one endorsement but a two-year series of editorials on patronage in the State Controller's office, each of which was answered on the air, giving the other side of the argument. The Legislature finally changed the system.

Endorsement of candidates was not believed to carry much influence at the top of the ballot, but people did carry their newspaper editorials to the polls to help them vote on lesser races. We heard from poll workers that viewers said they made notes of television endorsements and took the notes to the booth. Not many people could remember all of the names and races and propositions. Neighbors asked me about propositions. I made a list for about a dozen people regularly. That was private, not on the air.

We also heard from a few people we supported that our endorsement was appreciated, but they'd just as soon we didn't do it because we had to put on a spokesman for the other guy, who was a raving idiot, and voters might be influenced. However, it was a chance they were willing to take, as long as we, the station, were going to do editorials, a Constitutional right we intended to exercise, encouraging discussion of issues and candidates. We thought endorsements were good because in most cases we could interview the candidates in person, which a multitude of voters not could do.

Few people probably ever had the opportunity to hold the same job at a metropolitan newspaper and a TV station. I actually knew of no other veteran of both posts. They were much the same. There were no other veterans of both who belonged to the National Broadcast Editorial Association. There were only about 65 of us in the country. Enough to attract a President to meet with us. I had occasional contacts with the newspaper version, and we even talked a joint meeting, but it didn't happen.

The Fairness Doctrine was eliminated during the Reagan Administration. It seemed a step toward real freedom for broadcasters. As the new millennium neared, a few fringe broadcasters abandoned the most basic rule of twentieth-century journalism, to be honest, fair and tell both sides, while accusing the regular news channels of slanting the news. Yes, it was that devious.

Was this a violation of the First Amendment that guarantees free speech? No. Was it unfair, dishonest? Yes, and the Constitution gave them the right to be so. If it was libel they could be forced to pay. Unfairness is not libel. Most political criticism is not legally libelous.

Newspaper people and broadcasters, were continually accused of being liberal. I'd say that many were, because while they were reporting news they often saw the underside of life, and reporters knew it was not entirely peopled by shiftless succulents and criminals. They saw people with family or work problems, disease and accidental tragedy, people of "normal" background who did not know how to work their way up in a rewarding capitalist system.

I did discover in the editorial world that strong political emotions often were not part of careful study of details. Finding out the other side tempered strong opinions.

It was well known that publishers or station owners were mostly conservative, but they allowed bipartisan reporting because they knew it was based on reportorial experience, and hiding the bad was not good and usually not feasible.

An interesting byproduct of editorializing was that it created a continuous flow of visitors who had something to sell: an idea, a person, a cause. The editorial office was a stopover for people intending to run for office, or, as with Howard Jarvis for example, hunting free air time for his tax proposition. From Governors to U.S. Senators, we saw them all at our door, and we often went to theirs.

The web has created a new world. Where will the digital revolution in news go? The contents of the stew pot will change, and the result is certain to be a surprise.

On the Air

When Bob Wood Wood went to New York, he was followed as manager by Ray Beindorf, who had been KNXT's sales manager, then Bill O'Donnell, who had been manager of the CBS radio station in Chicago, and Russ Barry from CBS in New York. When they were absent, they named a staffer to read the editorials. The consensus, which I could not differ with, was that I was not air quality. But, merely being on the air was accepted by the public as proof that someone, almost anyone, was famous and worth listening to. I saw people arrive in town and launch personal campaigns to become visible and therefore famous. Getting reply time, rebutting editorials, was free time.

My personal experience doing the editorials on air, during the last year I was at KNXT, may have proved the experts right about my airworthiness. After eleven years, I was on. It was interesting, but I had no ego that craved air time.

The crew who took part in tapings were curious how I would do the first time. The booth announcer told a million TV audience who was on camera. Then the stage manager signaled "go" by dropping his hand under the camera lens, and I was on.

I stared at the camera, and stared, and finally smiled and waved a hand and said, "Helloooo."

When the laughs were over, the director in the booth said let's be serious, and he called for a take two, and from then on being on air was routine. The Press Club kept news on the set behind the bar. My appearance got no comments. Forty years later, the old tapes I have are not bad. I'd say A+, at least. Humility helps.

I had gone on the air because a new manager from New York didn't want to do editorials himself and said I would. I warned him I was no good, and he said "do 'em."

The new manager was in the wrong job. He fired three of the six department heads. He left me alone, but only after trying one of his imports as a reader.

Performances during tapings could vary. One would be up, another dull and down, even if they were done minutes apart. An old pro, KNXT's weatherman, Bill Keene, agreed. He sometimes taped a forecast after doing one live on the six o'clock news, so he could go home early and not sit around waiting for the eleven o'clock news. It worked if no change in the weather was expected. Keene said he sometimes found a big difference in the otherwise almost identical reports. We couldn't explain it.

On-air people, reporters, talked about the "recognition factor," which in their part of television was substantial. People in stores or restaurants or anywhere might stare, even say hello. I didn't care about that, though it was interesting to see heads swivel when I walked into a market or gas station.

When I started doing some of the editorials on the air, people around the station began treating me differently, as though suddenly I was "important." A young woman named Nora who worked in engineering stopped me in a hall and gave me a hug. I wanted to say, "It's only me, the same guy who worked here eleven years."

The most surprising thing of that nature occurred when Ann and I retired and moved to Vista in San Diego County. We went to see a musical at the Vista outdoor theater.

Before the show, we had dinner in the restaurant on the same property. The waitress paused, looked at me intently for a couple of seconds, then said:

"I used to watch you do editorials on KNXT in L.A." It had been fifteen years ago.

A letter came to the station from a high school classmate we had not heard from after she moved to Oregon. She wrote that she had been visiting her mother in Yucaipa, in Riverside County, was walking by a television set, heard a voice she recognized, looked and found out where I had gone to work.

That kind of on-camera incident happened only one more time. I was retiring from a few jobs on Boards of Directors of public agencies in San Diego County. While doing paperwork (one must file papers to *quit* a public office) a woman who was helping studied me a minute and finally asked if I had been on TV. She remembered the face, but not the circumstance: Thirty-six years later. In San Diego? It could have been me. In the early days, motels had cable service that showed competing stations from L.A. We had watched my taped KNXT editorials while in a San Diego motel.

Jerry Brown and Equal Time 250

When Jerry Brown first ran for public office he had some opposition. About 250. There was speculation that this was a record number of candidates for any office anywhere.

There have been two Federal edicts which attempted to force the holders of broadcast licenses to meet someone's definition of "fairness."

The Fairness Doctrine meant that licensees had to be fair. If you were not fair, the Feds would see that you were. Complaints came from all sides of the political game. Guidelines were ad hoc, seat of pants, the way the wind blew and only as good as the last FCC decision. Finally, the Federal Communications Commission dumped the Doctrine.

The Equal Time Law (not its formal name) was easier to understand. Whatever time or rate a station gave to one candidate for political office had to be available to all others seeking the same office. This was a law, not a regulation. Congress approved an exception to permit some televised debates.

At KNXT, Editorials generated fairness activities by taking sides in controversies or by endorsing candidates. Replies to editorials satisfied the fairness test. Editorials were not exempt from the Equal Time Law. Put a candidate on the air and other candidates were entitled to Equal Time. News broadcasts were generally exempt from both the Doctrine and the Law.

Gradually, over a few years the News Department began to forward calls about either one to me. I dealt with the Fairness Doctrine almost daily, and frequently conferred with Legal. As a result, I could explain the Doctrine and the Law to people who called. That history of handling complaints led a studio cameraman to visit my office on a Friday afternoon, four days before a regular election day.

The cameraman said the Program Department had just finished taping a half-hour special on religion to be aired on Sunday, two days away. When the man who was interviewed left the studio he handed a pamphlet to the cameraman. It urged a vote for the man for a seat on the Community College Board.

The show had nothing to do with the election or the Community Colleges. But, the cameraman, alert to legal things, gave me the pamphlet. He said the program would be broadcast on Sunday, two days before the election. He wondered if the Equal Time Law might apply? If so, he thought I might want to talk to someone about canceling that particular Sunday broadcast.

Definitely, I said. We couldn't put him on the air Sunday before election day. It would be an undisputed setup for the Equal Time Law, and we'd have to invite Jerry Brown and 250 others to appear on the air, each one for half an hour Sunday or Monday.

Well, said the cameraman. You have a problem. We had taped the same guy the previous Friday, and he appeared on the air last Sunday – five days ago.

It was one of those Oh My God moments. The cameraman left the office while I started calling the station General Manager, the Program director, and then Bill Whitsett at Legal in Television City. The rules were well known, but we had never been forced to apply them. After we put the candidate on the air, the other candidate, in this case 250 candidates, had seven days to request equal time.

The show with the candidate had been broadcast the previous Sunday. So far we had no requests for Equal Time.

Any candidate wanting free time had until midnight Sunday – two days away – to call us.

The Equal Time Law had been triggered. All we could do was sit silently sweating and hoping that there would be no request from any one of the 250. If one applied, we would be obligated to notify the others. We were looking at 250 times half an hour. There wasn't that much time before the election, even if every minute of each day and night went to putting candidates on the air. All station time could be turned over to candidates until the polls closed on election day. Regular programming would be scrapped.

After talking with Bill Whitsett in Legal, and while waiting for whatever might happen, I gathered information so we could put a package together and present it to the FCC and show them precisely what we faced. It would be impossible, and we would request relief of some kind.

The law had been changed by Congress to allow Presidential debates, so we did not have to put ten or twenty candidates, in some years, on the air. There would not be time to change the law for this pending disaster. But, FCC could have to decide something.

First, we needed to know the actual time involved. We did a stopwatch run of the tape that had appeared on the air the previous Sunday. Thirty minutes did not mean that the candidate was on the air for 30 minutes. There was an opening, an announcer telling what was coming up, plus time for the show's host to talk. The only time that counted was when the candidate's face was on the screen or when his voice could be heard if the camera was on something else.

After replaying the tape, I estimated we could be hit for 17 minutes of candidate time on air. That was around 250 quarter hours, roughly 60-plus hours of TV time, featuring an army of candidates. Saturday and Sunday around the clock would be only 48 hours. We waited for a "time bomb" to go off.

By the deadline to make requests, we had heard from no one.

We told the guest who had taped a second show on Friday before election that his show was postponed a week. On "his" Sunday we did a re-run of an old program. No reason was given.

It sounds nonsensical, but it was potentially real. Jerry Brown was elected. I didn't meet him until he ran for Governor and came to my office at KNXT. I did not mention the equal time excitement. And, yes, the Equal Time Law is still on the books.

Otis and Company

Norman Chandler, publisher of the Times, was called "Norman" by everyone. Even in the company newsletter, "Among Ourselves," called by some, "Among our Slaves," he was "Norman."

His son, Otis, had been very visible, a guy who worked in the same places we all did, or at least close enough that we crossed paths and greeted each other, and he remembered our names. When Otis became publisher of the Times, it became obvious that his training did not include assembling a broad brain trust, and that left him prone to blind spots, which in turn hurt good employees.

Buffy, Mrs. Norman, had an office in the Times, smaller and not close to that of Publisher Otis. She was a forward person, announcing herself with certainty that would not be challenged when she raised money to build a great Music Center. Years later, I was aware from a source inside the family circle that she was so ill she could not leave the house in Hancock Park. We shared the same doctor, but not ailments. .

Otis talked about Norman Chandler's dream of an expanding newspaper empire, one dominant newspaper chain from Santa Barbara to San Diego. After two of the four downtown L.A. papers folded in 1962, Otis said to me and probably to others, "My God, what would it be like if we (Times) were the only paper in town?" He was concerned that they would be perceived as not caring about the community if they didn't cover every bit of conservative evangelicalism that made "news" in the disappearing Hearst papers.

Otis, at the retirement for a veteran news executive, explained in surprising detail the benefits that would be bestowed upon this long-time, loyal servant, though he didn't use those exact words. Maybe Otis had heard that someone said the man was being cast out with nothing, which was not the case.

Medical benefits had been openly criticized in the past. They were a considerable help, but generally allowed three days a year, which could not be accumulated. Walter Ames, who was television columnist at the Times, complained publicly that he worked there 16 years, then had a heart attack and got three days of sick leave. When I became an Assistant City Editor I learned that executives would receive up to six months medical time off. On a different side, a reporter attempted suicide, we thought. CE Jim Bassett sent me to the hospital, some distance away in another city, to do whatever was needed to help. I spent the day there. Peggy Cook, our wise old hand on the District Attorney's beat, wanted to retire and confessed that she had lied about her age and was really 65, not something younger. She needed to clear up the record to receive Social Security. I was told to go help her get the retirement. I checked SS, and they took care of her problem. Social Security said lots of people lied to employers about age.

Otis came to KNXT a few times. We had a private dining room, as the Times did, and our chef, a tiny little gray haired gal named Thelma, was a marvel. Governors, Senators, a Cardinal. She pleased a big audience. I had used the Times' chef and dining room for the Mirror, while Chief Editorial Writer, to have lunch for the editors with newsmakers and political candidates.

When I went to KNXT, Otis called asking to see a tape of a show about hunting. I got a copy from Television City, where the CBS network's main offices and some of many Southern California production facilities were located. He had to come see us, because it was a two-inch tape, and the machine to record or play that size tape was not portable. We watched it in a vacant office at KNXT and engineering ran the tape. The hunting program included a piece about a hunter trying to fire a fatal bullet into a large deer that was wounded and incapable of using its legs to get up, but was sitting upright on the ground., The hunter fired a pistol into the animal's body, it flinched, but continued to sit up. The trophy head was preserved. The hunter fired again, and again. It was brutal. Otis, a big game hunter with some mounted animal heads in his Times publisher's office, asked "Why do they have to show that?" I was never a hunter and had no answer, but it was reality.

He told me one day in his office that he was "offended" when Dr. Frank Stanton, the President of CBS, approached Otis after both had attended a Board of Directors meeting for a major airline, and asked for help on a major battle with Congress over our broadcast of "classified" Pentagon Papers. News people nationwide were upset by the threat to put Dr. Stanton in jail for contempt of Congress. CBS and Stanton were getting support from newspapers, broadcasters and members of Congress. I told Otis I thought Stanton regarded the CBS stance as a freedom of the press matter, an industry thing, not a personal problem of Stanton's. I was stunned by Otis' reaction, because a couple of years earlier the Times was in from the start when the news business put a closed circuit TV system in the Sirhan trial in 1969. Now, Otis's thinker corps failed him when journalism organizations were involved. The CBS President did not go to jail.

Otis talked about the future of newspapers, and wondered how long they could continue. Printing and delivery were big costly pieces of the business, and were outdated in his view in the Sixties, long before the arrival of the digital age. He once said while visiting KNXT, "I wish I had your distribution system." He was decades ahead of Kindle and I-pad.

My encounters with Otis were not unusual. He always seemed glad to see and visit with people from the papers after he retired, and welcomed reporters to his auto museum in Oxnard. He came to the Old Farts Society, a Times-Mirror alumni lunch group, and gave a prize of twenty-five thousand dollars to the winner of a contest he sponsored and OFS judged. He offered to continue with the twenty-five-grand prize annually if the OFS would change its name, which he did not care to be connected with. He thought it was a bit too informal or undignified, and I agreed. But the gang thumbed their noses at him, and he withdrew the offer. It was a loss to no one except young reporters who might have won the prize each year. Otis' think tank failed him. They did not know how to deal with organizations of news people. The organizations ranged from job-hunter groups to fronts for business look-alikes, and their names might be invented to appeal to corporate expense watchdogs or occupational sectors. Otis did support some of them by his presence, or substantial donations to coventions. All were distant acquaintances, at best, and important causes might not cross his desk, even if the paper belonged. Overall, Otis made mistakes in personnel, as any boss does, but he let those he picked run their part of the show. First, he was a reporter. Standing around talking with other Times reporters when he was working with them, Otis was said to have told them, "Reporters don't make enough money." I hey loved that, but he made no big changes until the matter of hiring an east coast movie critic at a relatively big salary exposed the Times as not generous. More bad advice.

Sirhan Sirhan, Cameras Only as Needed

Superior Court Judge Herbert V. Walker was aware from the start that American justice was on trial. The recent history alone was almost unbelievable.

A defendant of mixed Middle-Eastern nationalities, Sirhan Sirhan, assassinated a likely Democratic Party nominee for President, Robert F. Kennedy, in front of witnesses in a Los Angeles hotel.

The victim was the brother of President John F. Kennedy, who had been assassinated five years earlier in Dallas by Lee Harvey Oswald.

The President's assassin, Oswald, was himself shot to death in front of witnesses, while in police custody, by Jack Ruby.

Ruby, a nut, was convicted, but won a new trial because he was not granted a change of venue. Ruby contracted cancer and died before his new trial could be held.

Feeding on the historic violence of these crimes were publicity-prone conspiracy theorists who led a gullible public to believe that anything was possible, including unidentified conspirators who might strike again.

These were "publicity cases," an informal description which meant that special preparations could be required for press coverage, legal assistance, official judicial notice and even extra juror pools.

The legal system asserted its authority quickly to keep control of The People vs. Sirhan Sirhan. Superior Judge Arthur L. Alarcon issued a gag order forbidding those involved in the case to discuss it publicly.

Superior Judge Herbert V. Walker was picked to try the case, but where? The judges and the Sheriff were firm regarding security. The Sirhan trial courtroom had to be near the jail where the defendant would be housed. They could not risk transporting this prisoner on the streets every day from a new County Jail a mile away in downtown traffic.

Criminal courts were on the eighth floor of the old Hall of Justice. The old, and full, County Jail at that time was in the top few floors of the Hall of Justice, starting just two stories above the courtrooms, one floor above hideaway jury rest areas.

It was risky using an old courtroom with four eight-foot windows facing public streets eight floors below. Those windows would be

covered by solid steel panels. The corridor between the public elevator and the courtroom required enough space to handle a daily crowd.
Everyone would be searched before going into the courtroom. The "foreign" press insisted on being there.

That was the easy part.

Months before the trial could begin, the court received over a
hundred requests for seats from newspaper and broadcast reporters.
Artists and authors also wanted in. The courtroom had about fifty
seats. Demand kept growing.

Judges Walker and Alarcon sought help with courthouse seating.
The judges were told that local Press Clubs were mainly social organizations, not equipped to advise on trial seating priorities. Somebody
in the courthouse found out about the Radio and Television News
Association of Southern California, an organization that included stations from Santa Barbara to San Diego. There was a meeting which I
heard about later. The judges suggested to RTNA that, because they
(RTNA) knew the people and their needs as journalists, RTNA could
advise the Court who needed the fifty seats. No luck. I was told that
someone on the "other side" (the court) referred to "toothpaste sales-
men," a common derogatory term (and there were many) nationwide
for television people in general.

RTNA said that making choices for seats was a hot and thankless task
which judges had created for themselves by banning cameras broadcasts a
year before, a formal action by the State Judicial Council. KNXT had futilely
tried to stop the ban,.

Cameras were allowed in some other states for years without problems
but California banned broadcasting of trials. That was a year after the U.S.
Supreme Court, with no evidence, ruled that the presence of a camera in a
courtroom was "inherently unfair" to a defendant. That was the notoriou
"Estes" decision which granted a new trial to a small-time Texas swindle

who, having won a new trial, did not even bother to plead not guilty in his new trial. He went to prison.

The camera ban, inherently prejudicial, remained, though it apparently is not applicable if judges decide it is not inherently unfair. They are still banned from the Supreme Court's presence during oral arguments, but radio recording is OK there. I suppose every lawyer who gets to practice before SCOTUS will want a full record, including sound or pictures if TV is admitted to oral arguments. It's a pride thing. And SCOTUS no doubt would expect the legal teams to show off. Orals are not like a routine trial. Who loses if cameras are excluded, but radio recording is allowed? I'd suggest that a single camera shot from across the room would eliminate the show-off, if the participants can't be identified. Of course that might not solve a problem of a Justice who wanted to show off. They exist. Maybe it is better that the public not see SCOTUS at work.

A new idea, closed circuit television, was suggested as a way to provide additional seats for Sirhan. That would require a camera – possibly forbidden by the state's Judicial Council action, and by the U.S Supreme Court in Estes. When my non-journalist son asked "What is the big deal about closed circuit television? It's very simple," I said, "Politics. The Supreme Court KNOWS somehow that cameras are bad."

I knew both judges from years covering trials as a newspaper reporter, but in 1968 I was in a different world, writing "station editorials" at CBS-owned KNXT, Channel Two. More and more I was spending time on First Amendment controversies, including coverage of trials with modern electronic devices.

It was Judge Walker's burden to be sure that the world saw the Sirhan trial. He wanted an open trial that would not deny access to domestic or foreign news media. The public might have no seats, therefore would "hear all about it" from the printed press, or radio and TV reporters wielding pencils. The public's only visual access would be drawings by artists using tools not often used in news coverage since the Civil War.

Judge Alarcon was not opposed to the press. He was smart and friendly, a slim WWII infantry dogface who served in Europe and emerged as a staff sergeant. He told me he survived one day by ignoring a lieutenant's order to jump a stone wall in front of an enemy machine gun. He was a former Deputy District Attorney, a well-known prosecutor.

Alarcon and I had worked on Freedom of the Press matters with a select committee of newsmen, judges and lawyers. One of the lawyers we worked with was Warren Christopher, later Secretary of State. Another was Seth Hufstedler, who would soon become State Bar Association President, and whose wife was a judge on the Federal Circuit Court of Appeals. Alarcon and I had traveled together in local counties, encouraging formation of other Bench, Bar, Media Committees. He was a senior judge of the Federal Ninth Circuit Court of Appeals when he died in 2015. We had kept in touch most of those years.

Judge Walker was possibly the most experienced of the small group of Criminal Court judges. He was a large man, imposing, noted for heavy eyebrows that made him look angry, not at all like the pleasant person we in the press knew well. He would have to run an error-free proceeding in which attorneys for the defense would probably try to expose legal weaknesses that could be grounds for appeal if Sirhan were convicted. That was not a big worry. Walker would be sure the legal questions were resolved correctly and he would maintain order if attorneys got noisy. I don't know who, if anyone, in the court system knew that Judge Walker had a heart ailment. I learned of it soon after the trial. He had trouble walking to his car from a dinner. Heart attack. Later, when I took my wife and son to see Walker and his wife, Alice, at their home in Glendale, he mentioned it while talking about something else, but dismissed it as not serious, just uncomfortable sometimes. He died in late 1976 at age seventy-seven.

News people told Judges Walker and Alarcon they wanted no part of deciding who got inside to cover the Sirhan trial, and they also did not like the idea of rotating seat holders so everyone saw part of the trial. Pool reporting, in which reporters decided who would represent them all and share the information, would be unsatisfactory for an international news group.

Still searching, Judges Walker and Alarcon invited the California Freedom of Information Committee to meet with them at the Hall of Justice. The CFOIC had gone statewide in 1968 and was growing in new directions with friendly cooperation from the State Bar and the Judicial Council.

The CFOIC meeting included the two judges, Walker and CFOIC veteran Alarcon; Ray Spangler, publisher of the Redwood City Tribune and recently national President of the all-media newspersons' organization with thirty-five thousand members now known as the Society of Professional Journalists; Frank Haven, Managing Editor of the Los Angeles Times; Clayton Brace, ABC Vice President and General Manager of KOGO-TV San Diego; Richard Fogel, Executive Editor of the Oakland Tribune, and I from KNXT, the CBS-owned TV station in Los Angeles. (The other founder of CFOIC, Roy Heatly, had moved to a Sacramento TV station.)

TV people wanted a real camera, like one which we knew had been hidden behind a specially constructed wall in the Estes case in Texas. The Supreme Court blasted that idea. Estes had become known for cables around the courtroom floor, cables that had been present at a preliminary hearing. The camera was hidden for the trial.

Small "industrial" cameras were coming into wide use for security. We talked about whether the Judicial Council would allow that kind of TV, not for broadcast but to enlarge the courtroom. That would let the world "see and hear" the trial through the eyes and ears of reporters bearing only pencils and pens, which should satisfy the Judicial Council's goal in banning broadcasts of the trial. The press and TV were willing to help this indirect coverage so we could get a camera in the door and prove it was not disruptive. From our standpoint, it was a poor compromise, but all we could hope for. Judges Walker and Alarcon wanted it. We did not expect any opposition from lawyers on either side, and not from Sirhan, who wanted the trial to tell his "story."

CFOIC said we would pay all costs and personnel. We hoped for approval, but got only a "suggestion" from Judge Walker:

"Let us see what you can do."

It was an invitation to demonstrate closed circuit.

Outside the judge's chambers, the CFOIC group paused to decide how to proceed. That took only a moment. We all knew each other. Clayton Brace, from San Diego, said to me:

"You're the only television guy here from LA. It's up to you. Let us know what you need." The others said the same, and everybody who was called did help over the next three months. First, I had to get approval from KNXT's manager, Ray Beindorf. He called New York. The next day he had the word: Dr. Frank Stanton, CBS President, said "Make it work."

Ray let me spend a majority of the time for about three months working on the project. It was a simple technological job. But, we had to satisfy judges who had announced, in clear, if uninformed, decisions that cameras did not belong in courtrooms. By the time we finished, about fifteen KNXT employees had been involved, plus others from KNBC Channel Four and KABC-TV Channel Seven, and more from the L.A. Times' Haven, CBS Television City, and Spangler and Fogel in Northern California. We asked the national Radio TV News Directors Association to find out if a closed circuit had been used anywhere. Live broadcast of trials was allowed or encouraged in some other states. Usually cameras were in the back of a courtroom, with a camera operator. Closed circuit? "Never been tried," was the word. "Not to enlarge courtrooms." The small camera quality was bad. It had a ghost – a shadowy picture called "vidicon lag" that appeared when a figure on the screen moved.

At the station (KNXT in this case) a few of us in news and engineering talked about what was needed. That would depend upon the courtroom. On-site examination of Judge Walker's courtroom showed that, to be completely hidden, a small camera could fit in the box that now held the motor and controls of a window air conditioner. An ordinary louvered metal cover hid the machinery and was the outlet for cool air. How could a camera shoot through that cover? A hole for the lens? Covered by glass? Camera controls? What could they do? Pan? Zoom? No, this was not a mystery show on TV which used barrel-sized studio cameras, in color. We could have one camera, one view, and avoid showing the jury.

Heading the ideas group was Eddie Miller, KNXT's chief engineer. He called a couple of days later. Miller and his assistant manager, Norm Cobb, waited in his office. When I walked in I saw a TV monitor on his desk. It showed my feet walking in. Miller and his gang had put together a hidden camera in a plywood box that was on the floor. They borrowed a louvered screen to cover the camera. The lens was against the louvers and they were out of focus, almost invisible. We were ready for the judge.

We took over Judge Walker's courtroom for a couple of days. Usually, I made arrangements with Harold "Freddie" Frediani, the Court Clerk, to find times when the court calendar was clear. Miller's engineers and a carpenter from CBS Television City removed the rear air conditioner unit about eight feet above the floor, set the camera in position to show a picture of the lawyers and judge, and put a monitor on a counsel table.

Judge Walker liked it. He called after a day or two and we arranged a date a couple of weeks later for the entire Judicial Council, more than twenty judges from all over CA, to see it after they had a regular meeting in L.A. Judge Walker turned the courtroom over to us and offered no guidance. He would not be there.

Ed Miller's engineers set up the latest model. Engineer Bob Lawson said we had a little problem. Black cloth around the camera, inside the plywood box, had pulled loose, and we could see light from outside the building when standing at some places in the courtroom. Should they pull it out and fix it? I wondered who among the Judicial Council members might snoop?

"We only get one chance," I said. Lawson's guys redid it.

The next afternoon Engineer Bob Lawson and I greeted the Judicial Council, about twenty of them, at the gate separating the courtroom audience from the counsel and judge. I told them that the camera was in, it was working now, and we hoped they liked it. We opened the gate, and the guests responded by wandering around, looking for a camera. No camera.

I said to follow me and led them to the judge's chambers. They crowded in and found two monitors (supplied by KNBC) on Herb Walker's desk, showing the interior of the courtroom. Our guests were not talking much. They went back out to search the courtroom, even looking under chairs. I signaled Lawson and he pulled a ladder up from behind seats in a back corner, climbed up and removed the cover of the rear window air conditioner, exposing the small camera.

They still weren't saying much. Superior Judge John Cole had not even said hello when they arrived. Our sons had been in the Northridge Indian Guides tribe maybe five years earlier. A year after that a neighbor of mine died. An early-teens son worried his mother because he didn't want to go to school. The boy did say one day that he might like to be a judge. Mother didn't know why. I took the boy downtown to the courthouse to meet John Cole and learn about "a day in the life of a judge." That fatherless family moved away soon. I had not seen Cole since.

Judge Cole had the only meaningful comment from the Judicial Council. After Bob Lawson exposed the hidden camera, Judge Cole said:

"I knew it couldn't be there. That cover has been up there for fifty years."

I said, "It's brand new. It was finished yesterday in the prop department of CBS network, and painted and dusted to look old."

The dirty old controls were original. The judges made no other comments. They left to go home, all over the state.

Never did Herb Walker tell me that we, or he. had Judicial Council authority to do anything. He just said – at decision points -- to go ahead and do whatever we had discussed. We already had formal approval where it counted, or we would not have gotten this far. It happened at a brief hearing on routine pre-trial matters. It was not in a regular courtroom, but in a "secure" courtroom borrowed for the day, a room which had no view of the outdoors streets or buildings. Present were Sirhan and his two lawyers, and the District Attorney's staff. They had been told what was proposed. Sirhan approved closed circuit and so did his counsel. That was our "must" for the record.

Weeks later I was at a Board Meeting of the national Radio TV News Directors Assn. in the Beverly Hilton when my secretary called. Walker wanted me in his office. I drove down town. The judge said, "Let's go ahead with it for trial." I went back to the RTNDA Board meeting in Beverly Hills and told them what we were going to do. These TV newsmen from around the nation were not impressed. Some were already using film or tape cameras in courts. Colorado TV stations had been filming trials since 1954.

Surely the California Judicial Council had to be involved. No judicial authority was going to flout the Estes decision of the Supreme Court, but Walker needed help to satisfy the world press. This would not be a broadcast. We would transmit a signal by wire. We dangled a long coax cable out the eighth-story window behind the camera to someone who reached out a fourth floor window and pulled it in. The cable could be seen from the street below for the duration of the trial.

ABC engineers came to hook up the TV wire from the eighth floor window to the monitors on Four. County carpenters installed shelves on a wall for three special studio monitors. Speakers were mounted beside each monitor facing a room full of standard courtroom folding chairs, maybe 100. County employees installed another system to Judge Walker's courtroom to record all audio separately on a machine beside his bench.

On the eighth floor a "modesty" booth was installed. Everybody going in the courtroom would be searched by a male or female Deputy Sheriff. Besides weapons, visitors would also be checked for miniature recorders and cameras. Someone told Judge Walker that a miniature recorder could tape the audio easily by simply laying the recorder on the audio cable anywhere on the fourth floor. No direct wire contact was needed. There was no bailiff inside that auxiliary courtroom, just trial watchers.

"Is that true?" the judge asked about audio recording on the fourth floor. "Yes." I said.

"How can we be sure nobody sneaks a recorder in?" he asked.

"Search 'em, just like you will everybody going in the courtroom upstairs," I said.

So, they built another modesty booth on the fourth floor, staffed by male and female deputies, though not full time, just as needed during the day.

How many people used the auxiliary courtroom? That depended mainly on what would be going on. Court trials often have minutes or hours when nothing is happening that is news worth repeating. The crowd varied a lot, from a handful to few dozen people. They also let a few people from the public watch on the fourth floor, including a group of law school students, I was told. I took my wife and her friend on a tour when they were downtown. They saw a routine court hearing in progress with Judge Walker and some lawyers a few days before the Sirhan trial began. My guests were not impressed.

The hidden camera worked well. A second, backup, camera was in the window box. There were little additions. Microphones were set up on the counsel tables to be sure their words were heard. Judge Walker decided to wear a lavalier microphone whenever he was on the bench, so his words would be recorded on the audio record he was keeping.

The judge told us that they needed a bigger picture. The camera was above and behind jurors, so their faces would never be shown. The picture took in the witness chair, the judge's bench, but not the far end of the counsel tables. We had to go to a wide-angle lens. We rented one. I arranged insurance, to be paid by CFOIC, in case that lens disappeared.

More trouble. A wide-angle lens is great for focus. That brought the louvers on the air conditioner cover into focus. We asked Judge Walker for permission to cut a small hole in the cover, about an inch high and six inches wide. No problem. The hole was a gate that could be swung inward so nothing was in front of the lens. The camera was covered with black velvet cloth that reflected no light. Nobody noticed it anyway. Almost.

One morning midway through the trial Freddie called me at KNXT:

"Your damn camera isn't working," he said. "Get down here and fix it. The jury is waiting,"

I got a little more out of him. There was a picture, but something was wrong, it was out of focus. It did not sound like an engineer would be necessary. I told Freddie to alert a guard at the judges' parking lot. I'd be there in 10 minutes. It was about eight minutes, door to door, down the Hollywood Freeway. I went to the eighth floor where a few people were standing outside. A deputy who let me in was expecting a "mechanic." Freddie, alone except for a bailiff, was at his desk reading something and merely nodded.

A hasty look at the camera was enough. The gate on the camera cover was closed. During the night someone had tampered with the gate, maybe while trying to wipe off "old" dust. It was fixed in a minute. Freddie called a deputy on the fourth floor. The picture was OK.

Of course, a project that complicated, even if relatively simple technologically, had some after effects, although it received virtually no local publicity. We were playing it cool, hoping not to indicate that we were pressuring the courts, or that the courts were doing anything unusual to circumvent a Supreme Court decision.

I was not present in the eighth-floor courtroom except half of one day to see what difference might be evident in the auxiliary courtroom. Sound was better with closed circuit. I was told that before the voir dire questioning of jurors by attorneys began, the jurors were informed of the presence of a camera. A lavalier microphone, consisting of a thin wire and a microphone, was hung around the neck of each juror as his or her questioning began. It became routine rapidly, and Judge Walker wore his lavalier every day when he took his chair.

Mary Neiswender, a journalism classmate from USC, covered the trial for the Long Beach Independent. She was assigned a particular seat on the eighth floor, good for the entire time, and glad of it. She thought she would have been excluded at least part of the trial if there had been no auxiliary courtroom. She had to leave the courtroom a few times during trial days to call Long Beach and update her running story in the Independent. "Her seat" was waiting, empty, when she went back to the courtroom.

Suddenly, a lot of folks became closed circuit fans, without seeing any news stories in local L.A. newspapers. A woman in the Midwest, probably St, Louis, wrote requesting a memento of the courthouse for her collection of Bobby Kennedy things. I think I sent her pictures of the setup. A journalism prof wrote about it in a textbook.

I was invited to explain the project at a convention of the Society of Professional Journalists in Memphis. The Sheriff of Memphis, Bill Morris, asked me to survey the courthouse there for possible application at the trial of James arl Ray for the murder of Martin Luther King. I did look in the probable trial ourt, but Ray pleaded nolo contendre and there was no trial. Morris already ad a security camera watching Ray in jail. Archeologists in L.A. wondered if a tle camera could be used to help the public see what their diggers were do-g in a big hole in the LaBrea Tar Pits. It would not help much. The camera eeded to concentrate on small areas which changed frequently.

Closed Circuit was used again in Northern California, but was soon utdated and forgotten because the State Judicial Council decided a TV amera and a newspaper's still camera could be admitted if a judge was greeable.

Probably the best result was the use of closed circuit on a big scale in he Moussaoui 9-11 (punishment/death penalty?) trial in Virginia Federal istrict Court (see Legal Wars chapter) in 2006. The unrelenting opposition Federal judges to cameras in "their" courts surrendered to practical needs o serve the public. A Closed Circuit was allowed into a Virginia courtroom o families, not the public at large, could watch a live broadcast in several ates. I heard nothing about that until much later, but Associated Press ad carried a story in Virginia. (See Legal Wars chapter). The AP story I saw d not mention the Sirhan trial, although the Virginia judge knew what we ad done. A friend who knew about our Sirhan Sirhan closed circuit system iggested that I write to her relative, the judge in the Moussaoui trial, and tell er what we did. I wrote to the judge and to the defense counsel. I explained ur system, offered any help, but said it was simple and an engineer could do easily. I heard nothing, then years afterward accidentally heard about the irginia system. In both cases, the public interest was decisive.

ade to Black

September, 1976, I attended a White House reception for broadcast edito-alists, hosted by President Ford -- who was not there, though we members of the Broadcast Editorial Association had already seen him at a handshake affair. That morning I arranged to attend the daily Press Secretary's briefing for the White House correspondents, and took Jim Foy along. Foy was Editorial Director of KNBC in L.A. When we left the President's reception that afternoon and walked outside the Old Executive Office Building, I told Foy that I'd had it with editorial writing and I was going to quit when we got home. I could not imagine doing the same thing for another decade before reaching retirement age.

Thus ended a twenty-five-year year career in journalism, in November, 1976. My final broadcast was endorsement of an Orange County candidate for Congress. He won.

Before leaving KNXT I got a call from Gene Fuson, Editorial Director of KFZWB radio. He heard I was leaving, and would I mind if he applied? I said I'd recommend him. He got it.

During a call with a senior exec in New York a few months later, I was asked, "What did he (the manager) tell you?" "About what?" "When he let you go?" I told the New Yorker I wasn't fired, I had quit. Why? I was part of a discreet inquiry to confirm local newspaper stories about the latest station manager, who alienated many people. Then I heard they had a new manager. The new manager married Gov. Jerry Brown's sister.

See that Camera?

Probably around 1982 I was working near downtown and got a phone call from Judge Peter Smith. He was trying a publicity case, a TV star as plaintiff. A TV news camera was set up in the back looking over the heads of jurors and recording the bench and witnesses. Pieces were being played on evening news. A newspaper's still camera was on a tripod against the outside of the rail, and a photog was on a chair behind it, occasionally moving the camera to get a different picture. The cameras were mentioned in press coverage a little at first, to explain that the Judicial Council had changed Rule 980 to permit recording and still shots.

"Don't you want to see what you guys have done?" Pete asked. I said I'd be right there. TV fans stood in line to get in and see Carol Burnett. A bailiff at the courtroom door looked at my press ID and said to follow him inside. An aisle seat was reserved for me by Judge Smith.

The crowd inside was paying no attention to either camera. They were watching Burnett testify that a scandal magazine had libeled her. I left at the next break and thanked the judge.

I continued to work elsewhere in interesting and busy non-journalism jobs. We retired at age 66 to San Diego County in 1989, an idle existence which lasted ---- at least two months.

First, I went to a homeowner board meeting. They had a vacancy. Then the airport had a vacancy. Then ...

When "retirement" ended by 2010 I had served in public agencies as an elected office holder or appointee to Boards and committees at the local, County and State level. The agencies were involved in County Regional Planning; running a busy commuter airport; running local, county and state water agencies; border crossings with official visits to the Tijuana City Council, and the reverse when they came here; unending legal matters with several Indian tribes whose leaders, over decades in court, became good friends; "classified" border security systems; the Port Authority; freeway and public transit construction; droughts and probable flooding of certain roads. "Normal" travel routinely went to Sacramento, Las Vegas/Hoover Dam (Colorado River Compact), El Centro and Mexican water systems from the Colorado to Tijuana. This does not touch upon continuing battles with the City of San Diego, which never gave up trying to get the other cities and independent water agencies to pay their (San Diego) bills for water.

-0-

My still young looking wonder woman, a volunteer at the Cal State Univ. San Marcos library all of that retirement time, was diagnosed with Parkinson's in 2011 and died on a holiday trip to AZ about four years later, age 90, in early 2014, ten days before our 68th anniversary. We did everything, from Bangor to Berlin, Hong Kong to Monaco, Zurich to Hilo in one summer. She was still trim and lovely, a funny, dazzling partner. One does not recover from such a loss. I weep every day. Two brilliant granddaughters ages 19 and 26, with amazing parents who were married at 19, help me focus on the future.

Photographs are included to bring their own special light on a few Gangster"s Butler stories.

Judge Herb Walker looked angry, perhaps, but was a kind friend and fellow camera fan.

The author, Howard Williams, was chairman of a Los Angeles Press Club dinner honoring retiring Inspector Ed Walker, the LAPD press relations officer. Radio and TV's policeman Joe Friday, Jack Webb, center, also was helped for years by Walker.

The kitchen knife killing of Mickey Cohen's bodyguard by a movie star's daughter was part of a series of stories that seemed to have no end. The Lana love letters (that is her at the Coroner's inquest) led to this book's bizarre "Butler" story.

Our author was a "pundit" on Channel 2, or thought he was.

Four pictures show the interior of Judge Walker's courtroom where the Sirhan camera was hidden.

FBI Director J. Edgar Hoover's letter "Proves" the Author and two other newsmen were not spies.

Mickey Cohen sent notes to Ann Williams' wife about her new baby.

The giant "classified" Hughes helicopter was "hidden" beside major public roadways.

Dead bodies, not always those of Baja fish, made Gangster Mickey Cohen dangerous to be around.

Art Buchwald and Jack Smith, LA Times columnists, finally met at a Press Club dinner.

BY MICHAEL A. LEVETT
Times Staff Writer

Former Superior Court Judge Herbert V. Walker, who sentenced both Sirhan Sirhan and Caryl Chessman to the gas chamber, died Saturday night in Newport Beach.   *L— 11-20-76*

The 77-year-old retired jurist was visiting his son's home when he suffered a fatal heart attack, a family spokesman said.

Walker's 16 years on the bench and a reputation for being tough but fair culminated in 1968 with his selection to preside over the trial of Sirhan, the man accused of shooting Sen. Robert F. Kennedy.

Before the trial he opposed an attempt to bargain for a life sentence for Sirhan, insisting that a trial was required for the public to learn all the facts in the case.

Sirhan was the 20th man Walker sentenced to the gas chamber. The sentence was later changed to life imprisonment.

He was one of eight judges who sentenced Chessman to death for robbery and rape.

Among the stocky, bushy-browed jurist's well-publicized trials were those involving Confidential magazine and boxer Art Aragon.

Judge Herbert V. Walker
Times photo

And in 1967 Walker conducted an unprecedented hearing on the constitutionality of capital punishment. He found the death penalty to be constitutional.

The judge was born in San Francisco and grew up playing in jail—his father was jailor in Hanford.

He was graduated from USC law school in 1928 and was California deputy commissioner of corporations until 1943.

That year he joined the staff of the Los Angeles district attorney and later replaced Grant Cooper as chief deputy district attorney. Cooper later served as Sirhan's defense counsel.

Walker spent five years as chairman of the hearing board of the Air Pollution Control District and in 1953 he was appointed to the Superior Court bench by then-Gov. Earl Warren.

At the time of the Sirhan trial Walker was the senior member of the Superior Court's criminal panel.

His tough reputation often led attorneys to challenge him for prejudice, but the Criminal Court Bar Assn (composed of many of the same lawyers) honored him in 1964.

"His standards of fairness and justice have been in the highest tradition of judicial responsibility," the association said.

Walker retired shortly after the Sirhan case in 1969.

He leaves his wife, Alice, a son, Herbert, and two daughters, Kathleen Brocklehurst and Elizabeth Zentner.

Funeral arrangements were incomplete.

EVENING

NEWS

FINAL CITY

APRIL 5, 1958   4★   MA 5-2311—145 S. Spring, Los Angeles 53 — TEN CENTS

ER'S GIRL
ER'S SUITOR

Cheryl, 14, Stabs
Johnny Stompanato,
Former Cohen Aide

BY HOWARD WILLIAMS, Staff Writer

Actress Lana Turner's 14-year-old daughter is in jail today for stabbing to death her mother's lover, Hoodlum Johnny Stompanato.

Stompanato, 43, often called the "Adonis" of Mickey Cohen's former gang, was slain with a butcher knife about 10:15 last night.

He died almost immediately on the floor of the pink bedroom of the actress in her home at 730 N Bedford Drive, Beverly Hills.

Beverly Hills Police Chief Clinton Anderson said the slaying apparently came as the climax to a bitter quarrel between the actress and

EXTRA

The Weather
SUNNY—Sunny and warmer. Some
gusty northeast winds. High tomorrow 74, low tonight 50.

LOS ANGELES · EVENING

MIRROR NEWS

FINAL CITY
N.Y. STOCKS

Vol. X—No. 154   In Four Parts   PART I   TUESDAY, APRIL 8, 1958   ·   4★   MA 5-2311 — 145 S. Spring, Los Angeles 53 — TEN CENTS

LANA'S LOVE LETTERS TO JOHNNY REVEALED

March List of Jobless Up 25,000

WASHINGTON, April 8
(AP)—The government re-
ported today unemploy-
ment rose by 25,000 in
March. This took the total
to 5,198,000 — the highest
in 16½ years.

The regular monthly re-
port of the Commerce and
Labor Departments also
showed a 321,000 rise in em-
ployment for March, taking
the total of those at work to

Mickey Cohen Bares Actress' Torrid Notes

Tender and passionate love notes Lana Turner wrote to Johnny
Stompanato were told to The Mirror News today by Mickey Cohen.
Mickey told The Mirror News he would not disclose all the letters.
"The ones I am giving out are love letters, the endearing kind,"
Mickey said. "The others I am keeping back might be construed in
a different way."

"My dearest, darling love," Lana wrote to Stompanato Sept. 19
from Copenhagen, Denmark.

"I do wish it could be bright and brilliant,
but somehow I am not quite up to it. Because
all I want to write and say, is I Love You.
GOD! It was so wonderful to hear your dear
voice again, Daddy!"

"It already seems like months since we've been

Japanese Fear 'Hot' Pacific

My sincerest best wishes to both you and your newly arrived little doll. Hope to see you Ann, and the baby some day.

Mickey Cohen

Howard Scott Williams

UNITED STATES DEPARTMENT OF JUSTICE

FEDERAL BUREAU OF INVESTIGATION

WASHINGTON 25, D. C.

September 17, 1951

*Mr. Lyle C. Wilson
Manager, Capital Bureau
United Press Associations
National Press Building
Washington, D. C.*

Dear Lyle:

I wish to acknowledge your letter of September 4, 1951, transmitting the rather detailed statement of Mr. Howard Williams of your Los Angeles office.

As Mr. Nichols told you over the telephone, after checking on the matter when the facts were called to the attention of the Bureau by the military authorities in April of 1950, the details were furnished to the Department, and under date of May 17, 1950, the Bureau was instructed by the Criminal Division to make a full investigation of the incident growing out of photographing an experimental helicopter. This investigation was made and full facts were submitted to the Department last year and the Bureau was advised on July 25th that the case could be closed after consideration by the Department of Justice and the U. S. Attorney's office in Los Angeles.

While our reports reflect Mr. Williams' activities in connection with this incident, nevertheless we are more than happy to supplement our file by including therein Mr. Williams' report, and I can very well appreciate Mr. Williams' interest in getting this matter cleared up. I think that you can safely tell him that the whole matter is closed and it need give him no further concern.

With best wishes and kind regards,

Sincerely yours,

Edgar

MAMMOTH XH-17 HELICOPTER, designed to lift
heavy artillery and tanks and carry them short dis-
tances, was rolled out of Howard Hughes' Culver City
plant today for the first time. T'...
shows giant 126'...
...deliver power from two turbojet en...
...en ground test...

The Gangster's Butler

Columnist to Be Honored

'Art Buchwald Night'

Art Buchwald, the famed syndicated columnist of the N.Y. Herald Tribune, will be guest of honor and speaker at a gang dinner, Wednesday evening, March 13.

The nationally-known newsman will give an informal talk on some of his newspaper experiences and perhaps will touch on such subjects as "how to write a column" in French.

Buchwald is "a local boy who made good" in the newspaper world.

He is a former student at USC where he majored in English and wrote for the campus newspaper, the Daily Trojan, and the humor magazine, the Wampus.

After his college training, he became a staff member of the Paris edition of the N.Y. Herald Tribune. He started reviewing movies and later was graduated into writing a column.

He is the author of a number of books, and his column now appears in hundreds of newspapers throughout the country, including the Los Angeles Times.

Howard Williams of the L.A.

ART BUCHWALD
Famed Columnist to Speak at Press Club Gang Dinner, March 13

County Medical Association, 8-Ball Final editor and a former classmate of the guest of honor, will be host for the evening.

Pub-Rel Class for PC Members

Charles Katzman, PC educational director and head of the news communications division of UCLA graduate department of journalism, has organized a class in public

and television news services as well as various aspects of newspaper and editorial work.

Special "Workshop" sessions on how to write releases and stories

Please Let Him Park Your Car

The attendant in the Press Club parking lot depends on your tips and your cooperation. On busy nights, the attendant must park the cars in such a manner that large number of cars can be accommodated.

The attendant does not leave the lot until it is empty or keys are returned to members or left at the bar when they cannot be located. Don't give him a bad time when he insists on parking your car.

L. A. newspapermen find Sunkist citrus out of this world, too.

Made in the USA
Las Vegas, NV
12 March 2021